Teaching for Intellectual and Emotional Learning (TIEL)

A Model for Creating Powerful Curriculum

Christy Folsom

To Neema,
(Central Park)
Happy Teaching
Christy Folsom

ROWMAN & LITTLEFIELD EDUCATION
Lanham • New York • Toronto • Plymouth, UK

Published in the United States of America
by Rowman & Littlefield Education
A Division of Rowman & Littlefield Publishers, Inc.
A wholly owned subsidary of The Rowman & Littlefield Publishing Group, Inc.
4501 Forbes Boulevard, Suite 200, Lanham, Maryland 20706
www.rowmaneducation.com

Estover Road
Plymouth PL6 7PY
United Kingdom

British Library Cataloguing in Publication Information Available

Library of Congress Cataloging-in-Publication Data

Folsom, Christy, 1947–
  Teaching for intellectual and emotional learning (TIEL) : a model for creating
powerful curriculum / Christy Folsom.
      p. cm.
  Includes bibliographical references.
  ISBN-13: 978-1-57886-872-8 (cloth : alk. paper)
  ISBN-10: 1-57886-872-6 (cloth : alk. paper)
  ISBN-13: 978-1-57886-873-5 (pbk. : alk. paper)
  ISBN-10: 1-57886-873-4 (pbk. : alk. paper)
  eISBN-13: 978-1-57886-924-4
  eISBN-10: 1-57886-924-2
  1. Education—Standards—United States. 2. Education—Curricula—United States.
3. Affective education—Curricula—United States. 4. Educational
accountability—United States. I. Title.
  LB3060.83.F65 2009
  371.3—dc22   2008028822

⊚™ The paper used in this publication meets the minimum requirements of
American National Standard for Information Sciences—Permanence of
Paper for Printed Library Materials, ANSI/NISO Z39.48-1992
Manufactured in the United States of America.

Contents

Preface

To what extent were the whys and hows of learning and thinking an explicit focus and subject of discussion in the classroom?

—Seymour Sarason

Seymour Sarason (1982), a noted psychologist and educator, made an interesting observation. After visiting hundreds of classrooms, he noticed a pronounced lack of discussion about thinking and learning. When he asked the teachers why they did not discuss thinking and learning with their students, they reported that they had not been trained to talk about thinking or learning. Furthermore, even if they knew how to carry on these conversations, there was no time in the curriculum to do so.

MISSING PIECES

In my work with teachers, I made the same observation. As a teacher in a gifted and talented pull-out program, it was clear that most students had not been taught about their thinking and learning. These were bright and capable students. While some were underachievers who put little effort into their classroom work, many others had never received a grade lower than an A. Whether they were underachievers or A students in their classrooms, many students lacked the thinking skills that would help them become more self-regulated learners. The students often had extensive knowledge in different areas, but few strategies that would help them organize or apply their knowledge. Therefore, an important part of the pull-out program was teaching thinking skills that included problem solving, creative thinking, and the self-management skills of setting criteria, making decisions, planning, and self-evaluating project work.

We used the work of J. P. Guilford (1977) and Mary Meeker (1979) to frame the teaching of thinking skills. Guilford was a psychologist who developed the structure of intellect theory (SI) in the mid-twentieth century. Meeker, one of Guilford's students, later developed an educational application of his theory that includes assessment and learning activities that used strengths in intellectual processing to overcome weaknesses.

The pull-out classrooms were colorful places. Meeker's color-coding of the five thinking operations in Guilford's structure of intellect theory that included getting information, using memory to make connections, evaluating, and using convergent and divergent thinking provided a visual framework for teaching students about their thinking and learning. This framework helped students become aware of their thinking within the context of a wider range of thinking skills. While students learned the self-management skills of decision making, planning, and self-evaluation involved in project work, they saw these skills in relationship to research skills, critical and creative thinking, and problem-solving strategies.

After several years of successful teaching, the pull-out program in the district was replaced with a consultant model for serving gifted students. Now, little time was spent teaching students in pull-out classes. Instead, the teachers in the gifted and talented program met with classroom teachers to help them meet the intellectual needs of gifted children within their own classrooms. These meetings focused on how to differentiate curriculum for a particular student, how to make sure students had reading and math materials at an appropriate level, and how to differentiate and expand curriculum to better meet the needs of the gifted students in the classroom.

Project work that provides opportunities for students to develop a wide range of thinking skills seemed a good place to start. Curriculum that integrated the teaching of thinking skills with content had been successful in the pull-out program. The students were challenged and they learned in a variety of disciplines and developed skills that they were not learning in their regular classrooms. I felt that these teaching strategies would be successful in general education classrooms. I had taught in a fifth grade classroom before coming to teach in the gifted program, and students at all ability levels were motivated by the challenge of making decisions, planning, and self-evaluating in organizing their project work.

Some of the classroom teachers included project work in their curriculum. Yet, they did not teach thinking or self-organization skills in any specific way. While these were important skills for all students to learn, they were essential for gifted students. If the needs of gifted students were to be met in the general classroom, the critical thinking skills involved in decision making, planning, and self-evaluation were needed to raise the level of learning for those students.

Many educators in the field of teaching thinking concur. Marzano (1993) states that the processes of decision making, planning, and self-evaluation "render any activity more thoughtful and more effective" (p. 158). According to Marzano these skills are necessary for higher-order thinking to take place. The noted expert in critical thinking, Richard Paul (1995), advocates education that features "active, independent, self-directed learning" where students are "active participants in their own intellectual growth" (p. 45).

Setting and using criteria to make decisions about projects is a starting point in helping students think about their thinking and consider standards in making decisions. The importance of learning the self-organization skills of decision making, planning, and self-evaluation are noted by Doll (1993). In writing about curriculum, he points out that "there is nothing more important to the human being than the setting, experiencing, and evaluating of goals, plans, and purposes" (p. 170).

As I helped teachers plan to teach these processes within their curriculum, I quickly recognized that they were unfamiliar with discussing thinking skills that the students needed to learn. While it was difficult to communicate about teaching thinking skills, it was more difficult for the teachers to see the importance of making these processes visible by discussing them with the students.

A NEED TO KNOW

I needed to know more in order to effectively help the teachers. It was time to go back to the classroom to better understand how the strategies and processes used in the gifted program could be transferred into a general education classroom. During the 1993–1994 school year, I returned to teaching fifth grade. In addition to the basic skills of reading, writing, and math, I planned curriculum that included the teaching of thinking skills, focusing on the self-organization process, to my fifth grade students through social studies and science project work.

I observed the students' learning. As they set criteria for decision making, planned their projects, and evaluated their own work, they became more focused and responsible for their learning. Students with behavior problems tempered their behavior as they delved into projects that they themselves had planned. Students who went to the special education resource room received help from the special education teacher who came into our classroom to help her students as well as others research information and edit the writing. Other students, identified as gifted, thrived as they researched subjects in more depth using a variety of resources. All students thrived as they built models, wrote scripts, designed costumes and gathered props, and rehearsed for presentations.

Metacognition was an important component. Students became more conscious of their learning as they discussed the thinking involved in their work.

As students consciously applied thinking processes in their assignments and projects, they became more empowered as learners. They demonstrated what Mary Meeker once said, "They owned their learning."

Yet, I needed to know more. The knowledge I had gained in gifted education helped me develop curriculum, differentiate instruction, and plan learning experiences that benefited the wide range of learners in my fifth grade classroom. While teaching in my own classroom, I continued in my consultant role as the gifted and talented teacher. I worked with teachers, helping them plan and adapt curriculum for gifted students in their classrooms. As I worked in this dual role using what I had learned in gifted education, it became even clearer that there was important knowledge to which classroom teachers had not had access.

FILLING THE GAP

Frustrated with what I was experiencing, I determined to find out what was missing. I enrolled in the doctorate program at Teachers College, Columbia University, focusing my research on the teaching of thinking and discovering how to help general education teachers acquire the knowledge needed to teach thinking skills to their students. How can teachers learn to integrate the teaching of thinking skills into their classroom curriculum? How can they use project work to teach their students self-organization skills? What will help teachers discuss thinking and learning with their students? How can teachers be encouraged to include the explicit teaching of thinking into their curriculum?

In short, how can we fill the gap that exists between gifted and general education? The TIEL Curriculum Design Model, and subsequently this book, emerged from that question.

Acknowledgments

I would like to thank the four teachers, Erica Leif Denman, Ted Kesler, Stacy Silver, and Brian Aherne, who welcomed me into their classrooms on a weekly basis for an entire school year. I appreciate their time, the hard work they did with their students, and the valuable feedback during the research and writing process. I would like to thank Greg Folsom for his meticulous work and long-suffering patience in formatting the text and transforming the many figures found in the book from teaching tools to printable documents. Thank you to John Leistler for his insight, suggestions, and encouragement. His inspired teaching fully illustrates teaching for intellectual and emotional learning. And, thank you to Dr. Jane Schumann for her confidence in the TIEL Model, her valuable feedback, and the push to get this project finished.

Foreword

Daniel Pink, in his new book on the whole mind, emphasizes the point that the knowledge society is giving way to the creative society, a place where people will need the skills of design, empathy, symphony, and connection over the skills of traditional thinking. In other words, working effectively will require using creative abilities in tandem with people skills. Christy Folsom's book is a clarion call to educators to take up this same challenge in schools, to make them learning communities where meaning is built through self-organized projects.

The book represents an important tool for teachers and teacher candidates in planning and implementing meaningful instruction for their students through project-based approaches. Begun as a dissertation project by Folsom in which she worked with four teachers intensively across a year—meeting and talking about their practices—it has blossomed into a guide for all educators on teaching for intellectual and emotional learning (TIEL). The book is organized into different chapters that begin with the framework that the teachers will use to elevate their work with students—the TIEL Wheel, a scaffold to assist in designing, implementing, and assessing curriculum and instruction in classrooms. It continues with chapters on consciousness, that of the teacher and learner to the processes of thinking and feeling, on communication, on curriculum, and on connections, moving from the abstract theoretical ideas about teaching to the level of application in everyday practice.

Driven by Folsom's recognition of a problem, the book details a solution that is aligned with her perception of what is needed by students and teachers. She states: "Whether they were underachievers or A students in the classroom, many students lacked the thinking skills that would help them become more self-regulated learners." This problem was further complicated by the fact that teachers also lacked the skills to transform this lack of ability in students, thus creating an ongoing dilemma for enhancing meaningful learning in schools. Teachers in her study lamented that they had not received adequate instruction in connecting concepts of thinking to practical teaching in the classroom. Therefore, they also lacked an understanding of how to help students self-organize. Moreover, they learned through classroom experience about their deficits in addressing social and emotional issues that students brought to school.

Folsom begins the book with a historical overview of American education, nesting her argument for project-based learning in the progressive movement championed by John Dewey in the 1940s. She then offers a rationale for a qualitatively different curriculum today—our flat world where outsourcing is commonplace, our global economy where we are interdependent and must compete in the world, and the emergent primacy of technology that insists on the ability to think in an age of information explosion.

Strongly influenced then by the work of Dewey on project-based learning and J. P. Guilford on cognition, the TIEL Wheel is divided into ten segments that represent five cognitive and five social-emotional processes, qualities of mind balanced by qualities of character. These qualities in turn are transformed into desired skills for students to learn. The qualities and skill sets correspond to each other in important ways. For example, the thinking process of evaluation is matched to the character quality of ethical reasoning. Skills needed for evaluation include analysis, decision making, and judgment, while ethical reasoning calls for fairness, honesty, and thoughtfulness. The thinking operations include cognition, memory, evaluation, convergent production, and divergent production. The qualities of character include reflection, empathy, ethical reasoning, mastery, and appreciation, each with corresponding skill sets.

Folsom takes this model and applies it to classroom practice in multiple modalities. It becomes a bulletin board, a laminated reference in the classroom, the primary tool for curriculum development and design, the catalyst for professional development work, the basis for student development of project ideas and assessments, and a major tool for teaching metacognition and guiding teachers in self-reflection. The author shows examples of student work and teacher plans that authenticate the application of the model to these various tasks. She even presents revised work to illustrate the role of reflection in learning. As such, the model becomes an indispensable tool for teaching and learning in classrooms that value thinking and feeling as equal partners in learning.

As an antidote to the current climate of teaching and learning in schools as an exercise in test preparation, this book is a refreshing reminder that learning matters more than achievement and that teaching is more than using data to decide on which skills to emphasize in worksheets. Folsom has created an educational vision that has high practical value even as it has strong theoretical roots in our educational history. It offers a concrete way for teachers to help students learn at higher levels but also to develop the character traits so necessary to being able to function in twenty-first-century society. For gifted educators, it offers a blueprint for making differentiation in classrooms real and palpable. For general educators, it affords a vision of enhancing the learning level for all students in an even-handed way. The book should be required of all who supervise teachers as it provides a primer to meaningful teacher growth and change over time.

Joyce VanTassel-Baska, EdD
Jody and Layton Smith Professor in Education
College of William and Mary

Introduction

This book is about teachers learning to teach thinking and social-emotional processes through project-based curriculum. Teaching for intellectual and emotional learning (TIEL) represents thinking and the qualities of character important in social-emotional learning and provides a structure for designing a project-based curriculum. The TIEL Curriculum Design Model is a tapestry woven from experiences in learning and teaching, from practice and theory. While the TIEL framework includes both thinking and social-emotional processes, and both will be addressed, the focus of this book is on teaching the self-organization skills of decision making, planning, and self-evaluation within the context of project work.

THEORY AND PRACTICE

The TIEL Model embodies what I have learned from teaching over the decades in various areas of education. My classrooms have held a wide variety of students. Some classrooms were bustling with preschoolers just beginning their formal journey through school. Others held elementary or middle school students who were deaf, struggling to learn language and speech. In general education, my classrooms were filled with elementary students, including special education and gifted students. In gifted education, my pull-out classroom invited gifted talented students for a few hours a week. Now, my classroom holds university students who are themselves preparing to become teachers. For all the variety, students have generally learned best when I taught thinking skills through project-based learning.

The TIEL Curriculum Design Model is constructed from theory as well as practice. The TIEL Model rests on three sets of shoulders—J. P. Guilford, whose

1

work has influenced gifted education; Mary Meeker, who made Guilford's work educationally practical; and John Dewey, the giant in general educational philosophy whose thinking was grounded in practice.

AUDIENCE

This book presents teaching and learning experiences needed by all students. The book is for teachers, administrators, teacher educators, and teacher candidates in the field of general and gifted education. Parents who are navigating the educational system will also find this book helpful as they look at the teaching and learning their children are experiencing in school. Young students, who will probably not read the book, will benefit when the adults in their lives do.

For teachers, TIEL is a reminder of why they became teachers in the first place. The TIEL Model provides validation for ways of teaching that teachers know are best, but often get lost in the bureaucracy and current demands of the educational system. This book will help teachers see possibilities and give them tools that help them realize those possibilities.

Administrators who entered the field of administration to improve learning opportunities for students will appreciate this book. The TIEL Model helps administrators achieve the balance needed in the teaching and learning going on in their schools. It can help them build a community of learners and teachers who work together to challenge all their students.

Teacher educators need this book to teach future teachers how to develop curriculum that includes the teaching of thinking and social-emotional learning. Future teachers need to know how to develop curriculum that will help their students strengthen thinking and social-emotional processes within rigorous content. At the same time, this book will help future teachers become prepared for the complex teaching and learning needed by their students in the twenty-first century.

The concepts represented in the TIEL Curriculum Design Wheel have helped me in teaching students in every age group and field of education. I hope that this book validates the work that good educators are doing and helps them see greater possibilities for increasing the teaching of thinking and social-emotional learning in classrooms every day.

ORGANIZATION OF THE BOOK

To illustrate how the TIEL framework addresses both intellectual and social-emotional processes, I will focus on the experiences of four teachers and their students. This book tells how the TIEL Curriculum Design Model assists teachers in five important areas—codification, consciousness, communication, curriculum, and connections.

- The TIEL Model provides *codification* of the thinking and social-emotional skills that are the new basic skills.
- The TIEL Model helps teachers develop *consciousness* of a wide range of skills students need to learn.
- The TIEL Model gives teachers a language to *communicate* about thinking and social-emotional learning with their students.
- The TIEL Model provides a structure for designing *curriculum* that leads to complex learning.
- And finally, the TIEL Model helps teacher candidates make *connections* across disciplines and from teacher education coursework to their classrooms.

Part I: Codification

The first part explains how the TIEL Curriculum Design Wheel graphically names and organizes fundamental thinking operations and qualities of character. Here I explain how historical changes in educational needs have resulted in a variety of codifications and how the TIEL Model provides a new codification that is needed for the educational needs of today.

Part II: Consciousness

The second part follows Ted, a third grade teacher, as he becomes conscious of the many opportunities in his classroom to teach the self-organization skills of decision making, planning, and self-evaluation through project work.

Part III: Communication

Part three explores how the TIEL Model facilitates metacognitive discussions of learning and thinking in the classroom. While each of the other parts includes the work from the one research year, this part covers a three-year span. It is based on Erica's experiences in her first three years of teaching as she and her students learned to communicate more clearly about thinking and learning as she taught fourth and fifth grades.

Part IV: Curriculum

The fourth part tells the story of how Stacy, a fourth grade teacher reluctant to try more complex ways of teaching, brings project-based learning into her classroom. Stacy transforms how she develops curriculum to include the teaching of self-organization skills of decision making, planning, and self-evaluation.

Part V: Connections

Part five shares the experiences of Brian, a second grade teacher, as he adapts the teaching of self-organization skills to meet the developmental needs of his students. In the process, he uses the TIEL Model to make connections from his practice to the theory he learned in teacher education coursework, connections across subject areas, and connections from teacher to student and from student to student.

Appendix: Methodology

The appendix includes the methodology of the research on which this book is based. The research involved teaching the four selected teachers, through a year-long professional learning intervention, how to integrate the teaching of self-organization skills into project-based curriculum. Baseline assessments determined what teachers and their students knew before the professional learning process began and final assessments determined what had been learned about teaching decision making, planning, and self-evaluation at the end of the school year.

Each part of the book includes examples drawn from the case studies of the four teachers who participated in researching the use of the TIEL Model to teach self-organization skills to their elementary school students through project work.

I

CODIFICATION

cod·i·fi·ca·tion (kod'ə fi kā'shən), *n.* 1. the act, process, or result of arranging in a systematic form or code

—Webster's Unabridged Dictionary

Codification is the process of systematically organizing concepts and providing a vocabulary for understanding and communicating abstract ideas. Codification of educational ideas has occurred throughout the history of education in America. When social, political, and economic changes lead to new methodologies in education, new codification is required to facilitate implementation.

CHAPTER 1: CODIFICATION OF THINKING AND SOCIAL-EMOTIONAL PROCESSES

Why is new codification that addresses the teaching and learning requirements of today needed? In the twenty-first-century global economy, both educators and noneducators point out that students need not only a command of basic literacy and math skills, but also the ability to problem solve, think critically and creatively, and work collaboratively with others. New educational needs require new codification. This chapter recounts the changing codification of education from Horace Mann, who founded American public education, to current standards that describe a more complex way of teaching and learning. Understanding the shifting needs in education helps place the concepts of teaching for intellectual and emotional learning (TIEL) within a historical context.

CHAPTER 2: WHAT IS TIEL?

What is *teaching for intellectual and emotional learning* (TIEL), and how does it codify the intellectual and social-emotional skills that need to be taught today? This chapter explains the fundamental intellectual components and qualities of character represented in the TIEL Curriculum Design Wheel and how this is made accessible in the classroom.

1

Codification of Thinking and Social-Emotional Processes

If the challenge of the twentieth century was creating a system of schools that could provide minimal education and basic socialization for masses of previously uneducated citizens, the challenge of the twenty-first century is creating schools that ensure—for all students in all communities—a genuine right to learn.

—Linda Darling-Hammond

"What were you *thinking*?" "If you would just think about it a little harder." "Come on, think!" "How would you feel if . . ." As teachers and parents, we are familiar with these questions and exhortations. We have used these phrases as well as others in an effort to coax a reasonable response from our students or children. Yet, what do we expect them to say? What do we mean by thinking? What are some basic intellectual and social-emotional skills we want children to have?

EDUCATIONAL HISTORY

Concerns for how to help students develop intellectual skills have been an important goal at least since Socrates, who discovered that many of his contemporaries, like our students and children, could not rationally defend their own statements (Paul, 1995). Throughout our own, relatively recent, educational history in the United States, both the intellectual and social-emotional aspects of learning have been addressed in various ways, with differing amounts of emphasis, by educators with diverse points of view.

In the late nineteenth century, debates raged over what organization of content would guide the intellectual and moral training of students. At

7

mid-twentieth century, when social-emotional concerns received priority, the field of curriculum theory emerged with the promise to clarify the confusion over what to teach and how to teach it (Kliebard, 1992). Recently, a steady stream of educational reforms bearing new standards for both students and teachers has spilled into the new century. These standards include reference to intellectual learning and to some extent social-emotional learning. At the same time, a new emphasis on character education has emerged.

Yet, in this first decade of the twenty-first century, thinking and social-emotional learning are still not commonly discussed in most classrooms. While many of the standards for students and teachers developed in the late 1990s make reference to thinking or intellectual skills, most teachers do not have the preparation needed to integrate the teaching of thinking into their daily curriculum.

WHY DO WE NEED NEW CODIFICATION?

The teaching of thinking and social-emotional learning has ebbed and flowed throughout twentieth-century American education. Yet, the educational needs in the twenty-first century demand that these two core areas of learning and teaching must become more focused and more effective for all students and all teachers.

A Flat World

Thomas Friedman (2005), a Pulitzer prize–winning foreign affairs correspondent for the *New York Times*, has written a book that helps set the context for education in the twenty-first century. Friedman describes a flat world reconfigured through technological advances that allow one part of the globe to be instantly connected to another. While we are reminded of this each time we are connected to a call center in India or the Philippines, we may be less clear of the far-reaching implications.

Friedman (2005) provides some historical connections to help. As the transport of goods by the railroad during the 1860s shifted the economy from an agrarian to an industrial one, today's technology, allowing transfer of knowledge work across oceans and continents, is creating another drastic economic shift. Jobs that require a high level of skill in math, science, and engineering go to the most qualified in any country in the world. Our situation is similar to that of the industrial revolution, which brought about wide changes in "the role of individuals, the form of governments, the way we innovated, the way we conducted business, the role of women, the way we fought wars, the way we educated ourselves, the way religion responded, the way art was expressed, the way science and research were conducted" (p. 46).

Qualitatively Different Education Needed

Preparing strong individuals who can collaborate and connect in the global economy requires a qualitatively different kind of education. Schools need to more consciously foster abilities and characteristics involving a wide range of intellectual skills and qualities of character. Friedman (2005) points out that students need intellectual skills that include decision making, creativity, problem solving, imagination, pattern recognition, adaptability, and the capacity to be self-directed. In addition, students need social-emotional characteristics that include collaboration skills, a sense of social responsibility, empathy, tolerance, and the capacity to trust and the honesty to be trusted.

There are other reasons, however, to prepare students intellectually and social-emotionally besides providing well-rounded workers in the global economy. Taking a more local point of view, Jane Rowland Martin (1995) points out that children are coming to our schools without the foundations in thinking and social-emotional skills they need to succeed in school or deal with the complexities of daily life. She argues that schools must provide these foundations that were formerly more consistently built at home. Whether the vantage point is global or local, intellectual skills and social-emotional characteristics are needed.

Change and Codification

New needs require new codification. When needs change, a new system that uses new names or a rearrangement of familiar terminology becomes necessary. As computers became increasingly available, a new codification was needed to help the average person find his way around the new technology. Recognizing the need, Bill Gates invented new codification that millions of us use daily when we switch on our computers. With pictures and words, we are able to navigate systems that were previously only accessible to professional computer programmers.

Codification helps disseminate new concepts, establishes a needed language, and facilitates communication. Throughout history, economic, technological, social, and political transformations have driven educational change. At each juncture new codifications have been established to provide new terminology, or terminology used in new ways, that address these changes.

It is important to know where we have been in education in order to understand where we need to go. To help place the TIEL Curriculum Design Model within a historical context, this chapter briefly explores some of those junctures and how intellectual and social-emotional aspects of education have been addressed and codified at various points in American educational history. The chapter also provides a window on how the teaching of thinking became severed from general education.

THE NEW PUBLIC SCHOOLS AND CODIFICATION
OF MORAL BEHAVIOR

In pre–Civil War America, Horace Mann and others took up the challenge of establishing universal education. Mann drew his philosophy of education from "Jeffersonian Republicanism, Christian moralism, and Emersonian idealism" (Cremin, 1961, p. 9). Mann adopted Jefferson's idea that freedom depended upon a citizenry with the ability to make wise decisions. Yet, America was diverse even in the early half of the nineteenth century, and wise decisions are best made on the basis of shared values. Therefore, an important role of the school was to help establish a community of citizens who shared common ideals.

Preparing Citizens with Common Values

Schools needed to prepare individuals who were able to exercise "self-discipline, self-government, and self-control" (Cremin, 1961, p.11). To prepare students who were ready for their role in a free democratic society, Mann focused on the moral aspect of schooling. This meant inculcating students with moral values. Mann believed that with such education, wise decisions and an ideal America would follow.

The McGuffey reader provided a kind of codification for teaching and learning during these first years of public school that focused on moral development. The stories focused on patriotic history and a wide range of moral values. As students learned to read, they learned lifelong values of self-discipline and the importance of making good choices.

Horace Mann had worthy goals. He wanted schools to create a community that shared a common codification of moral values. Diane Ravitch (2000), educational historian, tells a story that shows the widespread influence of the McGuffey readers. When Theodore Roosevelt used the term "Meddlesome Matties" in referring to his critics, most members of that generation clearly knew what he was talking about. Many remembered the story from their days in school spent with their McGuffey readers.

Lack of Analytical Thinking

Moral values were more clearly codified than thinking processes in the early common school. Teachers taught subjects of reading, writing, penmanship, spelling, and arithmetic as they had been taught—largely through repetition and rote memory. Subjects were taught by young teachers who were often just a year or two ahead of their pupils in completing the few years that the common school offered.

Most teachers had little formal education in how to teach. Normal schools began preparing teachers after 1830, yet these preparation schools provided little more than a review of the subject matter learned in the eight years of common school (Paul, 1995). In the climate of rote learning, critical thinking skills were not expected. Richard Paul points out that then, and "even to this day," prospective teachers have not been expected to demonstrate ways of teaching students how to "explore the evidence that can be advanced for or against their beliefs, note the assumptions upon which their beliefs are based . . . nor have [prospective teachers] been expected to demonstrate ability to think analytically or critically about the issues of the day" (p. 43).

INDUSTRIALIZATION AND CONTENT: 1890–1900

The economic change from an agricultural to an industrial economy in the late nineteenth century resulted in our secondary system. While attending high school today is a necessity for even a modest economic foundation, at that time, high schools were few and far between. Almost every community had an elementary school by 1900 and there were many universities, but high schools were not common and they were controversial (Ravitch, 2000). The high schools that existed taught the classical disciplines of mathematics, Latin, and Greek, as well as the newer subjects that included science, history, and book-keeping. Yet, with increasing numbers of high school students requiring the skills demanded by an industrial economy, more high schools needed to be established.

Charles W. Eliot: Content and Intellectual Development

As a high school education became more of a necessity for a wider range of students, content needed to be codified. What subjects should be taught? Who should learn which subjects? Charles W. Eliot, the president of Harvard, wanted more high schools established in order to improve the preparation of the students applying to his university. Eliot even wanted to expand the subjects taught at the grammar school level to include "natural sciences, physics, algebra, geometry, and foreign languages" (Ravitch, 2000, p. 31).

Eliot reflected how many teachers feel. If only their students had been taught more in the earlier years, they would be better prepared for what they are to learn now. Yet, Eliot, who advocated electives, was less concerned with what subjects were taught than the intellectual development of the student. He considered the development of "mental power, the power to think, reason, observe, and describe" (Ravitch, 2000, p. 31) to be the most important function of education.

William Torrey Harris: Mental Power

In the process of creating high schools, a wider discussion was unfolding that included another question. Why should certain subjects be taught? To question the what and why of content was revolutionary at this time. Yet, in this era of progressive politics known as progressivism, it was inevitable that education would be influenced. In the late 1890s, as progressive ideas of education were taking hold, Eliot had an ally in his support of liberal education that focused on developing intellectual power.

William Torrey Harris, starting his educational career as an elementary teacher, became superintendent of schools in St. Louis in 1868 and was appointed twenty years later as U.S. Commissioner of Education. Cremin (1961) notes that Harris successfully merged his philosophy of idealism with the practicalities of running a school district and "ultimately nationalized the institution of the public school" (p. 15). Harris believed in the rigorous study of the disciplines in order to train students' memories and reason, yet he held a somewhat different view of mental discipline from Eliot. Eliot was less rigid about the subjects to be taught, proposing that students have electives from which to choose. Harris, on the other hand, thought that particular subjects were necessary to train the mind, including the "the three moderns—modern science, modern literature, and modern history" (Ravitch, 2000, p. 30).

SCIENTIFIC CURRICULUM: 1900–1930

It was against this background that the current system of education in the United States was designed. At the turn of the twentieth century, a major purpose of education was to prepare poor citizens and immigrants for socialization and factory work. During the 1890s, industrialization was in full swing with workers and their families abandoning their farms and home businesses for factory jobs in the cities. At the same time, waves of "tired, . . . poor, . . . huddled masses" were making their way to America seeking freedom from political strife in their homelands and opportunity in their newly adopted country.

Joseph Mayer Rice: The Media

There was great pressure on the social and political systems to provide social services for the newcomers and accommodate their children in schools. At the same time, in 1892, Joseph Mayer Rice, a physician-turned-journalist, set out on a project to investigate schools in twenty-six cities for a monthly magazine called *The Forum*. He found that teachers were inadequately prepared and predominantly used recitation, rote learning, and memorization as methods of teaching (Cremin, 1961).

His descriptions were vivid. He stated that one New York school was "the most dehumanizing institution that I have ever laid eyes upon, each child being treated as if he possessed a memory and the faculty of speech, but no individuality, no sensibilities, no soul" (Rice, as cited in Ravitch, 2000, p. 21). A St. Louis school, where Harris had been superintendent twenty years before, fared even more poorly. Rice reported a teacher saying, "Don't talk, listen. Don't lean against the wall. Keep your toes on the line" (p. 21). At a Chicago school, Rice listened to a teacher leading a group drill, saying, "Don't stop to think, tell me what you know!" (Cremin, 1961, p. 5).

Colonel Francis Parker: The Practitioner

On the other hand, Rice saw what he considered to be exemplary schools where children were motivated and learned without coercion. One of these schools was the Cook County Normal School headed by Colonel Frances Parker, who began teaching in a country school at age sixteen. Following service in the Civil War, Parker returned to teaching and discovered his dissatisfaction with the public schools of the day. After reading contemporary literature on education, he traveled to Europe to learn the latest educational innovations (Cremin, 1961).

Rice wholeheartedly approved of the methods he observed in Parker's school. Children used the acres of land adjacent to the school to make observations of nature and record their findings. The curriculum was correlated—we now say integrated—in order to help students see the connections among various subjects. Children worked in groups and had responsibility for teaching younger students. Rice became an avid supporter of this "New Education," which he observed in six of the thirty-six schools he visited. Rice's findings contributed to the twentieth-century curriculum battles described by educational historians and provide background for understanding the lack of substantive change in teaching that continues to this day (Cremin, 1961; Cuban, 1993; Kliebard, 1995; Ravitch, 2000).

Scientific Curriculum

As the century turned, the whats, hows, and whos of education continued to be questioned. What curriculum should be taught? Who should receive what curriculum? And how should that curriculum be delivered? Just in time to facilitate this discussion, the fields of psychology and mental measurement were in their beginning stages.

In 1905, Alfred Binet and Theodore Simon of France developed an intelligence test that American educators realized could assess achievement as well as intelligence (Tannenbaum, 1986). Originally commissioned by the French government to determine which children needed special education, Binet and Simon soon found their test adapted to new uses. Lewis Terman of Stanford

University transformed it into the Stanford Binet intelligence scales. The test has undergone many revisions and is still used today to screen for high intelligence and learning disabilities. The tools and terminology of measurement were in place that would allow American education to be carried out much differently than before.

Multiple Faces of Progressive Education

Progressive education had several very different faces and several codifications. Cremin (1961) describes progressive education as the education arm of political progressivism at the turn of the twentieth century in America. Just as politicians and private citizens were trying to make social changes that addressed taxation, business reform, and housing for the poor, many educators wanted to see similar social progress in the education system.

On the surface, the differences in some versions of progressive education are vast. It is hard to believe that the child-centered, experience-based pedagogy that Rice observed in Parker's school and the pedagogy supported by the mental measurement movement would both be described as scientific and fall under the name of progressive education. Yet, *progressive* refers to "changing, improving, or reforming" (Webster's Dictionary, 2006) the status quo. Educators, however, had widely varying views on how change might be accomplished and with those views came a variety of codifications.

G. Stanley Hall: Child Development Movement

G. Stanley Hall was a leader in the child development movement, one branch of scientific education. Codification included child study, natural order, developmentalism, differentiation, and, of course, the word "scientific." According to Cremin (1961), Hall's main influence on education was to "shift the focus of teaching to the student" and place a "new emphasis on the scientific study of feelings, dispositions, and attitudes" (p. 103–104) that he felt had an important place in education.

After receiving the first doctorate in psychology ever awarded at Harvard in 1878, Hall went to Germany to study the work of educational reformers of the time. He greatly admired Francis Parker and made regular visits to Parker's school in Chicago. He strongly agreed with Parker that "the child is the center of all education" (Campbell, 1967, p. 119). When Hall became president of Clark University in Massachusetts in 1889, the college became a center for developing pedagogical practices based on the study of the child.

Teachers were advised to "keep out of nature's way" (Lerner, as cited in Ravitch, 2000, p. 73). Instead of set curriculum, teachers needed to take their cues from the children. While, historically, education fit the child to the school, Hall believed that educators trained in scientific methods could fit the school to the child (Cremin, 1961). He also believed that many children did not have the intellect for education and required curriculum that was differentiated to suit their limited capacities. According to Hall, school was to fit the child, but not all children in the same ways.

Franklin Bobbitt: Social Efficiency Movement

Franklin Bobbitt took the notion of differentiation to a new level. Influenced by the new emphasis on efficiency that Frederick Winslow Taylor was bringing to factories, Bobbitt created a different form of scientific education based on measurement. The codification used in the social efficiency movement included order, educational engineering, mental measurement, and needs. In 1912, Bobbitt published "Elimination of Waste in Education," an article in which he adopted the language of manufacturing to discuss schools. Students were "raw materials" to be formed into "products"; schools were "plants"; and administrators were "educational engineers" (Bobbitt, as cited in Kliebard, 1995, p. 85). Bobbitt's enduring influence on education is easy to recognize in the emphasis on testing, measuring, and quantifying that holds a solid place in the operation of today's schools.

Bobbitt proposed that education prepare students for life. He maintained that one of the greatest sources of waste in education was providing a liberal education, such as that supported by Harris and Eliot, to students who had neither the ability nor the opportunities to use such knowledge. Those who were college bound could benefit from such curriculum, but he maintained that all others needed to be prepared for the kinds of lives that they would lead.

Bobbitt traveled to various school districts in the country to ferret out waste in high schools. Even in schools that had a wide range of vocational courses for both boys and girls, Bobbitt was able to find evidence of waste. If girls were enrolled in commercial courses such as stenography and bookkeeping, Bobbitt found it wasteful for them to take algebra and geometry courses. If they were enrolled in domestic science, he questioned why they were also enrolled in physics and chemistry (Ravitch, 2000).

Education that prepared students for their future vocations and social roles required a great deal of sorting. Psychology and mental measurement provided the means to assess the individual educational needs of each student. The Stanford-Binet test revised by Terman was most frequently used to determine the kinds of courses in which students would be enrolled. Binet believed that intelligence could be developed, yet his contribution to mental measurement would be put to a very different use. The new testing tools developed by psychologists would establish the validity of the social efficiency movement and change the conception of what students needed.

The social efficiency movement in education was harder on African American students as it provided a "scientific" reason to maintain segregated schools. Ravitch (2000) points out the devastating effects of efficiency and differentiation on black students, who lived predominantly in the segregated South in the second decade of the twentieth century. While black leaders and parents called for studies in the disciplines for their children, they were dismissed as not being progressive in their thinking. The social efficiency movement provided "scientific evidence" for maintaining levels of education that would prevent African Americans from acquiring the knowledge and skills that could help them emerge from poverty.

William Heard Kilpatrick: Project Method

The project method was popularized by William Heard Kilpatrick, a professor at Teachers College. After growing up in Georgia, he was a student of Dewey's at the University of Chicago in 1898 and later at Teachers College, Columbia University, in 1907. After his classes with Dewey at Teachers College, he said that studying with Dewey had changed his thinking. Unlike others who wrote about educational theories and practices, when Kilpatrick discussed the project method he explicitly spoke of both intellectual and moral development.

Based on a curricular connection between home and school, the project method had origins in vocational education. An agriculture teacher in rural Massachusetts discovered how he could connect schoolwork to his students' farm responsibilities. One example of a home-project could involve bringing a sample of cow's milk from home and testing it for bacteria at school or weighing and calculating the price of feed for livestock (Kliebard, 1995).

While social efficiency educators recognized in the home-project a way of replacing science subjects with projects, Kilpatrick saw it differently. The home-project, to Kilpatrick, offered the possibility of rejuvenating the concept from the child development movement that curriculum could emerge from the child. While the project method was not new and others had written about it, Kilpatrick wrote a highly praised article published in 1918 that described the project method and defined the terminology.

Kilpatrick (1918) became the spokesman for the project method, a way of teaching thinking through problem solving. According to Kilpatrick, a project was "any unit of purposeful experience, any instance of purposeful activity where the dominating purpose, as an inner urge, (1) fixes the aim of the action, (2) guides its process, and (3) furnishes its drive, its inner motivation" (p. 319). He strongly believed that, through solving problems in a social setting, students could develop their intellectual abilities as well as moral character (Cremin, 1961). Kilpatrick's (1918) codification included the terms project, experience, purposeful, to do, to make, to enjoy, solve problems, group and individual projects, intellectual, and moral.

The project method, one tenet of several facets of progressive education, took on a life of its own. It was no longer a method, but a curriculum. Unfortunately, Kilpatrick began to see the project method as not simply a means to teaching a subject, but as a replacement for the subject itself (Kliebard, 1995). Throughout the 1920s and 1930s, this message spread as schools across the country revamped their curricula and rearranged classroom furniture to accommodate project curriculum. In 1934, the largest school district in the country, New York City, adopted project curriculum under the name Activity Curriculum. In a mammoth project by any definition, seventy-five thousand students experienced the project method in their classrooms (Cuban, 1993).

John Dewey: Synthesizer

When progressive education is mentioned, John Dewey's name usually comes to mind. Yet, he referred to Francis Parker as the father of progressive education. Dewey drew heavily on what he had observed in Parker's school, where his two children were enrolled, to develop his own theories of education. Dewey did not completely espouse any of the branches of progressive education. As Kliebard (1995) points out, Dewey "synthesized and reinterpreted" (p. 26) ideas that supported his own ideas about teaching and learning.

Origins of Ideas

For Dewey, the other progressive movements were not options to join but a buffet of ingredients from which to choose. The tenets of social efficiency were the antithesis of Dewey's thinking, but he drew ideas about child-centered learning from Stanley Hall, his former teacher at Johns Hopkins University. He used ideas of social change and social justice from Lester Frank Ward, a sociologist who believed that the human mind allows us to intervene in our own lives by the ability to make choices and plan, thereby not leaving us to the whims of evolution (Cremin, 1961).

Dewey also drew from outside the scientific approach to education. Dewey's interest in placing thinking and intelligent organization at the center of curriculum development reflected the ideas of mental discipline that were largely being eradicated by the social efficiency movement. Dewey's codification was vast. Nevertheless, a few examples are thinking, experienced-based learning, occupations, child-centered, project work, planning, decision making, character development, intellectual growth, and reflection (Dewey, 1938, 1964, 1991).

Codification

While Dewey's ideas have been in and out of fashion, many are common practice in some of today's classrooms. He advocated that a child's education be child-centered. This would include experiential hands-on learning, project-based learning, and opportunities for children to plan their work. His vision of education included fostering collaborative learning among children, building relationships with the community, and preparing students with the thinking skills and social-emotional characteristics needed to maintain a democracy.

Some of Dewey's terminology referred to methods of teaching the content of disciplines, while others made reference to outcomes of learning. For example, experienced-based learning was the starting point for building larger concepts within the disciplines. A former teacher at the Dewey school reports that as they learned about grains, the students cooked cereal. In learning about the farm, six-year-old students planned and constructed "a miniature farm, including a house, a barn, and cultivated land made out of large blocks, twigs, and soil" using rulers to "make the model to scale" (Mayhew & Edwards, 1936, pp. 80–84).

Blind Men and the Elephant

Dewey's writings on education are so voluminous and multifaceted that applying his work can be an experience similar to that of the blind men who investigated the elephant. Some educators grab the tail of one idea and see all of education as one long and sturdy rope. Others grab an ear of a different educational method and see all of teaching as a giant fan. Classroom applications can become focused on one aspect of Dewey's philosophy of education and miss the larger whole of his description.

The misinterpretation of child interest as a foundation for constructing learning is an example. Dewey has been criticized for the lack of focus on teaching organized content in schools and in schools of education (Hirsch & Trefil, 1987; Ravitch, 2000). Yet, Dewey (1938) spoke clearly against the extremism of progressive educators who rejected traditional education in its entirety. He gave an example to make his point:

> Many of the newer schools tend to make little or nothing of organized subject-matter of study; to proceed as if any form of direction and guidance by adults were an invasion of individual freedom, as if the idea that education should be concerned with the present and future meant that acquaintance with the past has little or no role to play in education. (p. 22)

While children's interests were to be taken into account, a teacher could not leave subject matter solely to the accidents of child interest. Dewey believed that the teacher's role was to purposefully and intelligently plan curriculum (Dewey, 1938, 1964).

CONFUSION AND COMPLAINTS: 1940–1957

Through the 1940s and 1950s, the field of education experienced a level of confusion extreme even by its own standards of argumentation and chaos. By the 1940s, progressivism had reached maturity. The language of progressivism was the mainstream language used to refer to schools, teaching, and learning. Cuban (1993) states that "by 1940 . . . varied forms of progressivism had become accepted by most citizens and professionals as the modern form of public schooling" (p.152).

What was new had become old and, therefore, subject to overturn. Cremin (1961) reports that 1955 marked the end of the progressive movement with the closing of the journal called *Progressive Education*. He says, "Somehow a movement that had for half a century enlisted the enthusiasm, the loyalty, the imagination, and the energy of large segments of the American public and the teaching profession became, in the decade following World War II, anathema, immortalized only in jokes" (p. vii).

Tightly closed classroom doors undoubtedly contributed to the demise of progressivism. Even during the popularity of progressivism, many teachers continued to teach in ways that were comfortable for them. Many did not completely follow the "architecture of teaching methodology" (Cuban, 1993, p. 153) outlined by progressivism. Cuban's research on how teachers taught during the years from 1890 to 1940 revealed a range of teaching styles and ideologies even in school systems with the reputation for having the most progressive schools.

Attacking Dewey

As progressivism came under attack from educators and parents in the post–World War II era, much of the blame was leveled at Dewey. One writer of the time said that "Dewey's pragmatism had removed all intellectual and moral standards from the schools" (Ravitch, 2000, p. 344). Yet, intellectual and moral development were the foundation of Dewey's "well-thought-out conception of education" (Paul, 1995, p. 44). Clearly, teachers and administrators had grabbed a limited piece of the elephant if an observer did not see evidence of deep critical thinking and opportunities for teaching moral development in a classroom aligned with Dewey's pedagogy.

There are several opinions on why Dewey's ideas did not receive widespread traction in schools. Paul (1995) states that the ideas of Dewey were "bastardized" (p. 44) into something that was never intended. Darling-Hammond (1997) points out that progressive education required that teachers have a great deal of pedagogical skill and content knowledge to be successful. Progressive education required that teachers meet two challenging goals that had not yet received widespread attention. They were to be attentive to student needs and use student-based strategies while, at the same time, teaching "high levels of disciplined understanding in content areas" (p. 12).

Kliebard (1995) offers another explanation. He points out that Dewey's "emphasis on intellectual inquiry and social regeneration at all levels and by all segments of the population made it too vague and imprecise" (p. 154).

Teaching for intellectual inquiry and social regeneration requires knowledge that teachers did not have. To be successful, Dewey's pedagogy required that teachers have an understanding of how to elicit thinking to build understanding of content, scaffold the complex thinking involved in inquiry and project work, and help students develop qualities of character.

Access to Knowledge of Thinking

To fully apply Dewey's theories, teachers and teacher educators needed access to knowledge about the intellect that would help them succeed with a complex pedagogy. Yet, in the 1940s, a more complete understanding of cognition was just beginning. In the 1920s, Edward Thorndike presented the idea of connectionism, which explained that the brain worked like a machine with many unrelated connections, but this did not provide help with pedagogy. Thorndike and others who were interested in how the intellect worked focused mostly on testing levels of intelligence that supported the social efficiency view of education.

In 1950, J. P. Guilford (1968, 1977) gave an address at the American Psychological Conference that had far-reaching effects on how intelligence was viewed. During World War II Guilford had carried out research that resulted in the structure of intellect theory that presented intellect as multifaceted. Others, Binet, Thorndike, and Thurstone, believed that intelligence was more than one entity, but Guilford's work codified multiple mental aptitudes, including creativity. While the Stanford-Binet test focused on one aspect of intelligence, Guilford's work opened up the possibility of finding talent that was not identified through existing intelligence testing. Those interested in gifted education paid attention.

Gifted Education

As progressive education declined during the World War II years, there was a similarly diminished interest in gifted education. In his chapter covering the history of gifted education found in *Gifted Children*, Tannenbaum (1986) reports that gifted education was at "its lowest ebb during World War II and immediately thereafter" (p. 15). The advent of intelligence testing had facilitated the development of programming for gifted students in the first half of the twentieth century. Schools for the gifted were established, notably Leta Hollingworth's Speyer School in New York City in 1936, as well as the Stuyvesant School for boys in 1902 in the same city.

Programs for gifted students, or "fast learners" as Hollingworth (1926) insisted, took a variety of forms. Prior to 1920, provisions for gifted students predominantly involved grade skipping or acceleration. Yet, with new knowledge from the field of psychology about individual differences and how children learn, programming for the gifted focused on enrichment instead of accelerating through curriculum at a faster pace.

In several areas of the country in the 1920s, enrichment for advanced students took place in the regular classroom. This was known as the contract method with students working on independent projects under the oversight of the classroom teacher (Tannenbaum, 1986). Another programming option was ability grouping that placed advanced students from a geographic area in full-time special classes within certain schools or, in some cases, special schools. In the 1930s, enrichment within the regular classroom became the preferred method for serving advanced learners. Yet, Tannenbaum points out that even when interest was high there were relatively few opportunities for gifted students.

By the 1950s there was concern that the intellectual talents of gifted students were being underdeveloped. A report by the Educational Policy Commission stated concern for the "social waste" (Tannenbaum, 1986, p. 15) that came from neglecting intellectually advanced learners and made suggestions for meeting the educational needs of this group of students. A 1954 national survey of high schools indicated interest in challenging gifted students. Concern for addressing the talents of advanced learners was again in the spotlight.

At the same time, others, not representing gifted education, were equally concerned about the lack of intellectual pursuits in the public schools. A new view of secondary curriculum emerged that satisfied both the quantitative requirements of social efficiency and the project aspect of activity-experience. Life adjustment curriculum, adopted by the majority of states in the mid-1940s, focused on preparing high school students for the social and vocational aspects of life but gave little attention to the intellectual aspects of school. Life adjustment proponents sought to replace traditional subjects with courses in "home living, vocational life, civic life, leisure life, and physical and mental health" (Douglas, as cited in Kliebard, 1995, p. 214).

Rejection of Anti-Intellectualism

The 1950s began with a severe reaction to the anti-intellectualism that this latest curriculum innovation represented. Professors in the academic disciplines castigated public educators in general and teacher educators specifically for underestimating the abilities of American students and limiting their opportunities for intellectual development. The economy was again undergoing major changes following World War II with more demand for well-educated people to fill the professional jobs. From a purely practical point of view, parents concerned with the lack of rigor in their children's education and the implications for opportunities in the new job market joined the chorus of dissent.

World War II had brought about a new respect for intellectual endeavors. President Franklin Roosevelt surrounded himself with advisors referred to as a "brain trust." In addition, citizens in the United States were well aware of the scientists who had created the atomic bomb and the escalating postwar technology race with the Soviet Union. With education in the throes of ideological confusion, increased interest in intellectual development for all students found concrete support with an important event during the second half of the decade.

THE SPUTNIK TRANSFORMATION: 1957

The 1957 launching of Sputnik by the Soviet Union quickly transformed the discussion of the educational crisis into action. The government was prepared to invest great amounts of money to turn the listing educational ship around. However, instead of giving the money to educators to fix the curriculum problems, the money went to those in academic departments of science and math at major universities.

The most talented students were sought to complete college degrees in the areas of math and science, but educational expectations were raised for all students. Hyman Rickover (as cited in Ravitch, 2000), credited with development of the atomic submarine and a vocal critic of the education system, believed that each child should be educated to the highest level. He observed, "Even the average child now needs almost as good an education as the average middle- and upper-middle class child used to get in the college-preparatory schools" (p. 362).

Subjects became the new codification. Efforts over most of the twentieth century to limit or alter the teaching of subjects such as English, science, math, history, and languages came to an end (Kliebard, 1995). While the focus of government intervention was initially on math and science, the disciplines in the humanities also received funding to develop new curriculum in those subjects. One notable example is a social studies curriculum entitled *Man: A Course of Study*, developed by Jerome Bruner (1966), that utilized inquiry teaching, an interdisciplinary approach, and project work.

New ways of thinking about teaching and learning were codified. In the 1960s, the terms *critical* and *creative thinking* became a common part of the educational lexicon. Hilda Taba (1962) developed a model of teaching that involved inductive thinking. Using this method, students organized information and made generalizations by making multiple observations, developing categories, and then doing deeper research into one of the categories. She also researched the use of questioning to elicit critical thinking in students.

In spite of the progress made, the new ways of teaching could not be sustained on a widespread level. The training for teachers did not keep pace with the curricular innovations that involved knowledge of subject matter and complex ways of teaching that were involved (Darling-Hammond, 1997). In addition, teachers could close their doors and continue their own ways of teaching much as they had done throughout the first half of the century (Cuban, 1993).

REVOLUTION AND CODIFICATION: 1960–1980

Focus on intellectual development of students that followed the launching of Sputnik was brief. By the mid-1960s through the mid-1970s, most of the gains that had been made in raising the intellectual level of American education were lost. The attention of the country was diverted to the Viet Nam war, the civil rights movement, protests on college campuses, and multiple political assassinations that, in rapid succession, took the lives of John F. Kennedy, Malcolm X, Martin Luther King Jr., and Robert Kennedy.

Educational Kaleidoscope

Educational memory was growing shorter. In the 1960s, within the ten short years that had seen progressivism's official passing, education passed through the furor over life adjustment curriculum and the intellectual gains following Sputnik's influence to arrive at the introduction of the open classroom. Inspired by the British primary schools and books such as *Summerhill* by A. S. Neill, open classrooms promoted schools "that would free children's imagination and creativity from deadening routines, tyrannical authority, and passive learning" (Cuban, 1993, p. 151). It was a concept that connected well with the social reconstructionist attitudes of the 1960s.

Open education had a brief lifespan accompanied by the requisite rearrangement of furniture. However, instead of merely removing the bolted chairs and desks from classroom floors as in the 1930s, entire walls were removed this time. New schools were built without walls between the rooms. Learning centers were set up, boxes of manipulatives for math were put on the shelves, audio equipment and filmstrip projectors were arranged for student use, and desks and chairs were organized into groups (Cuban, 1993).

Imagine the state of schools as the civil rights movement gained momentum. A minority of teachers struggled to establish open classrooms and find other like-minded teachers for support (Cuban, 1993). Some retained other progressive practices that included project curriculum. Other teachers in poor urban schools taught traditional curriculum using outdated textbooks.

Others, especially those teaching in high schools, continued their teacher-directed, teacher-centered pedagogy, while others were implementing life adjustment curriculum. Still others continued to implement teaching practices and materials that came out of the Sputnik era. At the same time, schools were still testing and tracking students into vocational, middle, or college-bound tracks.

Civil Rights Movement

The civil rights movement had an enormous impact on schools. With the *Brown v. Brown* decision in 1954, the Supreme Court agreed that school segregation was unconstitutional, opening the door to school integration as well as integration throughout society. Integration was slow and painful in the South, but the Civil Rights Act of 1965 empowered the courts and the federal government to demand more timely compliance in integrating schools. Integration gained speed.

The dual education system in the South had prevented poor black children from receiving the higher quality education available to white children. Yet, there was little understanding of the implications this would have on schools. Few plans had been made between the 1954 Supreme Court decision and the 1965 Civil Rights Act to accommodate the unprepared students who would enter schools. Schools were not prepared for the influx of impoverished, poorly prepared students that entered the schools during this time.

At the same time, many African Americans continued the migration from the South to northern cities that began in the 1940s. This became the new "urban crisis" (Ravitch, 2000, p. 383), as their children entered schools for which they had little preparation. Classrooms in the poorer urban schools that enrolled these children were often already overcrowded and lacked sufficient resources. High school students were tested and placed in low level or vocational tracks or life adjustment classes, when what they needed was rigorous instruction in basic skills of reading, writing, and mathematics (Ravitch, 2000). Younger students, also needing basic reading, writing, and math, entered open classrooms without the self-management skills required to navigate the choices.

The cost of the 1960s was becoming clear by 1975. Many schools had become chaotic as respect for teachers declined and discipline eroded. Many middle-class families had fled the city schools and moved to the suburbs. SAT scores had dropped significantly since 1963. The SAT panel reported that students were not able to read thoughtfully and critically, nor were they able to write well. College entrance requirements had been lowered and fewer students enrolled in advanced math and science classes (Ravitch, 2000).

GIFTED EDUCATION: 1950–2000 AND BEYOND

Concern for the intellectual quality of education for all students intersected in the late 1950s when both advanced and normal learners benefited from the curriculum innovations of the Sputnik era. During the late 1960s into the 1970s, however, the attention of educators became focused on disadvantaged students who lacked basic skills (Tannenbaum, 1986). While general education entered a "back to basics" movement, education for the gifted again received attention in the mid-1970s.

Guilford's 1950 Paper

Guilford's 1950 paper on creativity opened the possibilities of finding advanced children beyond the confines of the IQ test. Research increased on how to best serve the gifted, including ability grouping, acceleration, enrichment classes, and social concerns of gifted children. In 1969, a provision for funding for gifted education was added to the Elementary and Secondary Education Act. With newly available funding, those in gifted education focused on developing curriculum, teacher education, and preparing leadership for the field that continued throughout the 1970s (Tannenbaum, 1986).

Growth of Gifted Programs

With the infusion of federal money in the 1970s and 1980s, gifted programs were established across the country. A popular model was the pull-out enrichment program where groups of students met with a teacher once a week for a few hours or a whole day. Students studied topics with the whole group or carried out individual research projects on topics of personal interest. When funding for gifted programs declined in the early 1990s, pull-out programs were often replaced with consultant models in which the teacher of the gifted worked with classroom teachers to assist in differentiating curriculum.

From their inception, gifted programs have included an emphasis on the teaching of thinking skills and social-emotional development. Enrichment curriculum has included adaptations of Bloom's (1956) taxonomy, Meeker's (1979) application of Guilford's work, Joseph Renzulli's enrichment triad model (Tannenbaum, 1986), Gardner's (1985) multiple intelligences, and Sternberg's (1988) triarchic theory of intelligence. While each of these theories and frameworks found early homes in gifted education, some are now applied in general education.

Intellectual Intersection

The attention to intellectual development found in gifted education is beginning to intersect with general education in several ways. Carol Ann Tomlinson (1999) and others from gifted education have developed ways to differentiate curriculum in the regular classroom to meet the learning needs of gifted students. Others who work in general education have created curriculum development methods that assist teachers in developing curriculum that helps challenge the thinking of all learners. Grant Wiggins and Jay McTighe (1998) have developed Understanding by Design and H. Lynn Erickson (2006) focuses on concept-based teaching.

STANDARDS AND ASSESSMENT: 1990–2000 AND BEYOND

In the first decade of the twenty-first century, we have new codification that addresses standards and testing. During the era of social efficiency, Rugg (as cited in Cremin, 1961) described education as an "orgy of tabulation" (p. 157). In our current educational environment with the emphasis on testing, today's educators may relate to that statement. With echoes from the early 1900s and the 1970s, the No Child Left Behind Act of 2001 begins with a focus on disadvantaged children, "The purpose of this title is to ensure that all children have a fair, equal, and significant opportunity to obtain a high-quality education and reach, at a minimum, proficiency on challenging State academic achievement standards and state academic assessments" (2002).

While teacher preparation, curriculum, and instructional materials are all part of the No Child Left Behind Act, from a teacher's point of view, the focus has been on the assessments, measurements, and accountability systems. Many teachers find themselves treading water, barely staying afloat as they deal with test prep, test sophistication, walk-throughs, and value-added, that quantitative difference between the present and previous test score. Many ask, "How did this happen?" It has been coming for quite some time.

A Nation at Risk: 1983

The country faced a call to arms when *A Nation at Risk* was published in 1983 by the National Commission on Excellence in Education (NCEE). In an interesting disconnect between the federal government and the general public, Education Secretary H. T. Bell (as cited in Fiske, 2008) expected this report to "paint a rosy picture of education" (p. A27) and quiet those who claimed that education was in serious trouble.

Considering the state of education leading up to that time, it is unsurprising that the commission found little evidence of excellence. Using the militant language of the cold war, *A Nation at Risk* proclaimed that America had committed "an act of unthinking, unilateral educational disarmament . . . [by] squander[ing] the gains in student achievement made in the wake of Sputnik" (NCEE, 1983, p. 5). The report outlined the deficiencies in the education system and admonished educators at all levels, as well as parents and students, to take a serious role in changing the direction of education. *A Nation at Risk* began a new generation of educational reform.

Decade of Reform

The late 1980s and through the 1990s was a busy decade for school reform. In 1990, the first President George Bush and the nation's governors established national goals for education entitled Goals 2000. This laid the groundwork for Goals 2000: Educate America Act (1994) that was signed into law by President Bill Clinton on March 31, 1994.

Also in 1990, as globalization of the economy was beginning, the first Commission on the Skills of the American Workforce released a report on the declining jobs for low skilled workers (NCEE, 2000). As 2006 drew to a close, the National Center on Education and the Economy (NCEE) published another warning document. Drawing from Friedman's book, the *new* Commission on the Skills of the American Workforce issued a report entitled *Tough Choices or Tough Times* (NCEE, 2006) outlining the challenges that globalization present to our education system.

These reports express alarm about education not unlike earlier alarms that have punctuated the history of education. Societal and economic changes, now as then, require that our children have additional knowledge and skills to succeed in life. The need for better teaching methods and new education structures led to three waves of school reform during the late 1980s and throughout the 1990s.

The first wave included new emphasis on coursework and testing mandates, the second addressed improvements in teaching and teacher education, and the third focused on the development and use of more challenging standards (Darling-Hammond, 1997). Each wave of reform brought with it new codification embedded in new standards that guide teacher education and student learning.

There is good news in all of this. After several decades, attention to the teaching of thinking through curriculum and instruction, largely missing in general education since Sputnik, has reappeared in teaching standards for general and gifted teacher education and learning standards for P–12 general education students. The descriptions of each of these standards make clear the importance of teaching rigorous content and thinking skills.

Standards for Teacher Education

During the second wave of reform, standards became the new codification. The National Council for Accreditation of Teacher Education (NCATE), in cooperation with a variety of education associations, established new criteria for assessing programs in 2000. Through NCATE, standards were developed for teacher education programs to assure that teachers are prepared to design curriculum and instruction that include the teaching of rigorous content as well as thinking skills and social-emotional development.

Standards for elementary teachers fall under five categories: foundations of development, learning and motivation, curriculum, instruction, assessment, and professionalism. The curriculum standards state that candidates will "know, understand, and use fundamental concepts" in specific subject areas that include English language arts, science, mathematics, social studies, the arts, health, and physical education.

In the area of instruction, one of the standards focuses on thinking processes and states that teacher candidates understand and use teaching strategies that encourage the "development of critical thinking, problem solving, and performance skills" (NCATE, 2000, p. 8). Social-emotional growth is addressed in one of the professional standards stating the importance of establishing relationships with parents. Social-emotional factors are implicitly addressed in standards that mention collaboration, social interaction, and motivation.

P–12 Learning Standards

While standards were being developed to assess teacher education, states were developing learning standards that clarified what students from preschool to high school were to learn. The New York State Standards are an example of student standards that, like the NCATE Standards, emphasize both content and thinking skills. Each of the New York State Social Studies Standards begins, "Students will use a *variety of intellectual skills* [italics added for emphasis] to demonstrate their understanding of [each social studies content area]" (New York State Education Department, 1996). Standards in other content areas also include thinking. "Students will apply the knowledge and thinking skills of mathematics, science, and technology to address real-life problems and make informed decisions" (1996).

Standards for Gifted Education

New standards have codified knowledge and practice in gifted education. While the teaching of thinking skills and social-emotional learning has had a long history in gifted education, quality of preparation and implementation has differed widely. In 2006, the National Association for Gifted Children (NAGC), in collaboration with the Council for Exceptional Children (CEC), established national standards through NCATE for programs preparing teachers of the gifted. Several standards address both the cognitive and affective aspects of teaching advanced learners. One instructional standard states that teachers will "apply higher-level thinking and metacognitive models to content areas." Another standard that addresses cognitive elements states that teachers will "provide opportunities for individuals with gifts and talents to explore, develop, or research their areas of interest or talent." Social-emotional factors of learning are addressed in several standards.

Codification for All Teachers and All Students

The standards for both teachers and learners have led to a preoccupation with standardized testing that has caused many to grow weary of standards. Yet, embedded within the standards are the keys to raising the level of teaching and learning for all students. The codification of thinking and social-emotional learning that many educators in earlier times struggled to incorporate into their methodologies are found in standards for both general and gifted education. This codification includes critical thinking, problem solving, performance skills, intellectual skills, social-emotional (factors), metacognition, and higher-level thinking.

These intellectual skills have been found at the heart of the burning questions in American education since Horace Mann. Why should we teach intellectual skills? How can we best teach intellectual skills? Who should learn intellectual skills? While these questions have not yet been sufficiently answered, now, in the twenty-first century, we need to consider additional questions that address intellectual and social-emotional aspects of teaching and learning. How do we balance the teaching of intellectual skills with the responsibility to help students develop qualities of character within the teaching of meaningful content? How do we make such complex teaching and learning accessible to all teachers and students?

SUMMARY

After surveying more than a century of school reform, debate, and theoretical argument, it is clear that it is much easier to rearrange furniture and remove walls than to make comparable adjustments to thinking and to the teaching practices that flow from that thinking. Horace Mann's vision of education included both the moral and the intellectual. Historically, however, education has been dominated by a dialectic point of view stating that there are only two purposes for education—intellectual development or social aspects of education (Taba, 1962, p. 21).

Those who constructed methodologies based on either viewpoint developed codification that reflects their philosophy. The viewpoint that intellectual development was to be accomplished through the teaching of basic skills and selected disciplines with less concern for "education for democratic citizenship, moral values, . . . or social problems" (Taba, 1962, p. 21) dominated American education in the nineteenth century.

With the turn to the twentieth century, those who held the second viewpoint, that the learner must be considered and that "education has a constructive role to play in shaping the society" (Taba, 1962, p. 22), instituted a wide variety of progressive reforms. Dewey and others saw the importance of both intellectual and moral aspects of education, while yet others used the emerging field of mental measurement to sort students into educational programs that focused on either the intellectual or the social. Rarely did the two viewpoints come together in classrooms.

Following the launch of Sputnik, both general education and gifted education benefited for a brief time from interest in intellectually based curriculum. However, that focus was largely lost in the chaos of the 1960s as schools adjusted to serving educationally disadvantaged children in the aftermath of desegregation. While general education focused on basic skills, the teaching of thinking and social-emotional learning continued to be important elements in gifted education programs. New standards for teachers and students in both general and gifted education, established during the late 1990s and the first decade of the twenty-first century, include both intellectual and social-emotional learning.

In summing up educational history and looking toward the future, Linda Darling-Hammond (1997) has said, "If the challenge of the twentieth century was creating a system of schools that could provide minimal education and basic socialization for masses of previously uneducated citizens, the challenge of the twenty-first century is creating schools that ensure—for all students in all communities—a genuine right to learn" (p. 5).

At this point in history, the right to learn must include both intellectual and social-emotional purposes. What is needed now are ways to make the elements of this complex teaching and learning accessible to all teachers and all students.

2

What Is TIEL?

When traveling in unfamiliar territory, you need a new map. The intellectual and social-emotional demands of our rapidly changing world require that educators traverse new teaching terrain. Students from elementary to graduate school need to develop a wide range of intellectual skills that have often received limited attention in classrooms. These include the self-organization skills of decision making, planning, problem solving, creative thinking, and self-directed research, as well as the ability to search and use their memories. At the same time, compassion, social responsibility, and ethics need to be taught and nurtured. While these are certainly not new mountains and valleys in the educational landscape, crossing them has been infrequent and inconsistent.

Learning these intellectual skills and social-emotional characteristics is no longer optional. In the world in which our students are being educated, this topography can no longer be left only to that rare teacher who seems to naturally incorporate the deeper intellectual and social-emotional aspects of learning into his or her teaching. All teachers and their students need access to fundamental knowledge that can promote thinking and emotional learning.

CODIFICATION OF COMPLEX TEACHING AND LEARNING

TIEL stands for *teaching for intellectual and emotional learning*. The TIEL Curriculum Design Model (often referred to simply as the TIEL Model) codifies intellectual and social-emotional processes that are necessary in complex teaching and learning. The TIEL Model provides educators with a map that guides them in developing curriculum, instruction, and a learning environment that better prepares students with the complex skills they will need in the expanded educational and vocational landscape.

The TIEL Model is a tool that scaffolds the complex teaching and learning required in our newly flattened world. The TIEL Model brings together intellectual and social-emotional elements of teaching and learning that lie at the core of the complex pedagogy that has been described in both gifted and general teacher education literature (Darling-Hammond, 1997; Dewey, 1964; Hargreaves, 1997; Martin, 1995; Ornstein, 2003).

Complex teaching and learning involves the conscious integration of intellectual and social-emotional processes with subject matter. Complex curriculum is rigorous and relevant including opportunities for students to make decisions, plan, organize, and self-evaluate. Metacognition is another important aspect of complex teaching and learning. Metacognition involves helping students think about and understand their thinking and learning.

However, complex teaching and learning is not solely about intellectual skills. Complex pedagogy devotes equal attention to social-emotional learning. This "nurturance of the spirit" to which Darling-Hammond (1997, p. 31) referred must be skillfully woven into the tapestry of intellectual learning. Teaching that includes both intellectual and social-emotional aspects of learning can help children develop into "humane and decent people" (p. 31) who can make ethical decisions, show empathy to fellow human beings, and appreciate the differences of others.

The TIEL Curriculum Design Wheel

Teaching for intellectual and emotional learning is graphically represented by the TIEL Curriculum Design Wheel (often referred to simply as the TIEL Wheel). The color-coded graphic codifies intellectual and social-emotional components required for complex teaching and learning. This visual representation of the components of thinking and qualities of character provides a visual and semantic scaffold for complex teaching and learning (see figure 2.1).

Like most maps, the TIEL Wheel provides important visual and verbal information. The titles, *Thinking Operations* and *Qualities of Character*, identify each half of the model. The TIEL Wheel is divided into ten segments that represent five cognitive and five social-emotional processes. Ralph Waldo Emerson (1990) has said that "character is higher than intellect" (p. 91). Therefore, I chose to organize the TIEL Wheel with the five sections that represent qualities of character placed in the upper half of the model and the five cognitive or intellectual processes placed in the lower half.

Each of the ten sections includes a title naming the thinking operation or quality of character that is represented. *Evaluation* is an example of a thinking operation, while *ethical reasoning* is an example of the corresponding quality of character. Listed under each title are several subskills that students need to

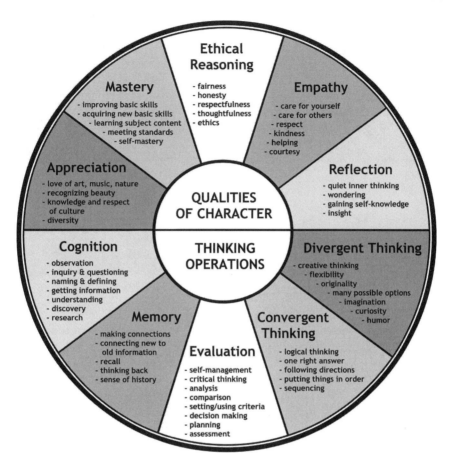

color key:

pink	Cognition & Reflection
blue	Memory & Empathy
green	Evaluation & Ethical Reasoning
yellow	Convergent Thinking & Mastery
orange	Divergent Thinking & Appreciation

Figure 2.1. TIEL Curriculum Design Wheel (detailed).

learn and that teachers need to teach. For example, within the thinking operation *cognition*, some of the subskills are observation, inquiry and questioning, naming and defining, gathering information, understanding, discovery, and research.

Additional TIEL Visuals

In addition to the TIEL Wheel, a second graphic representation was effectively used by each of the teachers throughout the research described in this

Qualities of Character

Reflection	Empathy	Ethical Reasoning	Mastery	Appreciation

Quiet inner thinking
Wondering
Awareness
Gaining self-
   knowledge
Insight
	Caring for yourself
	Caring for others
	Caring about your work
	Kindness
	Helping
	Courtesy
		Fairness
		Honesty
		Respectfulness
		Thoughtfulness
		Ethical decision
		   making
			Improving basic skills
			Acquiring new
			   basic skills
			Learning subject
			   content
			Meeting standards
			Self-mastery
				Love of art, music,
				   literature, and
				   nature
				Recognizing beauty
				Developing knowledge
				   and respect of
				   cultures
				Appreciating diversity

Thinking Operations

Cognition	Memory	Evaluation	Convergent Production	Divergent Production

Inquiry & questioning
Observation
Gathering
   information
Research
Discovery
Naming
Defining
	Making connections
	Making memories
	Recall
	Thinking back
	Sense of history
		Self-management
		Critical thinking
		Analysis
		Stating evidence
		Setting & using
		   criteria
		Decision making
		Planning
		Judgment
		Assessment
			Logical thinking
			One right answer
			Following directions
			Putting things
			   in order
				Creativity
				Flexibility
				Originality
				Risk taking
				Seeing options
				Sense of humor
				Curiosity

color key: pink   Cognition & Reflection
               blue   Memory & Empathy
               green   Evaluation & Ethical Reasoning
               yellow   Convergent Thinking & Mastery
               orange   Divergent Thinking & Appreciation

Figure 2.2.   TIEL bulletin board charts.

book. A set of ten charts, corresponding to the ten segments on the TIEL Wheel, was developed and used in the classrooms (see figure 2.2). In various configurations, they were used to create TIEL bulletin boards that provided an additional vehicle to facilitate discussion among teachers and students as they integrated the TIEL Model into their thinking and learning.

PHILOSOPHY AND PSYCHOLOGY

The TIEL Wheel graphically brings together elements from the fields of psychology and educational philosophy to form this scaffolding. These are the dominant disciplines in the emerging field of critical thinking (Paul, 1995). The thinking operations in the lower portion of the TIEL Wheel originate in the structure of intellect theory developed by J. P. Guilford (1977). The thinking operations are *cognition, memory, evaluation, convergent production,* and *divergent production.* The social-emotional aspects of teaching and learning found in the upper portion of the TIEL Wheel are adapted from Dewey's (1964) writings. The qualities of character include *reflection, empathy, ethical reasoning, mastery,* and *appreciation.* These will be discussed in depth later in the chapter.

Mary Meeker (1979), as part of her work in adapting Guilford's model to educational uses, assigned colors to each of the five operations. The colors serve two purposes in the TIEL Wheel. First, they suggest relationships that exist between the thinking processes and the qualities of character. Second, the colors make the TIEL Model visually accessible to both teachers and their students. Artist Elizabeth Murray spoke of the "physicality of color" (Smith, 2007). She painted in bright, bold colors on large canvases shaped with rolling curves and sinking dips that give a sense of physical immediacy. Similarly, color brings the abstract invisible processes of thinking and social-emotional learning into the visible present and helps students understand their thinking and learning.

John Dewey

Both Dewey and Guilford contributed a great deal to educational theory during the twentieth century. Dewey, long associated with progressive education, taught at the University of Chicago at the turn of the nineteenth century and later at Teachers College, Columbia University. Dewey's many volumes of writings share his ideas about every aspect of education, including, but certainly not limited to, thinking, learning, teaching, development of social-emotional characteristics, and how all of these should impact how children are taught.

While Dewey's (1964) ideas have been in and out of fashion, many are common practice in some of today's classrooms. He advocated that a child's education be child-centered. This includes experiential hands-on learning, project-based learning, and opportunities for children to plan their work. His vision of education included fostering collaborative learning among children, building relationships with the community, and preparing students with the thinking skills and social-emotional characteristics needed to maintain a democracy.

J. P. Guilford

Guilford's main contribution to educational theory occurred during the mid-twentieth century as Dewey's life was drawing to a close. While Dewey was an educational practitioner with interests in both intellectual and social-emotional aspects of learning, Guilford was a psychologist and a researcher whose work focused on intelligence. During World War II, he worked with the United States Air Force Psychological Unit to help determine why so many pilots failed flight training. He helped in constructing aptitude tests that assessed multiple abilities found to be necessary in flying an airplane.

Guilford was a pioneer in seeing intelligence as multiple factors. The structure of intellect theory, a three-part theory that includes *contents, products,* and *operations (thinking processes),* emerged from Guilford's (1977) research. Examined separately, each of the three parts of the theory provides insight into the contents and processes involved in learning, performance, and production of new ideas and materials.

The TIEL Model utilizes the *operations* that define thinking processes. It is helpful, however, to have a basic understanding of the *contents, products, operations* to place the *thinking operations* in context and to more fully understand the TIEL Model. Therefore, I will briefly review the three major components. The operations will be discussed in more depth later in the chapter.

Contents

The *contents* dimension of structure of intellect theory describes the "kinds of information" (Guilford, 1977, p. 14) being processed. The four kinds of information, or ways of knowing, included in the *contents* component are *figural, semantic, symbolic,* and *behavioral.* These four kinds of content are reflected in Gardner's (1985) multiple intelligences theory.

Figural refers to information that is concrete or perceived. This first form of information involves actual objects or representations of actual objects such as a picture of an actual object. In Gardner's (1985) theory, figural information can be found in dance and sports, the body-kinesthetic domain; visual art, the visual-spatial domain; and working with living organisms, the naturalist domain.

Where figural refers to that which is concrete, *semantic* refers to the abstract. Semantic information involves language that expresses meaning as described in Gardner's linguistic intelligence. Since language forms a large part of the foundation for learning, much of schooling is focused on the mastery of semantic information and skills. The majority of a student's day is spent learning linguistically the reading and writing skills needed to learn in other disciplines.

Symbolic information "stands for something else" (Guilford, 1977, p .19). Numbers, letters, musical notation, or mathematical symbols when used in combination to represent a concept are examples of symbolic information. Symbolic information is important in the musical and logical-mathematical domains. Finally, *behavioral* information refers to understanding yourself and others. This area of Guilford's contents corresponds to the interpersonal and intrapersonal domains described by Gardner.

Products

Products describe the "kinds of structures that information takes" (Guilford, 1977, p. 25). As in the contents and operations parts of the theory, there are several kinds of products. These include *units, classes, relations, systems, transformations,* and *implications.* Any of the products can be found in any of the content areas. For example, a *unit* is one object in any of the contents. It can be figural such as an actual tree or a picture of a tree. It can be semantic, as in the word "tree" or symbolic, as in a graphic representation of a tree. *Classes* involve grouping similar objects into categories. *Relations* involve making connections between two or more objects. For example, a large circle is to a small circle as a large square is to a small square.

Systems refer to a number of units and relationships integrated into a whole. Guilford refers to systems as the most complex structure that information takes since it involves multiple units and relationships. School systems, buildings, governments, or a simple diorama are examples of systems. *Transformations* occur when an object is used in a new or unexpected way. *Implications,* the final product, involves vision or seeing what is not visible or not yet there. Much of Albert Einstein's work involved implications.

Operations

The operations component of Guilford's theory forms the lower half of the TIEL Wheel. The *operations* serve an intermediary role between contents and products. Tannenbaum (1986) explained that the *operations* are the different ways a learner processes any kind of information to develop products that can take many forms.

All three major components of Guilford's theory—*operations, contents*, and *products*—are valuable in understanding teaching and learning. However, the five operations—*cognition, memory, evaluation, convergent production*, and *divergent production*—provide a useful framework for understanding the fundamental thinking processes teachers need to address in their curriculum. The operations describe simply and clearly the processes used for learning within any content area or discipline. The following section will define the operations within the context of the TIEL Model.

A FRAMEWORK TO GUIDE COMPLEX
TEACHING AND LEARNING

While the underlying theories that form the TIEL Model are not new, connecting the concepts visually provides a fresh perspective on teaching and learning. In the following sections, I define each of the components of the TIEL Model in more detail, explain the relationship between each intellectual component and the corresponding quality of character or social-emotional component, and give examples of questions that can assist teachers in planning more complex learning activities for their students.

Cognition and Reflection

Reflection goes hand in hand with *cognition*. Dewey (1964) connected the intellectual skill of observation, important in acquiring information, to reflection.

He stated that "there can not be observation in the best sense of the word without reflection, nor can reflection fail to be an effective preparation for observation" (p. 196).

Cognition

Cognition, the process of getting information, includes the skills of observation, research, discovery, knowing, and understanding (Guilford, 1977). Meeker (1979) added "awareness, rediscovery, recognition of information in various forms, and comprehension" to the definition (p. 14). Cognition is about recognizing and obtaining information and, therefore, requires content. The TIEL Wheel, as a guide to designing curriculum, leaves no room for debate concerning the importance of meaningful content. Children need to observe, research, discover, and understand subject matter found in the disciplines of math, literature, science, social studies, music, and art.

The thinking operation, *cognition,* helps teachers think in new ways about how they plan for students to obtain information. Those learning to become teachers need to see planning not simply as the sequencing of interesting activities, but as a means to help students develop the intellectual skills of questioning, gathering information, observing, and researching while learning meaningful, coherent content. Each of these skills leads students to discovery, understanding, and knowing.

Using the TIEL framework as a guideline for curriculum planning helps teachers ask themselves important questions as they plan. How will I plan for students to gather information in ways that will help them develop understanding of this topic? What questions will I ask that will help students develop a variety of thinking skills? What questions might students ask about this topic?

Reflection

Reflection is the act of wondering, questioning, and contemplating. Dewey (1991) said that reflective thinking is "troublesome." It requires "overcoming the inertia that inclines one to accept suggestions at their face value" (p. 13).

Reflection involves components found in both the top and the bottom of the TIEL Wheel. When teachers are reflective they think holistically. They go beyond rational problem solving (Zeichner & Liston, 1996) to seeking solutions through intuition, emotion, and passion (Greene, as cited in Zeichner & Liston, 1996). Reflection helps you learn about yourself as you are learning about your teaching. Yet, reflection should not begin and end with the teacher.

Students also need to learn to reflect, to "suspend judgment until further inquiry" (Dewey, 1991, p. 13). The TIEL Wheel visually reminds teachers to plan opportunities for their students to reflect on their learning. How can I plan for my students to reflect on the information and concepts they are learning? How can learning this content help students learn about themselves? How can I help students reflect on the intellectual and social-emotional processes of their learning? How can I help my students develop the capacity to wonder?

Memory and Empathy

Empathy emerges from *memory*. To feel compassion for another means that "one must draw upon one's own capacity . . . one's own experience" (Jersild, 1955, p. 127). It is through remembering experiences of caring, either in reality or sometimes vicariously through observing the experiences of others, that we ourselves learn to be caring individuals.

Memory

Memory is the glue that allows us to use our experiences to learn. Ewald Hering, a nineteenth-century physiologist, describes memory as "a binding and unifying force" and says that "we owe to memory almost all that we either have or are" (as cited in Schacter, 1989, p. 75). Through use of memory we are able to recall, memorize, and make connections, combine information, and recognize relationships (Bloom, 1956, Guilford, 1977; Sternberg, 1985). While recall can be considered a "lower order use of the mind" (Paul, 1995, p. 55), the storage function of memory also allows us to make connections that are important in learning new information and higher level thinking.

Memory, when linked with understanding, is an important skill to build. However, much of education has centered largely on how much information can be accurately recalled and restated with little attention to students' understanding of the underlying concepts. For many educators, Bloom's taxonomy, with its hierarchical categories of thinking that begin with knowledge and end with evaluation, became a guide out of the lower level thinking rut. While memory was involved in the more complex thinking at the higher levels, it was the "major psychological process" (Bloom, 1956, p. 62) involved in the knowledge category. Seemingly relegated to the lower end of the thinking spectrum, memory work has been neglected in school to the extent that many students do not have a command of basic multiplication or addition facts.

Technology has further lowered the value of stock in memory. The technological equipment at our disposal has eliminated much of the need for developing recall abilities. Information is a computer click away through the Internet, and cell phones have rendered the memorization of phone numbers obsolete. Yet, all technology is not detrimental to memory. While many students have never memorized a poem, most have lyrics to their favorite songs well in mind, with continuous exposure through their iPod headphones.

The TIEL framework helps restore the importance of *memory* in the process of teaching and learning. TIEL helps teachers recognize that memory goes well beyond the recall of information and encourages a broader range of questions as teachers plan learning experiences for their students. How can this concept be connected to something that is familiar to the students? How can students develop their memory skills within this content area? How can I help students make connections between concepts and thinking processes across multiple subject areas?

Empathy

Dewey (1964) states that the development of human sympathy, or *empathy* and caring, is an important "aim of education" (p. 197). While memory serves us academically, it also forms the well of caring in each of us. We draw on our own experiences in order to feel compassion for others. As we empathize with others, the connecting cues to our own experiences are strengthened and our capacity for empathy increases (Hoffman, 1991). Noddings (2003) points out that sharing the suffering of others contributes to our own fulfillment as human beings. Paul (1995) states that "empathetic understanding [is] necessary for a reasonable approach to living in a pluralistic society" (p. 129).

An awareness of memory as an important source of our feelings for self and others helps teachers consciously link the intellectual skills of memory to the emotional development of empathy. This awareness can help teachers understand more clearly how the life experiences of students can profoundly influence their learning and behaviors in the classroom. Jane Rowland Martin (1995) discusses the importance of caring and compassion in her philosophy of the schoolhome. Part of teaching and learning must include helping students to care for themselves as well as others, and to care for their work as well as the environment in which they live.

Questions that help teachers reflect on the teaching of empathy and caring include: How can students develop empathy during this study? What experiences have students had that will help them develop empathy for others and for themselves? How can I help the students care deeply about their work and the environment in which they live?

Evaluation and Ethical Reasoning

Evaluation and *ethical reasoning* hold center stage in complex teaching and learning. Ethical reasoning involves the same evaluative skills of setting criteria, weighing options, and self-evaluation, yet it is anchored by consideration for others.

Evaluation

Evaluation includes the critical thinking and self-organization skills involved in comparing, judging, and decision making using sound criteria (Doll, 1993; Guilford, 1977; Paul, 1995) that is commonly termed higher-order thinking.

The opportunity to choose motivates, opens opportunity for exploring options, and promotes self-directed learning. Many have written about the critical thinking skills included in evaluation. Marzano (1993), in his discussion of mental dispositions, states that the processes of decision making, planning, and self-evaluation "render any activity more thoughtful and more effective" (p. 158).

The critical thinking skills that are part of the TIEL component of *evaluation* help students transfer what they learn. Perkins pointed out that "the conscious and explicit use of decision making, planning, and self-evaluation serves as a bridge transferring those same skills to situations in life outside of school" (1995). Bain agrees, stating, "When students learn how to analyze ideas, make decisions using criteria, formulate a plan to accomplish a goal, and evaluate their own work, teachers prepare them to evaluate how they think and behave well beyond the classroom" (Bain, 2004, p. 94).

The TIEL Model makes visible the self-management skills of decision making, planning, and self-evaluation that are often expected, but infrequently taught in any explicit way. Learning opportunities that explicitly teach these intellectual skills help students develop into self-organized learners. Other terms used interchangeably with self-organization are self-management, self-direction, and self-regulation.

Questions that guide teachers in planning include the following: Where can students make decisions within this content study? How can I teach students to set criteria that will help them evaluate their work? What projects will provide an opportunity for teaching students how to plan?

Ethical Reasoning

Ethical reasoning, or to use Dewey's (1964) term, "unswerving moral rectitude" (p. 197), is evaluation anchored by qualities of character. Making ethical decisions requires the same evaluative skills of setting criteria, weighing options, planning, or evaluating one's actions. Yet, for reasoning to be ethical it must be combined with qualities of character that include empathy and appreciation.

The TIEL framework reminds teachers to dig deeply into content and ask the following questions. In the course of this study, where can children become aware of decisions based on honesty, respect, and fairness? How can I use group project work to help students develop capacity for ethical reasoning? Where in this study can students learn tolerance for the ideas and beliefs of others?

Convergent Production and Mastery

Convergent production is focused on the one right answer. It is related to *mastery* through emphasis on the mastery of information that calls for one answer, the effect on self-esteem and character development when mastery is not attained, and intellectual and emotional self-mastery.

Convergent Production

Guilford (1977) states that convergent production is a kind of productive thinking in which only one answer is considered correct. *Convergent production* is the focused production of information and is also involved in "retrieval of items of information from memory" in order to answer questions or solve problems (p. 109). Logical and deductive thinking, important to critical thinking (Paul, 1995), are also included in convergent thinking.

Many have pointed out that linear sequential thinking focused on one right answer is the predominate form of thinking addressed in our school system. Indeed, much of a student's day is filled with work that requires correct answers in math, spelling, reading, social studies, and science, often with limited understanding of the content that is studied. The greater portion of standardized testing is concerned with right answers whether in the form of multiple choice or short answers.

Nevertheless, there are questions that can help teachers consider the multiple aspects of convergent production. What facts are important for students to learn about this topic? Where can students practice sequencing and organizational skills in this study? How can I help students develop logical thinking skills?

Mastery

Mastery, found within the qualities of character, is linked to convergent production. Because assignments, assessments, and standardized testing require right answers, mastery is most often associated with convergent production in school. Mastery in school is usually perceived as meeting externally imposed requirements. Grades and test scores are examples that reflect a student's ability to meet external expectations.

Teachers need to consider the relationship between mastering school skills and the development of social-emotional characteristics. Teachers need to be aware of the effect on students who do not attain mastery in their school work. Students who experience repeated failure come to believe they cannot learn. For many students, feelings of confusion, frustration, and defeat contribute to a loss of confidence in themselves (Weiner, 1999). Others, who have already mastered the skills and materials taught at their grade level, can also experience feelings that inhibit the development of social-emotional characteristics that students need to be successful learners and grow into humane and decent people.

Teachers, however, cannot give students self-esteem. Students build self-esteem when they feel empowered as learners. Giving unfounded positive feedback does not help students develop the self-empowerment that comes from understanding their own thinking, organizing their own learning, and developing critical thinking skills. Paul (1995) asks, "What good is education for 'self-esteem' if it is based on the false assumption that we can 'give' students self-esteem by continually giving them positive feedback—while we ignore the skills and abilities the possession of which gives them a real sense of empowerment?" (p. 44).

Teachers need to be conscious of helping students develop social-emotional self-mastery as well as academic mastery. Emotional self-mastery comes through the same skills and abilities needed to feel empowered as a learner. These skills include reflection and learning how to make fair decisions. When students experience the power of planning and using carefully considered criteria to evaluate their own work, they develop emotional self-mastery as well as make academic progress.

Teaching self-mastery includes taking advantage of teaching moments when students can learn how to show empathy and appreciation for others as well as for themselves. When students persevere in their assignments and projects without giving up, they are developing emotional self-mastery. Teaching students the skills and abilities that will help them know they can learn strengthens both their academic and social-emotional mastery.

Teachers who are conscious of the multiple meanings of mastery ask themselves the following questions. How can I help this student develop mastery in academic skills in order to help her develop self-confidence as a learner? How can I teach my students the skills they need to feel empowered? How can I encourage him not to give up? How can I support students' development of personal mastery in the area of social-emotional qualities?

Divergent Production and Appreciation

Divergent production connects to *appreciation* through creativity. Experiencing creativity leads to an increase in feeling comfortable with difference, whether it is a difference in cultures, people, or the natural world around us.

Divergent Production

Divergent production involves the production of information that results in generating alternatives with an "emphasis on variety and quality of output" (Meeker, 1979, p. 20). "Inventing, designing, contriving, composing" (Guilford, 1968, p. 78) are some of the creative behaviors that Guilford described. Divergent production includes creative thinking and risk-taking. It is the kind of fluent, flexible, imaginative thinking that students need to succeed in our complex world.

Divergent thinking and production are necessary for complex learning to take place. Creative project work provides opportunities for both intellectual skills and social-emotional processes to be developed. When students create a project, they are involved in research, decision making, planning, and self-evaluation.

Collaboration skills are learned when a group works together on a creative project. Group collaboration provides opportunities for students to learn empathy and appreciation for their classmates. Creative projects encourage the use of imagination to see alternatives in solving problems. Students learn in a real situation what it means to be flexible and to make fair and ethical decisions.

Maxine Greene (1988), a tireless advocate of giving students opportunities to imagine, says, "When people cannot name alternatives, imagine a better state of things, share with others a project of change, they are likely to remain anchored or submerged, even as they proudly assert their autonomy" (p. 9).

The TIEL Model clarifies the importance of preparing students with the capacity to think in ways that will not keep them "anchored or submerged." They need the reflective skills to recognize when change is needed and the divergent thinking skills to imagine a different way of doing things in their own lives or within the larger world.

Teachers need to ask themselves how they can help students develop the divergent thinking ability to "seek alternative ways of being, to look for openings . . . to discover new possibilities" (Greene, 1988, p. 2). How can I plan for students to use their creativity within this content area? Where can I teach students how to think flexibly and take risks? How can I provide a space for students to explore their imaginations? How can I design assessment that takes into account divergent thinking and production?

Appreciation

Appreciation and *divergent production* have a reciprocal relationship. Opportunities for divergent thinking help students acquire flexibility, risk-taking, and imagination. An ability to think openly and imaginatively helps students develop appreciation for a world of difference. Dewey described this quality as developing a love of beauty in nature and art. The TIEL Wheel expands this description to include cultures and circumstances of others that may be different from what we know. In a test-saturated school system where too few schools place priority on art, music, and drama, the TIEL Model reminds educators of the importance of helping students develop aesthetic appreciation (McNamee et al., 2008).

Teachers need to ask themselves how they can plan opportunities for students to learn appreciation. How can this study help students develop an appreciation for differences and diversity? How can I help students develop an appreciation for their own differences? How can art, music, and drama support the learning of content while, at the same time, helping students develop an appreciation for the arts?

Convergent and Divergent Thinking

It is useful to discuss the thinking operations of *convergent* and *divergent production* together. Some students prefer one of these kinds of thinking over the other. While some are excited about designing a new planet for an imaginary solar system, others would prefer another page of straightforward computation in the math book. When teachers understand these two thinking operations, they have more insight into the learning abilities of their students and they are able to help their students understand their own learning.

A balance of learning activities that involve these two kinds of thinking is needed in the classroom. Understanding convergent and divergent thinking helps teachers plan activities that include both kinds of thinking. Understanding both kinds of thinking supports the kind of balanced planning that allows teachers to assure their students that their intellectual needs are being taken into account. If a learning activity involves a kind of thinking that a student finds uncomfortable, the teacher can guarantee that the next activity features more of her favorite kind of thinking. At the same time, teachers are able to explain to students the importance of developing their skills in all the thinking operations.

Here are some examples of questions teachers can ask themselves to help them plan learning activities that provide opportunities for both convergent and divergent thinking. How can the students learn this content through both convergent and divergent learning experiences? How can I design assessment that takes into account both convergent and divergent learning? How can developing mastery help students develop appreciation? How can appreciation of a new topic help students develop mastery? The chapters to follow provide examples of how the TIEL components are used to plan curriculum.

ACCESSIBILITY

The TIEL Model addresses the two purposes of education, the intellectual and the moral or character aspects of teaching and learning, that have existed since the beginning of public schooling in America. While there have been times when each purpose has been emphasized in education, neither the teaching of thinking nor social-emotional learning has been easily applied with any widespread consistency in classrooms for all learners across all content areas. For these to become part of daily classroom life, teachers need access to the underlying intellectual and social-emotional structures that form the foundation of these two historical educational purposes. Yet, words alone have not proved sufficient. How can the thinking operations and qualities of character found in the TIEL Model be made less abstract and more accessible to teachers and students in the classroom?

Teachers understand how visual materials facilitate communication and support learning. Learning to read and write is supported by visible examples of the alphabet in a classroom; children are assisted in learning numerical sequencing by a number line on the classroom wall; and many teachers use a word wall to visually help students learn vocabulary and spelling found in text throughout all their subjects.

Learning the unfamiliar language of thinking and social-emotional learning of the TIEL Model is similarly facilitated by using visuals. Three different kinds of visuals are used to learn and teach thinking operations and qualities of character. These include bulletin boards and charts, TIEL Wheel posters, and puppets representing each of the thinking processes.

TIEL Bulletin Board

Each of the four teachers whose stories are told in this book created a TIEL bulletin board in the classroom to support the discussion of thinking and make it less abstract (see figure 2.3). The bulletin boards varied in size and placement in the classrooms. Each bulletin board was divided into five sections, each in one of the five TIEL colors—pink, blue, green, yellow, and orange.

At the top of each bulletin board section, the teachers placed two charts. One chart named the thinking operation and the other named the quality of character represented by that color. For example, at the top of the pink *cognition* portion of the bulletin board was one chart labeled *Cognition* and another labeled *Reflection*. Each chart included a list of subskills within each category.

color key: pink   Cognition & Reflection
                blue   Memory & Empathy
                green   Evaluation & Ethical Reasoning
                yellow   Convergent Thinking & Mastery
                orange   Divergent Thinking & Appreciation

Figure 2.3.   TIEL bulletin board in Erica's classroom.

The TIEL bulletin board facilitates metacognition. Students were able to discuss the thinking they used in their learning activities. The teachers referred to the TIEL bulletin board as they taught the students how to do research, set criteria, make decisions, plan, and evaluate. They used the bulletin board to help facilitate discussions of the relationships that exist between the individual self-organization skills found within the thinking operation of *evaluation*. For example, developing criteria for evaluation precedes assessment and provides a guideline for the project.

Relationships also exist between thinking operations. The bulletin boards helped the teachers point out these relationships to their students. For example, gathering accurate information through research, within the *cognition* operation, must occur before making effective decisions found in the thinking operation, *evaluation*. To maximize learning, teachers need to determine what the students already know about a topic, *memory*, before presenting new information, *cognition*.

TIEL Curriculum Design Wheel

In addition to bulletin boards, large laminated posters of the TIEL Curriculum Design Wheel help make the thinking and social-emotional processes visible. Each teacher had a large poster of the TIEL Wheel showing only the titles of the thinking operations and social-emotional processes (see figure 2.4). This simple colorful visual, without the subskills, was often located on a wall in the carpeted area of the classroom where teacher-directed lessons took place. Teachers and students could easily refer to the poster as they discussed thinking skills during the lesson.

TIEL Friends Puppets

The TIEL Friends puppets also make the thinking operations and qualities of characters understandable for children and teachers as well. Six puppets represent the five thinking processes. Each thinking process is represented by one puppet, except for *evaluation*, which is represented by two, because decision making occurs between at least two possibilities. Each puppet has yarn hair and clothes that match the color of the thinking operation it represents. Connie Cognition is pink; Molly Memory is blue; Elmer and Ellie Evaluation are green; Christopher Convergent is yellow; and Daniel Divergent is orange (see figure 2.5).

The chapters to follow provide examples of how the TIEL components, with the visuals, are used to plan and teach curriculum that includes the self-organization skills of decision making, planning, and self-evaluation.

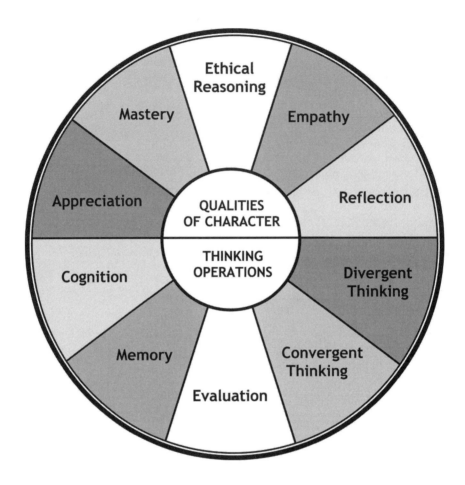

color key:
pink	Cognition & Reflection
blue	Memory & Empathy
green	Evaluation & Ethical Reasoning
yellow	Convergent Thinking & Mastery
orange	Divergent Thinking & Appreciation

Figure 2.4.   TIEL Curriculum Design Wheel (titles only).

Connie Cognition (pink)   Molly Memory (blue)   Daniel Divergent (orange)

Elmer & Ellie Evaluation (green)   Christopher Convergent (yellow)

Figure 2.5.   TIEL Friends puppets.

SUMMARY

The new educational landscape requires a new map. The TIEL Wheel provides a guide for the complex teaching and learning required in today's classrooms. Teaching for intellectual and emotional learning, the TIEL Model, brings together the intellectual as well as the social-emotional aspects of teaching and learning. Based on the work of psychologist J. P. Guilford and educational philosopher John Dewey, TIEL is made up of five thinking operations and five qualities of character. Three visuals—bulletin boards, posters, and puppets—make the abstract thinking and social-emotional processes represented by the TIEL Wheel more accessible to teachers and students. When teachers understand the components of teaching and learning represented by the TIEL Model, they are better able to understand their students' learning. They can plan curriculum balanced between the intellectual and the social-emotional components that lie at the heart of complex teaching and learning.

II

CONSCIOUSNESS

con·scious·ness (kon'shəs nis), *n*. 6. the mental activity of which a person is aware as contrasted with unconscious mental processes.

—Webster's Unabridged Dictionary

To prepare students to make decisions, plan projects, self-evaluate their work, and be aware of their thinking and how their actions affect others, teaching must be a conscious act. In order to teach thinking, teachers must be conscious of thinking processes, the range of thinking processes, and how to include the teaching of thinking into daily curriculum. Awareness of the social-emotional characteristics of students often comes more easily due to the immediacy of visible behavior. Understanding both intellectual and social-emotional components of learning and teaching helps teachers explicitly plan opportunities for both into their curriculum.

CHAPTER 3: CONSCIOUSNESS OF THINKING AND SOCIAL-EMOTIONAL PROCESSES

How do teachers become conscious of thinking and social-emotional processes? Teachers first need to become aware of the opportunities for teaching the self-organization skills that are already present in their classrooms. This chapter tells how Ted used the TIEL Curriculum Design Model to recognize these spaces and plan curriculum that gave his students new opportunities to understand their thinking and learning.

CHAPTER 4: TEACHER AND STUDENT UNDERSTANDING

What happens when teachers become more conscious of thinking and social-emotional processes? Teachers change their thinking and teaching, and students become more empowered learners. Because of Ted's changes in his teaching, the students were able to discuss planning, make decisions, and understand how to self-evaluate their project work.

3

Consciousness of Thinking and Social-Emotional Processes

> The mind needs ordered information to keep itself ordered. As long as it has clear goals and receives feedback, consciousness keeps humming along.
>
> —Mihaly Csikszentmihalyi

The TIEL Curriculum Design Model is a valuable tool that teachers can use to help students become more conscious of their thinking and learning. First, however, teachers need to develop a deeper consciousness of the opportunities to include the teaching of thinking and social-emotional processes within their curriculum.

Developing consciousness is not only for the novice who is beginning to learn to teach. Many experienced teachers can also benefit from becoming more conscious of teaching in ways that encourage thinking and social-emotional learning. When teachers have a deeper awareness of these processes, they are able to more purposefully include them into their planning. When teachers take full advantage of opportunities to teach thinking and social-emotional skills, they empower students as learners.

Teachers need help in developing an awareness of the opportunities that exist in their own classrooms to teach the thinking skills and qualities of character needed today. National teacher education standards and K–12 state learning standards include intellectual skills, critical thinking, and problem solving. While K–12 standards include little about social-emotional learning, teacher education standards more explicitly address social development and social interaction. Nevertheless, instruction on how to teach thinking and foster social-emotional learning has been limited in teacher education programs. Therefore, teachers often feel unprepared to teach thinking processes or to address the affective domain of education.

DEVELOPING CONSCIOUSNESS

Ted was just such a teacher. Ted's third grade classroom was best described as an intellectual sanctuary. Turtles were stacked one on top of the other sunning themselves in an aquarium by the window. A rabbit hopped freely around the classroom, the wire door swinging wide to freedom just beyond the cage. The gray bunny seemed to mirror Ted's philosophy of education—that one learns by experience and through having many options. A carpet defined a large section in the back of the room where colorful books spilled out from the surrounding bookshelves. Charts and posters, swinging from two clotheslines stretched across the back of the room, were held in place by wooden spring-loaded clothespins. This archaeology of learning hinted at the work—past and present—that went on in the classroom, while pointing toward the future. It was a comfortable and intellectually enriching place to be.

Ted was an accomplished veteran teacher. Yet, with all the richness in his classroom, he was not fully aware of what was already in place that could help him teach students thinking and social-emotional skills more explicitly. He was equally unaware of what he *could* be doing to help students become more empowered learners. The TIEL Model helped Ted recognize what he was already doing and what more could be done to teach intellectual and social-emotional processes more consistently.

TEACHING SELF-MANAGEMENT SKILLS

By all appearances, Ted was teaching many of the *evaluation* skills included in the TIEL Model. *Evaluation*, a central thinking operation in the TIEL framework, includes the important self-management skills of decision making, planning, and self-evaluation. When these skills are explicitly taught, students become more self-directed, more self-motivated and take more responsibility for their learning. They become self-regulated learners.

Previous Work

I went to Ted's classroom before beginning our work together to speak with him and his students about how decision making, planning, and self-evaluation were used in project work. There was order and excitement as students were completing the final projects of the year that culminated their study of immigration. When I saw the lists of criteria hanging in his room, I assumed that Ted was teaching self-management skills in project work throughout the curriculum. All he needed was a general vocabulary that would help him see the patterns in teaching thinking processes across all subject areas.

Then I looked more carefully. The evidence for criteria setting displayed in his classroom focused only in the areas of reading and writing. For example,

- How does a good piece of writing look?
- What makes a book "just right" for you to read?

However, there were no references in the classroom to the ongoing immigration projects. I asked the students about how they made decisions and plans in their classroom work. They were not aware that they were planning, evaluating, and making decisions in the immigration project. Similarly, the students were unaware that they made plans, evaluated, and made decisions in their reading and writing work.

Teacher Awareness

Teacher awareness leads to student awareness. Just as Ted needed a vocabulary of thinking and social-emotional learning, the students also needed the vocabulary to help them see that the thinking skills of setting criteria, planning, and self-evaluating that they used in their reading and writing projects were the same skills involved in the social studies project. When the teacher understands the opportunities to teach thinking and social-emotional processes throughout the curriculum, these processes can be clearly taught. When the teacher is aware, the students can become aware.

In order to teach his students more clearly, Ted developed consciousness in three important ways.

- He became *aware* of how he was presently teaching self-organization skills in his classroom.
- He came to recognize how self-organization skills can be taught through *project work* in all subject areas.
- He recognized the *value* of explicitly teaching self-organization skills through project work in any subject.

CONSCIOUSNESS OF SELF-ORGANIZATION SKILLS

The opportunities for teaching self-organization skills permeated Ted's teaching of the reading and writing process. While he was aware of his efforts to teach the children decision making, planning, and self-evaluation within the context of these subjects, the TIEL framework helped him see how these processes fit within a wider range of thinking processes.

Reading

I asked Ted about how he taught decision making, planning, and self-evaluation. He replied, "The strategies of self-organization fit into all my curriculum organization." Immediately he gave examples from teaching reading,

"I try to make them planful as readers. They keep a list of what books they want to read next, they write down what they've read and how much they've read, they keep that organized. . . . They plan out how much they should read in one reading session."

Ted explained how the self-organization skills of decision making, planning, and self-evaluation fit into the work he was doing in reading. Students were learning to plan by listing their goals for becoming better readers. The goals helped them determine what they wanted to read next. The students recorded their progress, carefully stating how many books they read. They used that information to plan how much they should read in the following reading period.

Writing

Similarly, Ted saw how self-organization skills fit into the teaching of writing. The students selected ideas to develop into stories. Next, they planned their writing using an outline or a web. That was followed by a period of writing, editing, and revising. After several consultations with the teacher, the students produced a final piece for publication. When all the pieces were finished, the class held a publishing party where parents and other guests helped them celebrate.

EXPLICITLY TEACHING SELF-ORGANIZATION SKILLS IN READING AND WRITING

In learning something new, we begin where we are. For Ted, this meant applying self-organization skills more explicitly to the work in reading and writing. Ted felt that he taught his students to be planful readers and writers. Yet, as he learned more about the *evaluation* component of the TIEL Wheel, he saw how he could include the students more explicitly in planning and evaluation.

Self-Organization in Writing

Ted often gave his students verbal instructions that served as the criteria to evaluate a writing piece. He then posted these instructions on posters in the classroom (see figure 3.1). Now, Ted decided to put this information directly into the hands of his students. He designed a worksheet that both he and the students used for grading a final published piece of writing. *My Published Piece Grade* includes five criteria that the students used to determine if a piece of writing was ready to be shared (see figure 3.2).

- Is the writing of minimum length?
- Is the paper edited for spelling and punctuation?
- Is the writing focused on one topic?
- Is the writing piece interesting and complete?
- Does the writing look beautiful?

Writing Instructions

2 paragraphs
Spelling and punctuation
One topic
Interesting
Beautiful

Figure 3.1. Instruction chart for writing assignment.

Name_____ Date_____

MY PUBLISHED PIECE GRADE

[ ] My piece is at least three-fourths of a page if typed, more than a full page if handwritten, three poems or more, five jokes/riddles or more.

[ ] My piece is edited: correct spelling, periods, question marks, capital letters, commas.

[ ] My piece sticks to the topic that I set out to write about.

[ ] My piece sounds interesting and complete.

[ ] My piece looks beautiful.

You can earn 3 points for each, for a total of 15 points.

If You Earn	Your Grade
13-15 points	√+ ☺
10-12 points	√+
7-9 points	√☺
4-6 points	√
3-4 points	√- or Do Over
< 3 points	0 or do Over

Figure 3.2. *My Published Piece Grade* evaluation worksheet.

The students evaluated themselves on each criterion using a scale of one to three points. The bottom section of the evaluation sheet explains the total number of points required to earn a particular grade. Grades were expressed using a system that includes checks, check pluses, and check minuses.

Self-Organization in Spelling

Ted also designed a way to help students self-evaluate how they used spelling strategies. The worksheet, *What Do Good Spellers Do?*, included a list of strategies that a good speller would use (see figure 3.3). Preceding each

---

Name_____ Date_____

WHAT GOOD SPELLERS DO

Put a √ if you are already doing it, and a G (for Goal) if you
    know that it's something you need to work on.

[ ]   I try to spell unknown words.

[ ]   I do my best to get it right.

[ ]   I listen for sounds in the words.

[ ]   I learn how to spell words that I use in my writing.

[ ]   I use resources to help.

[ ]   I think of another word it may be like.

Based on your checklist, write a reflection about your
spelling.

_____
_____
_____
_____
_____
_____

Figure 3.3. *What Do Good Spellers Do?* evaluation worksheet.

strategy is a place to write a check if the student was already doing it or a G to indicate a goal that needed work. There is also a place for students to write a reflection about their spelling. As an example, "I use resources to help me spell words. I need to listen better to the sounds in the words."

CONSCIOUSNESS OF SELF-ORGANIZATION SKILLS IN OTHER SUBJECTS

Opportunities to teach self-organization skills exist throughout the curriculum. In science, students can plan an experiment. In social studies, students can decide how they will design a project. In math, students can evaluate whether a math problem is right or wrong as well as decide which strategy to use in solving a problem.

Immigration Study I

In the spring of the year before the research began, I visited Ted's classroom. The class was concluding their study of immigration and the students were finishing their projects. I asked, "How did you teach the students to make decisions and plan their projects?" His answer was vague. The students were to make cardboard sculptures having "something to do with immigration. It had to depict some scene about immigration." He explained that decision making consisted of *not* telling them what to make, but letting them "construct what they wanted from cardboard."

The immigration project involved three phases. First, the students completed the sculptures individually. Then they had to choose a partner and join their two projects together. The criterion Ted gave the students for choosing a partner was "to ask someone whose work would connect well with your work." For the final phase, the students in the newly formed partnerships wrote a story together about their joined projects.

Planning

There was little evidence of teaching the students planning skills in the first immigration study. While setting criteria is the beginning of planning, there was no visible sign of criteria for the projects in the classroom. Charts hanging in Ted's classroom reminded the students of criteria to consider in the areas of reading and writing, yet criteria for evaluation of the immigration projects were not similarly explicit. Instead, Ted gave the students very general guidelines that instructed them to use cardboard to "make a scene about anything they wanted about immigration."

Teachers often make the assumption that students know how to plan. While Ted could articulate how he taught planning within reading and writing, planning in other subjects was an undefined term referring to an unstructured, unexplained process. Some students, often those who come from higher socio-economic backgrounds and who have had ample opportunity to make choices and plans in their lives outside of school, are highly self-directed in the classroom. They are able to plan and organize their work. Other students, regardless of socioeconomic background, are less self-organized and need more explicit teaching.

Ted, like many teachers, assumed that students knew how to plan. As the students worked, Ted circulated around the classroom asking questions based on that assumption. He asked, "What are you planning to do? What are you planning to work on?" While Ted was not yet teaching the students how to plan their projects, the opportunity for teaching self-organization skills existed and he was opening the conversation.

Decisions in Immigration Study I

The students were unaware of any discussion of decisions. They did not have worksheets that would help them understand the process of setting criteria to use in weighing options. He had not led them through a specific planning process. Understandably, they later had difficulty at each subsequent juncture of the project where making a thoughtful decision with another person was required.

Tom reported that he and his partner, Sam, wanted to do different things. Tom explained their disagreement, "I wanted people. Finally we came up with something that was part of my idea and part of his." The student teacher stepped in to help them connect their work. She suggested, "Put half of your idea and half of his idea together . . . that would make sense, sound good, and is believable." She helped them consider how to best combine the two projects. The elements important to making a decision eventually came together but not in an explicit way that the students could understand, discuss, or readily apply in a later situation.

Implicit Teaching of Self-Organization Skills

The teaching of self-organization skills was implicit in the first immigration study. Ted was not yet explicit about teaching his students self-organization skills outside of reading and writing. He was not yet transferring the self-management processes of decision making, planning, and self-evaluation to hands-on project work in other subjects. There were no charts in the classroom referring to the immigration projects. There were no lists of criteria outlining how the immigration sculptures would be evaluated.

There were no visual reminders of the decisions that needed to be made in the course of creating the sculptures or writing the stories. No calendar or planning chart visually guided the students toward the final due date of the projects or the dates for completing intermediary steps. Yet, the students successfully finished and shared their projects, in spite of a world of untapped learning that remained just below the surface.

Ted believed, and rightly so, that the strategies of self-organization fit into all of his curriculum organization. He commented, "Every work structure I have in here involves choices."

Nevertheless, the immigration study showed that Ted was missing an opportunity in social studies to explicitly teach students self-organization skills through project work.

TEACHING SELF-ORGANIZATION IN THIRD GRADE SOCIAL STUDIES PROJECTS

When Ted felt comfortable with teaching self-management skills more explicitly within the context of reading and writing assignments, he began to include these skills in other subjects. Over the course of the research year, he planned two major projects in social studies. Again, one focused on immigration, the other on making papier-mâché globes to learn geography.

Immigration Study II

This immigration study was the first study of the research year. However, using the TIEL Model helped make this a very different experience for Ted and his students from the previous immigration unit. This was the first project-based social studies unit for which Ted explicitly designed self-organization tools.

Definition of Self-Organization Tools

Self-organization tools are worksheets designed by the teacher to teach students how to make decisions, plan, and evaluate their project work. As they work on their culminating project, the students use the self-organization tools to manage their work throughout the project. At the end of the unit, students use an evaluation tool to evaluate their work.

Definition of a Culminating Project

A culminating project comes at the end of a unit of study, serving both as an assessment tool and as a learning opportunity. A culminating project assesses the students' overall understanding of the content and processes involved in a unit of study. Ted's second immigration study and the later globe study are examples of culminating projects in which the work of the unit is centered in the project from the beginning. Students learn the content of the unit as they complete the project. Another kind of culminating project allows students to do additional research on a topic relating to the main subject of the unit. Erica's Colonial Life unit and the Mexico study in chapters 5 and 8 are examples of this kind of culminating project.

A culminating project is generally a large project that requires time. The project must be of sufficient scope for the students to need to set criteria, make plans and decisions, do research, and self-evaluate when the project is complete. A culminating project, therefore, involves hands-on learning that includes visual, written, and spoken components.

The visual component usually involves a hands-on product. One example, in the second immigration unit, is the student-designed collage of pictures and objects that showed the heritage of their families. Some examples of incorporating the written component into projects include labels for the visual component, journals, or an accompanying research paper. Finally, the project becomes a learning experience for fellow classmates as each student orally presents his or her project.

Setting Criteria

In the second immigration unit, the students participated in planning by setting the criteria for the final project. Using the TIEL Curriculum Design Wheel, Ted began with *cognition*. This thinking operation includes the skills of observation and getting information. He showed the students an example of a heritage collage made on a poster board. It included small bits of memorabilia that told about his family. After giving the students some time to observe the collage, he asked, "What do you see?" As the students shared, he listed their observations on the overhead projector (see figure 3.4).

Collage Criteria

- The collage tells about a person's heritage.

- The collage is layered.

- There are parts sticking out.

- There are many symbols and materials used.

Figure 3.4.   Criteria for heritage collage project, Immigration study II.

These observations became the criteria for evaluation of the completed collage. As the students used their observation skills, they developed criteria that helped them evaluate their final project. Instead of telling the students the parameters of the project, he brought the students into the process of constructing the parameters. Instead of directing the students, he helped them develop ownership of the project (see figure 3.5).

Name_____ Date _____

MY SOCIAL STUDIES PROJECT GRADE

My Project:

[   ]   It is layered. It is not just flat. It has parts sticking out.

[   ]   I thought about the placement and arrangement of the symbols. I show connections among them. I have good reasons for placing the symbols the way I did.

[   ]   My project came from my sketch. I revised my sketch.

[   ]   I used many kinds of symbols and many kinds of materials.

You can earn 3 points for each, for a total of 12 points.

If You Earn	Your Grade
11-12 points	✓+
9-10 points	✓+
7-8 points	✓
5-6 points	✓
3-4 points	✓- or Do Over
< 3 points	0 or Do Over

TOTAL POINTS:

OVERALL GRADE:

Figure 3.5. *My Social Studies Project Grade* evaluation worksheet.

Multiple Purposes for Setting Criteria

Criteria for evaluation can be used in multiple ways. Setting criteria with students at the beginning of the project, as Ted did with the sample collage, provides an engaging introduction. At the end of the unit, students use these criteria to evaluate. As Ted reflected on the immigration project, he discovered a third use. Criteria for evaluation can also be used as a plan to guide the project. He commented, "The only mistake I made is that while we were making the project I should have had this [the criteria sheet] out. The students needed the criteria that would be used to evaluate the final project when they began the project. The criteria for evaluation can be a guide throughout the project."

Improved Teacher Planning

Defining the end product at the beginning transformed Ted's planning. Beginning at the end in curriculum design has a long history. Wiggins and McTighe (1998) currently recommend that teachers begin their curriculum planning at the end. Others have also taught the importance of beginning the planning process at the end through establishing clear objectives that state what the students will know and be able to do by the end of a lesson or unit (Bloom, 1956; Mager, 1984; Tyler, 1949).

Ted changed the immigration unit from the previous year. At that time, the students were given little guidance in how to construct their projects. Beginning with what he expected at the end of the unit helped him plan the teaching of self-management skills. Determining the criteria for evaluation at the beginning made it possible to include the students in this stage of planning.

He recognized how important structure was in helping the students accomplish the goal. With the *Heritage Collage* as the end product, the immigration unit began to take on a structure that had a beginning, middle, and end. Beginning with observation of the collage, the students constructed criteria for evaluation. In the middle, the students interviewed their parents and grandparents about their heritage. They obtained photographs and objects that told about their family to create the collage. At the end, when the project was completed, the students returned to the original criteria to assess their projects.

Geography Study

Geography is important in the third grade curriculum. There are many things to learn about physical places in the world. What are the symbols that help us read a map? What can we learn from a globe? What are the continents? What is the climate in various parts of the world? When Ted began planning the geography study, he knew what he wanted for a final project. He had recently taken a class in teaching geography to children where the teachers created papier-mâché globes. Attempting such a large and messy project with students who still had great difficulty sitting calmly on the carpet was a clear in-dication of Ted's willingness to take risks. It also demonstrated his firm belief that learning must be meaningful for the students.

Selecting Content

Ted wanted to teach the students planning and self-evaluation skills in mak-ing the globes. While Ted knew the topic of his unit and the culminating proj-ect, he had much to decide about the specific content of the unit. He began the planning process with questions that helped him organize his thinking about the content.

- What is the topic of the unit?
- What information do I want the students to know?
- What big ideas do I want the students to learn?
- What are some possible learning experiences that will help students learn the concepts and information?
- What culminating project will demonstrate their learning?

To help with the planning, he recorded his ideas on a chart. What informa-tion do I want the students to know? Under information, he included time zones, seas, oceans, and rivers. Other information included divisions denoting distance and time, equator, prime meridian, and the international dateline (see figure 3.6).

Ted listed several questions reflecting big ideas for the unit. Why is it cold at the poles and hot at the equator? How do we get day and night? Why do we have the seasons? How does the earth move and what happens as it moves? How are the geographical components of the earth organized and named?

Criteria to Choose Content

After much consideration, Ted chose to focus on how the earth is organized and named. He based his decision on three criteria—the time available for the study, the age of the students, and the complexity of the project. He knew that the process of making papier-mâché globes involves a great many steps that would take a considerable amount of time for third graders. After considering these factors, he decided to save the study of the earth's movement, changing seasons, and the cycle of day and night for a science unit. Once Ted established a focus, all learning activities—planning, researching, constructing, painting, and labeling—were directed toward completing the papier-mâché globes.

Making the globes became an all-consuming project. Ted prepared photo-copies of unlabeled continents. The students cut out the shapes and researched maps and atlases in the classroom to determine the name and placement of the continent. He devised a planning worksheet with three columns to guide

What is the topic of the unit?	What information do I want them to know?	What big ideas do I want them to learn?	What are some possible learning experiences?	What is the culminating project?
World geography	3 time zones 7 seas, 3 oceans 1 major river on each continent Equator, longitude, latitude Prime meridian International date line Land formations: islands, continents, mountain ranges Axis	Why is it cold at the poles and hot at the equator? How do we get night and day? Why do we have the seasons? How does the earth move and what happens as it moves? How are the geographical components of the earth organized and named?	Mini-lesson Demonstration with models Possible mini-lessons: Map work Cutting out the continents Using atlases to label Plan and create the globe Evaluate the globe	Papier-mâché globes Labeled Painted Key or legend

Figure 3.6.   Globe project ideas chart.

the students' work (see figures 3.7a, b). The first column provided a place for the students to write the date when the step was finished. Next to the date were two sets of brackets. When a step was completed, the student placed a check in one; the teacher checked the other. The second column outlined the task to be done. In the third column students evaluated their work on that task using a system of checks.

Role of Experience in Learning to Teach Self-Organization Skills

Teacher experience plays a large role in determining how much students are included in planning a project. When teachers are knowledgeable about the

Name_____ Date_____

MY GLOBE PROJECT

Directions:
1. Give yourselves a grade of √ +, √, √ -, or 0 for each item.
2. Do each item in the order that they are listed on this page.
3. Do not skip any items.
4. You must have a teacher's initial before moving on to the next item. The teacher will also give you a grade for each item and explain why he or she agrees or disagrees with the grade you have yourself.

Due date for this project: _____

Date Accomplished and Grade	What I Accomplished	How I Accomplished It
[ ][ ]	I finished the **papier-mâché** for my globe	
[ ][ ]	I painted my globe **sky blue**	
[ ][ ]	I painted in the **equator** and **Prime Meridian** lines	
[ ][ ]	I prepared all the major **land forms** for all 7 continents	
[ ][ ]	I labeled at least 1 **mountain range** in each continent	

Figure 3.7a.   *My Globe Project* plan/evaluation worksheet (front).

[ ][ ]	I labeled at least 5 **countries** in each continent	
[ ][ ]	I labeled the **United States** of America and **New York**	
[ ][ ]	I colored my **land forms** using markers or colored pencils.	
[ ][ ]	I glued all my land forms in their correct places	
[ ][ ]	I labeled a **compass rose** on my chart: N for North, E for East, S for South, W for West	
[ ][ ]	I labeled the 4 **oceans** on my globe.	
[ ][ ]	I labeled the 10 **seas** on my globe	
[ ][ ]	I put my name near the **North Pole**	
[ ][ ]	I shared my work with others.	

Overall Grade, according to me:
Why:

Overall Grade, according to the teacher:
Why:

Congratulations on a job well done!

Figure 3.7b. *My Globe Project* plan/evaluation worksheet (back).

content, they are more comfortable with bringing the students into the process of setting criteria for the final project. Since Ted had taught the immigration unit the year before, he was more comfortable in allowing the students to participate in setting criteria for evaluation. Therefore, even though the culminating project was different, Ted was able to include the students in the planning.

On the other hand, the geography unit was new. Ted felt less comfortable in having the students participate in planning this project than in the Immigration II unit. Therefore, the planning worksheet for the globe project reflected *the teacher's* thorough planning, but it involved minimal student participation. To the students, the planning worksheet more closely resembled a list of instructions than a cooperatively designed planning tool that involved their thinking.

Nevertheless, it was an important beginning in planning a new project-based curriculum unit. For project work to be successful, the teacher needs to define the criteria and steps in his own mind before attempting to construct the plan with the students. The teacher must think through all of the items that need to be included in the production of the project. Ted determined the requirements involved in creating the globe and developed a worksheet that would guide the project. Just as in the immigration unit, Ted would be ready to involve the students more in the planning of a future geography unit.

CONSCIOUSNESS OF THE VALUE OF TEACHING SELF-ORGANIZATION SKILLS

Learning requires time. It usually involves an uncomfortable period of cognitive dissonance while less effective practices are replaced with new practices or while new practices are integrated with old. Because of the time commitment involved, teachers need to recognize the value of a new teaching skill or strategy before they can fully commit the time required to learn the skill sufficiently to change their practice.

Ted knew that opportunities for teaching students decision making, planning, and self-evaluation were infused throughout his curriculum. Yet, inexplicitly infusing opportunities does not have the same effect as naming the concept being taught, explaining why it is being taught, and explicitly teaching it as a skill. Did the students understand that they were engaged in a process called planning? As Ted led students through learning activities, were they aware of the thinking processes involved? Was Ted aware of the rich learning of process that lay invisibly below the surface of the activities he planned?

Belief and Practice

There is often a difference between belief and practice. As teachers, our strong beliefs in certain strategies can make us think we are actually teaching them. Ted believed strongly in the processes of self-organization and felt he was teaching these processes throughout his curriculum. Yet, the students showed little awareness of making decisions, planning, or evaluating their work, even though the first immigration unit was filled with opportunities to specifically teach these skills.

The TIEL Wheel is a tool that helps support teachers in the difficult task of learning new teaching strategies and incorporating them into daily practice. Understanding the fundamental thinking and social-emotional processes represented by the TIEL Model helps teachers bridge the gap between believing that they are teaching thinking and social-emotional skills and actually teaching these skills explicitly. When Ted became more aware of how to teach planning and decision making to the students, he recognized that he was not explicitly teaching these skills within project work outside of reading and writing. He also saw that he needed to be more explicit in teaching these skills within reading and writing. As his understanding of thinking and learning increased, he became more open to making changes in his teaching.

Understanding Thinking

For teachers to consciously include the teaching of thinking and social-emotional skills in their planning, they first need to become conscious of their own thinking. When teachers understand their own thinking and learning, they become better at understanding the thinking and learning processes of their students. As teachers understand the thinking of their students, they become better at planning for instruction.

Ted began this process by analyzing his own thinking involved in the decision to buy a car (see figure 3.8). First, he noticed that he used the thinking

Ted's Analysis of Decision-making Involved in Buying a Car					
Cognition	Memory	Evaluation	Convergent Production	Divergent Production	Emotional Considerations
Ask people Call insurance companies	Remember previous car-buying experiences	Set criteria Use criteria to evaluate options Insurance Coverage Cost Expediency	Organize information Logically arrive at decision	Generate options Risk-taking	Honesty Empathy Mastery Appreciation

Figure 3.8.   Ted's analysis of decision making in buying a car.

operation *cognition* in getting information. He asked other people for their opinions concerning the best car for the money. He also made calls to insurance companies to determine the premiums for various kinds of cars. He used *memory* to connect his newly acquired information to his previous car-buying experiences.

He used *evaluation* skills to set criteria that were important to him and that would help him make a decision about which car to buy. These criteria included cost of insurance coverage, cost of the car, and how quickly he could make the transaction. As Ted gained more information, he used *divergent thinking* to generate a number of options from which to choose. In making his choice, he used *convergent thinking* to logically organize the information. Returning to the thinking operation, *evaluation*, Ted used his criteria to weigh the options and make a final decision among the alternatives. Understanding how he used these processes in a real-life situation helped him understand how to design learning activities that included a wide range of thinking.

Making decisions, of course, is not a wholly intellectual process. Emotional factors also play an important part. Which car dealership had a salesman who seemed honest? How did each of the salespersons show respect for and understanding of Ted's situation? How did a salesperson's mastery of the financing give Ted confidence that he was making the right decision? Which car dealership seemed most appreciative of Ted's business?

Understanding Planning

Teachers need an understanding of planning in order to teach students to plan. When it came to planning, however, Ted was a self-proclaimed meanderer. He was happy with the response he saw in the students' learning when he began to teach them to plan, but there were no bounds to his excitement when he discovered how purposeful planning affected his teaching. The nonspecific approach to curriculum development he described in early interviews gave way to conscious, purposeful methods of curriculum design.

Know Where You Are Going

Ted described an important learning moment, when he discovered that the best way to get where you are going in a reasonable amount of time is to know where you are going in the first place: "I discovered that the final project must emerge first and foremost, which shapes the process and the learning outcomes. What helped me learn it was the drawn-out, meandering quality to my class's immigration study." This simple planning technique does not preclude creative twists and turns. It does, however, let teachers clearly see where they are in teaching a concept. It further allows teachers to make informed decisions about how far to veer from the goal and how to return to it.

TIEL Provides Balance

Teachers need to develop curriculum that is balanced between intellectual and social-emotional learning. Balance is also needed among the thinking processes. As Ted planned, he used the TIEL framework to "put things in the proper place." He commented, "It [the TIEL framework] provides a balance. My awareness of TIEL helps me provide a wider range of experiences and approaches for my students in each unit of study."

The TIEL Model helped Ted increase the variety in the learning activities he planned as well as establish a balance between intellectual and social-emotional processes. Using the TIEL Model helped Ted answer a number of questions as he planned. Are students gaining information? Are they connecting to prior experience? Are there opportunities for both convergent and divergent thinking? Are their places in the curriculum for students to learn self-organization skills?

CONNECTING THINKING TO SOCIAL-EMOTIONAL LEARNING

Ted's emerging consciousness led to more flexibility in his thinking. Most of the examples, to this point, concern Ted's increasing ability to teach the self-management skills of decision making, planning, and self-evaluation within the context of project work. However, as Ted used the TIEL Wheel to teach the skills included in the *evaluation* operation, he became more aware of the social-emotional aspects of teaching and learning in his classroom.

He began to ask himself several questions. How can these qualities be demonstrated in the classroom? How can appreciation, reflection, mastery, ethical reasoning, and reflection be taught in the classroom? How can I provide opportunities for students to develop these characteristics in the classroom? He began to see the connection between the intellectual and the social-emotional components and how intellectual skills can be used to develop social-emotional characteristics.

Self-Management

Ted discovered that helping a child change his behavior is also a project where a student can apply decision-making and evaluation skills. Mark was an inclusion student who had been "traded" from another class. Mark's previous teacher had become so exasperated that she requested that he be transferred to another classroom.

Mark required a daily behavior chart that rated his conduct during transitions, meeting times, group work, and individual work. Mark's behavior during each of these classroom time periods was rated from 1 (needs more work) to 5 (excellent). Ted generally filled out the chart in the rush of the day, giving it little serious thought. Mark would begin "growling and slamming things" and argue that Ted was not fair.

Changing the System

One day, Ted realized that he had to change the system. Since he was spending more time on the outbursts than on the chart, Ted decided to include Mark in the evaluation. Ted recognized that the skills of using criteria to make decisions during the planning stage of a project could also be applied to helping Mark evaluate his own behavior. Perhaps if Mark was included in the discussion, he would take more responsibility for his actions.

"Mark, help me fill this out." Ted pointed to the word "transition" on the chart.

"How did you handle the transition this time?" Ted asked.

"Good," replied Mark. Since Mark's self-evaluation did not fully take into account what had actually happened, Ted gently nudged his memory.

"Mark, I remember that while you were going from the table to the rug, you pushed Zoe and she complained about it." After Mark thought about it, he pointed to the column stating "needs more work."

Ted concurred, "OK. One (on a scale of one to three). Let's put that down." Ted was amazed that as he asked Mark each question on the chart, Mark was "not getting all riled." His need to be combative decreased. He began to gain some control over his own behaviors by being part of the evaluation process (see figure 3.9).

Thinking and Social-Emotional Learning

In working with Mark, Ted established an opportunity to use components from both the thinking operations and the qualities of character. As another

	3 Excellent	2 Almost There	1 Needs More Work
Transitions			
Meeting Times			
Group Work			
Individual Work			

Figure 3.9.   Mark's behavior evaluation worksheet.

teacher put it, "Ted helped Mark jog around the circle." Mark gained information from the chart (*cognition*) about the times of the day when he needed better control. The chart helped him focus on the skills he was trying to develop during each of these difficult times. In jostling Mark's memory, Ted helped him observe himself more accurately and become more thoughtful about his actions (*reflection*).

After Mark rethought his behavior, he answered the question about the transition differently. When he recognized that he needed more work in this area (*evaluation*), his honest self-assessment (*ethical reasoning*) was based more on reality. Fully understanding what he needed to change, Mark pointed to "needs more work," which in this case was the right answer (*convergent production*) and "transitions," the area in which he needed to develop *mastery*. Ted encouraged Mark to use *divergent* thinking to see his behavior from another point of view. At the same time, Ted used *divergent* thinking in considering other options for helping Mark learn self-management skills.

Authentic Character Development

Ted gave Mark an authentic opportunity for real character development. Kohn (1998) has taken a critical look at current programs in character education. He reports that many of these programs focus heavily on inculcating correct behaviors through "extrinsic inducements designed to make children work harder and do what they're told" (p. 181). In contrast, Ted's work with Mark represents what Kohn suggests character education is actually supposed to do—"engage [students] in deep critical reflection about certain ways of being" (p. 181). In allowing Mark to be part of the evaluation process, Ted did exactly this. He engaged Mark in critical reflection about his actions and how they affected others in the class.

Responsibility for Teaching

The TIEL Model helped Ted develop a deeper sense of reflection. One of the most remarkable of Ted's changes was a new awareness of the teacher's responsibility to purposefully teach underlying thinking and social-emotional processes. In an early interview, one of the students indicated that she was unaware that choices were available to her in the classroom. When I shared this with Ted, he immediately put the responsibility on the student, referring to her as a passive learner. He said, "She doesn't see that every work structure I have in here, she has to make lots of choices."

At that time, Ted saw the problem as the child's. While many of the more academically able students come to school as active learners familiar with making choices, Ted described those who struggled: "They tend to be the more passive learners, not making choices for themselves and seeing—did I achieve my goals," he explained.

As the year drew to a close, Ted's thinking had changed. There was a marked contrast in how he thought about teacher and student responsibilities in the teaching and learning process. His discussion of Daniel, who had difficulties with self-evaluation, was a good example. Ted commented, "Some of them [students] are in a haze like Daniel. Grading himself doesn't mean anything to him." Yet as he continued, Ted expressed a very different point of view from earlier discussions. He thought a minute and then identified the problem. Contemplatively, he said, "So that's that whole reflection piece. So now I realize that I have to teach him how to reflect meaningfully about his work."

Ted recognized and accepted this responsibility as the teacher. He no longer attributed the lack of skill to student passivity or resistance. He recognized that if self-evaluation is to be accomplished successfully, then the skill of reflection must be taught. He realized that as the teacher, he must teach it.

SUMMARY

The TIEL Model helps teachers become more conscious of thinking and social-emotional learning in their classrooms. Ted, an accomplished veteran teacher, was unaware of all the opportunities to teach the self-management skills of decision making, planning, and self-evaluation in his classroom. While he taught self-management skills in reading and writing, he did not make the skills explicit. The TIEL Model helped Ted gain an understanding of thinking and social-emotional processes. He learned how to explicitly teach students the self-management skills of decision making, planning, and self-evaluation in social studies project work. As he used the TIEL Model to guide his planning, he created learning activities that were more balanced across thinking processes, as well as between thinking operations and social-emotional learning. The TIEL Model also helped him see his responsibility to teach thinking processes and include social-emotional learning in his classroom.

4

Teacher and Student Understanding

> Because what happens is if you get past your goal like I did yesterday, you feel really proud . . . you feel as though you've gotten everything . . . like . . . you've gotten a lot done. And it's amazing!
>
> —Nan, third grade student, commenting on the planning calendar

As the year progressed, Ted and the students both experienced changes. Ted made connections between the thinking and character components represented by the TIEL Curriculum Design Wheel. Making these connections helped him meet the needs of his students in new ways, as happened with Mark and the behavior chart. He realized the importance of explicitly teaching his students how to make decisions, plan, and self-evaluate within the context of their projects. He became an intentional planner who purposefully designed learning experiences that helped students develop their self-organization skills. He talked less, but asked more questions to encourage the students to do more of the thinking.

At the same time, the students became aware of the thinking processes they were using in their work. They learned to plan, self-evaluate, and discuss their work in ways that were not evident at the beginning of the research year. This chapter includes examples of Ted's understanding of his teaching and examples that show the students' understanding of their learning and thinking processes.

TED'S UNDERSTANDING OF HIS TEACHING

Changing teaching practice is difficult work. Changing practice requires that the change in thinking become visible. In a classroom, the missteps and re-adjustments associated with learning a new teaching strategy are quite public.

Growth, occurring in fits and starts, is complicated by thirty students experiencing similar characteristics of growth as the teacher implements new ideas. Changing practice while juggling the daily life of the classroom and fielding the concerns of parents can be an enterprise filled with risk.

Importance of Explicit Teaching

Yet, Ted enthusiastically set out on the rocky road to changing teaching practices. As he began assessing his teaching using the criteria of the TIEL Curriculum Design Model, he saw the importance of teaching self-organization skills more explicitly. When he planned to teach a concept or topic, he asked himself where he could best teach students to make decisions and plan.

As he reflected back over the year, he said,

> We *do* decision making. I just don't think I made enough of the connections. We've been doing decision making all year, like in choosing their jobs. Choosing their desks. Choosing their homework partners. Choosing their rug spots. Choosing reading spots. It's all decision making. But I wasn't explicit. I didn't make enough connections from one to the other. I didn't highlight it enough.

Highlighting Thinking

Teachers need to highlight what they are teaching and make the thinking processes more transparent. Making decisions was ubiquitous in Ted's classroom. Yet, he needed to clearly link the concept of decision making, in whatever setting, to the criteria used for making that decision. For example, when Ted asked the students how they should choose someone to sit by on the rug, he suggested that they choose "somebody who is not going to bother me." The next step is to have the following conversation:

Teacher: What decision did you make?

Student: I decided to sit by Mary.

Teacher: What criteria did you use to make your decision?

Student: I decided to sit by Mary, because she pays attention and that helps me pay attention.

Critical Thinking

According to Richard Paul (1995), a pioneer in the field of critical thinking, setting and using "intellectual criteria and standards" (p. iii) to assess an idea, an opinion, a piece of writing, a work of art, or a prospective rug partner is the foundation of critical thinking. For students to learn to think critically, they need to be explicitly taught what they are doing when they make a decision.

The process of critical decision making needs to be taught specifically and consciously just as the names and places of continents are taught.

Intentional Planning

As Ted became a more intentional planner, the undefined, implicit infusion of decision making throughout his curriculum gave way to conscious opportunities for the students to explicitly make decisions, plan, and evaluate their work. He grew more skillful at naming the concept of thinking or social-emotional learning that he was teaching, explaining why he was teaching it, and explicitly teaching it as a skill. He spoke of "finding those pockets in the curriculum where the kids can maneuver, where they can have a voice—spaces in the curriculum where they can manipulate [their own] learning."

Using TIEL for Planning

The TIEL Model helped Ted with his planning. He commented, "It provides a structure for my planning instead of this groping in the dark." Ted was a published poet and he liked teaching poetry to his students. As he planned a poetry unit for the final weeks of the year, he very consciously considered the TIEL components.

In addition to planning for the students to use evaluation skills in assessing poetry, Ted now had a better understanding of the thinking and social-emotional processes involved in the learning activities he planned. Using the language of TIEL, he explained his planning,

> I did want to see some examples of divergent thinking. Imaginative products. I definitely want to see some evaluation. Self-assessment of their products. I already started these poetry breaks where they recite a poem that they memorize. I definitely want them to get to that part about learning from other good poets. Researching poets . . . being aware of what good poets do.

Poetry Study

Ted used the components of the TIEL Wheel to create the learning activities in the poetry centers. While any activity involves more than one TIEL component, Ted specifically planned each activity in the poetry center to focus on particular thinking operations and qualities of character. He developed a *Poetry Centers Checklist* that gave general instructions and a place for students to record their progress throughout the centers (see figure 4.1). He also made an instruction sheet describing the activities at each learning center (see figure 4.2).

The *Beautiful Language* center requires students to use *evaluation* to choose a poem and *divergent production* to illustrate the poem. Ted specifically planned two centers for the students to develop skills within the *cognition* component. *Poetic*

Name _____ Date _____

MY POETRY CENTERS CHECKLIST

Directions:

- Choose one center at a time.
- No more than four people are allowed at a center. First come, first served.
- You must work only at the center you chose for the entire poetry workshop time. (You may not switch centers until our next work time.)
- You must have a teacher's initials when you finish the work at a center. You have to show your work as proof.
- You must work at four more centers by the end of our gathering stage.

Centers

		Teacher's initials
[ ]	Beautiful Language	_____
[ ]	Poetic Windows	_____
[ ]	Poetic Objects	_____
[ ]	Pretend Poetry	_____
[ ]	List Poetry	_____
[ ]	Map of the Heart	_____
[ ]	Poetry Postcards	_____

* I understand that I am expected to create three or more original poems by the end of our poetry study for our Authors Celebration on Friday, June 19th.

Figure 4.1.   Checklist for poetry centers.

INSTRUCTIONS FOR POETRY CENTERS

Beautiful Language   Find poems that you like. From one of your favorites, select a phrase that you would like to illustrate on 11X14 paper.

Poetic Windows   While you sit and stare out the window, write what you observe.

Poetic Objects   Select objects from a grab bag and write descriptions of the object.

Pretend Poetry   Imagine that you are a rabbit (or other animal or object) and describe what it is like to be that animal or object.

List Poetry   Write poems that make lists, such as: Around the City.

Map of the Heart   Draw a large heart. Write inside the heart the things that matter most to you.

Poetry Postcards   From a bag of postcards select one. Look at it and write about it.

Figure 4.2.   Instructions for poetry centers.

Windows and *Poetic Objects* require students to observe and describe. In the *List Poetry* center, students use *divergent production* to develop their poems. When students use alphabetical order or size to sequence items in their list poems, *convergent production* is involved in their writing. The *Map of the Heart* center involves both *divergent production* and *reflection* as they write the things that matter most to them. In the final center, *Poetry Postcards*, students observe their postcard (*cognition*) and write whatever they would like about the card (*divergent production*).

Less Talking, More Thinking

Ted's teaching changed in another important way. Teachers are often highly verbal since talking is an important part of what teachers do. Ted used a great many words, especially when giving instructions. I shared a technique for introducing work to the students that I learned in a Mediated Learning demonstration given by Reuven Feuerstein, a noted educator in special education and gifted education.

Students Develop Instructions

Dr. Feuerstein was working with a student with learning disabilities. Instead of reading instructions *to* the student, Dr. Feuerstein gave him the worksheet and instructed him to look at it closely. After a short period of time, he asked questions that drew the information from the student. After trying the technique a few times, Ted commented, "I think the kids are a lot more focused and directed in their work now."

Becoming less verbal was one of the greatest changes that Ted saw in himself as a teacher. While the TIEL vocabulary gave Ted more words to use, he was actually using words less. He shared,

> I am now less verbal. I introduce worksheets with questions. [I ask the kids:] What do you think this is about? Have you seen something like this before? Why do you think we're doing this now? How does this apply to what we've already done? What do you think it's asking you to do? And I'm getting them to do a lot more of the talking or the explaining. And that all happens because I'm able to give out the form or the chart or the worksheet ahead of time. And I'm giving them the time to study it more.

Ted was surprised at the success he experienced when the students participated in developing instructions for their work. He commented, "They learn and listen much better to each other than they do to me. The more I can structure out of here, the better."

Self-Direction and Classroom Management

Feuerstein's technique encourages self-directed learning. Students are required to focus on the task they are about to do. The questions engage their thinking and help them figure out the instructions. The students are asked to observe, make connections to what they already know, and evaluate why they are being asked to do the assignment. As in the observation activity preceding the heritage collage, the students establish criteria for their work.

Feuerstein's method of focusing student attention contributes to good classroom management. Students often become immune to the words of the teacher. When this happens, they frequently do not listen well when instructions are given. When the teacher uses fewer words and asks good questions, the students' mental involvement increases. When student involvement increases, classroom management improves.

STUDENTS' UNDERSTANDING
OF THEIR THINKING AND LEARNING

As Ted taught thinking processes within his curriculum, the students became conscious of their thinking and learning. Ted made significant changes in how he planned his curriculum and instructed his students. While Ted became more explicit in the teaching of self-management skills, how were the students understanding and developing these new skills? Did the students understand that they were engaged in a process called planning? What did they think about self-evaluation? As Ted led students through learning activities, were they aware of the thinking processes involved?

The students' understanding of self-organization processes indicated the quantity and quality of discussion going on in the classroom. While Ted felt that the students had a fair understanding of self-organization processes, he agreed that the students were somewhat muddy in regard to using thinking language to describe it. Yet, when I interviewed the students after the globe project was completed, the students revealed a deeper understanding of their thinking and learning than their emerging use of language to describe it would indicate.

Successes and Challenges

The students were anxious to share both the successes and the challenges that they experienced in working on the globe project. They attributed their successes to several factors. Ted's help was particularly important, as well as the help with materials they had received from the other teachers in the classroom. In addition to Ted, there was a student teacher, a parent aide, and often an inclusion teacher in the classroom.

Daniel especially appreciated the help with smoothing out the papier-mâché, while Rosa mentioned how Ted had assisted her in placing the continents on the globe. Nan, grasping the larger picture of the work involved in their projects, mentioned how much time they had spent on the globe project.

She could see that the poetry project they were just beginning would also take time. She commented, "Well . . . Mr. Kesler helped . . . we studied A LOT . . . we spent . . . more than half of the time we were spending . . . like . . . about three months or so we would just totally work on our globes. And now it's with the poetry too."

Nan's third grade perception was not completely accurate. While the globe project stretched over three months, the students did not work exclusively on the globes. Since the poetry unit was started in the final weeks of the year, it was limited to a shorter time period.

Understanding Decision Making

The students talked about the decisions involved in their projects. In the globe project, they did not feel they had any decisions to make. Daniel explained, "He told us directions." Yet, as they thought about it more, they realized they could decide how to color their continents.

Nan, who alone gave any serious thought to the colors, described her thinking, "Maybe South America should be red because it's really hot." The students were not aware of any serious decisions that had included specifically set criteria. However, that the students recognized the absence of decision-making opportunities, in itself, reflected their growing awareness of the underlying invisible processes of learning.

Understanding Self-Evaluation

The students demonstrated an emerging understanding of evaluation. They connected their understanding of self-evaluation to prior experiences with peer evaluation. At the beginning of the year they had corrected math and spelling with a partner. They also corrected homework with a partner. Daniel explained,

> We write down our grade on a sheet of paper. We do it with the person next to us. Like I usually do it with Yousef, because we come [to school] around the same time. If I saw that he missed two things and only did three, I'd give him a ✓ and not a ✓+. And if he finds out I only missed one thing or did all of them, then he would give me a ✓+.

Unclear Criteria

Nan pointed to the green combination planning/evaluation sheet that Ted had made for the globe project. She explained that since they were evaluating the globe project "as the steps go by," she did not think they would do additional evaluation at the end. Recalling the planning aspect of the worksheet they used, she said, "There is something that tells us what steps we're going on."

Making sure that students understand what they are to do is a continual challenge for teachers. The students were unclear about the criteria by which the globe projects were to be evaluated. They were not sure what determined whether their work was "good" or "not so good." The hidden criteria embedded in each step were not clear to the students. For example: Place the continents *correctly* on the globe. What is the "criteria" word? What word tells you how to place your continents? What does *correctly* mean? Where should each continent be placed? What guidelines are on the globe to help you with the placement?

Mixed Feelings about Self-Evaluation

The students had mixed feelings about the process of self-evaluation. Nan sometimes liked doing her own evaluation, but often disliked it. She definitely did not like the discrepancy that occurred when the teacher gave a different evaluation.

> I don't really like it [evaluating]. I like to let the teacher get it over with. I don't like to know if I did something wrong. If I did something wrong, I have to figure it out. A lot of time we won't know what's wrong—we'll think it's right. And the teacher comes up to us and says, "This part is a little wrong." So if you get a bad grade, you ask, why is it wrong? So before, you thought that it was right.

Daniel had experienced the disappointment that comes with a discrepancy between the teacher's and the student's evaluation. His and Ted's evaluations for the immigration collage were far apart. One of the criteria for the "On your paper where it says, 'Is it layered? Not flat. It has parts sticking out.' Did you give yourself a 2 or a 3?" Daniel very quietly said he had given himself a 4. He had placed a tiny globe on his collage, so his collage was not flat. He looked at the criteria again and then his collage, as he continued reading the list of criteria. "Arrangement of the symbols." His voice trailed off as he said, "I thought I was going to . . ." Daniel, having given himself a 4 on each criterion, was extremely disappointed with Ted's evaluation of his collage. Later, when Ted sat down with Daniel and discussed the evaluation again, they were able to come to an agreement about the evaluation.

Daniel noticed that many of the students were not careful with their self-evaluations. He remarked, "Some kids don't really want to do it [self-evaluate] anymore, so they just go real fast."

According to Rosa, many students preferred to let the teacher figure out the evaluation, because "they can do it so much faster than us kids."

Individual Differences

Evaluating their own work helped the students gain an appreciation of individual differences. During the research year there was much more variety in the projects than the previous year. The students were discovering what teachers already know, that it is precisely these differences that make evaluation and assessment so difficult. Sharing their appreciation of differences, the students explained the wide variety of globes, "Everybody's was different . . . it can be totally different just because of different handwriting. Everybody's doesn't have to be the same. Everybody doesn't have the same eye color."

Learning Empathy

During the globe project, the students developed empathy for each other in their learning. Nan was an advanced learner with a great deal of independence, whereas Daniel struggled with all phases of schoolwork and had known only limited autonomy. Although very different as learners, Nan and Daniel supported each other in many ways. When Daniel told about his globe difficulties, Nan was quick to point out that all hadn't gone well for her either. She had neglected the spacing and squeezed all the continents into one area of the globe. Referring to the plan sheet, Daniel added, "It doesn't tell how to spell Atlantic Ocean—it just says put on the four oceans."

Nan was quick to offer support, "I didn't even know there was an Arctic Ocean. I just put on the Pacific, Indian, and Atlantic. I'm like—where's the fourth? There is no fourth. And Xavier tells me, "Yes there is. The Arctic Ocean." I'm like, Arctic? I thought that was part of the Atlantic, you know?"

Student Voices in Evaluation

If the students were sometimes unclear about how to evaluate, they were very clear that their voices were important in the evaluation. Nan stated their case,

> The teacher can't say, "Oh! You didn't do that right, you know, that's bad." First of all it would hurt the kids' feelings and none of them [the globes] are bad. . . . They're all good because everybody worked on them really hard. It's the child's opinion whether it's good or not. They decide I didn't do this right. I should have done that. Oh, I forgot that. But the teacher thinks everything is the way it should be, you know. [Each person] did their best.

Clearly Defined Criteria

Nan's comments underscore the importance of the teacher setting clearly defined criteria for evaluation and making sure the students understand the criteria. While no globe looked exactly like another due to color, handwriting, or small variations in shape, the globes involved convergent production. A globe has distinctive characteristics. Continents and oceans have specific locations and they need to be labeled with the appropriate names.

When teaching self-organization skills, teachers need to define what they want students to understand and be able to do. The criteria for assessment need to be clear. After the teacher "intellectually organizes" (Dewey, 1964) the criteria in her own mind and on paper, she can develop the criteria with the students. Some criteria, which all students are required to meet, are non-negotiable. Additional criteria can be developed that meet the particular needs of individuals or small groups of students.

Understanding Planning

The students reflected various levels of understanding of the process of planning. Rosa mentioned the calendar Ted had given them in an effort to speed completion of the globe project. The calendar explained clearly how many days were left and what would need to be done each day to complete the globes. Nan, who understood that planning for time management needed to occur at the beginning of the project, pointed out that the calendar was not given to them in the beginning of the project.

Each student saw the value of the calendar. They explained how they used the one-month calendar that clearly stated what was to happen with the globes between the 10th and 19th of June. Daniel appreciated that it told him when to start, even though the real starting point had been months earlier. Rosa wanted the calendar at the beginning of the project.

Nan saw the calendar as a way to manage time. She knew the globe project had gone well beyond a month. She wanted a calendar of the days they would be working on a project throughout the year. Nan believed that if they had used a calendar at the beginning, the globes would have taken less time. While the students received the calendar late in the project, it had given Nan a great sense of accomplishment with her work. She explained, "Because what happens is if you get past your goal like I did yesterday, you feel really proud . . . you feel as though you've gotten everything . . . like . . . you've gotten a lot done. And it's amazing!"

Planning and Problems

The students were unanimous in praise of the planning calendars that helped them organize the final days of the globe project, but they were less enthusiastic about the green planning sheet (see figure 3.7). Daniel did not feel the green planning sheet was adequate in helping him through the process of creating the globe.

He was currently redoing his globe because it was upside down with the continents in the wrong place. Rosa reported that her globe was right side up, quite by accident. "I did it straight like that, without knowing," she said rather incredulously. (Perhaps, she was trying to help Daniel feel better, because earlier she said the teacher had helped her place the continents.)

To Daniel the positioning of the globe was a very random event, over which he had little control. "It just sort of happens," he said. Even though the planning sheet stated what the students were to do, it didn't give Daniel enough information on how to do it. "I just didn't understand the plan at all," Daniel lamented. When he faltered in explaining what had happened, Nan helped by saying, "The plan didn't tell us exactly where everything goes. It just told us the steps. Now put on your pieces. Now paint your globe. Put on your equator."

Daniel was frustrated with his mistake that resulted in his globe being upside down. As his ideas became clearer about his problems with the globe, he explained what he would like to have known, "Where to put the continents in. The plan tells us what to do . . . but [it needed] a little bit more things. . . . I didn't know which way it was supposed to go. They didn't tell us that."

Problem Solving

Planning does not mean there will be no problems with a project. Students may assume that by planning their projects their work will turn out perfectly. While a plan is a point of departure, there is always a chance for problems to occur. When things do not go as expected, teachers have the opportunity to teach students real-life problem-solving skills. Through solving problems, students learn the importance of patience, imagination, and effort in turning a project around. In addition, through experiencing problems, students develop empathy for others who may be struggling.

Helping Students Anticipate Problems

Well-structured project work gives students an opportunity to look ahead and anticipate possible problems that may occur as they are working. As part of their planning, teachers need to anticipate problems from a student point of view in order to help their students look forward. Adding a section to the planning sheet entitled, "Problems I Might Have," provides a structure for helping students foresee problems before they occur. Teachers can ask, "What are some possible problems that might occur during this project? What could be difficult about this project? How can you prevent that problem from happening? If you have a problem that you did not anticipate, what will you do?"

Such questions help students develop the ability to look forward and see implications. When students are aware of possible problems, they can more effectively avoid them. If unforeseen problems do arise, students will not be surprised that problems happen. Anticipating challenges helps prepare students to assume the role of problem solvers. They learn to think of solutions instead of becoming upset and blaming themselves or someone else when they have a problem.

Looking ahead to challenges may have helped Daniel anticipate the difficulties with the spatial orientation of his globe. Thinking about problems in advance can help students feel that they have more control over their projects. Anticipating and solving problems about something they care about helps students build resilience that they need to face other problems within and outside of school.

Differentiating Learning Activities

Some problems the teacher must solve. The globes were still in production long past the expected time for completion. Since several students were struggling with the green planning sheet, it became clear that adjustments were needed. Ted modified the green planning sheet to include fewer items to complete and printed it on white paper. Using the revised sheet, all of the students could learn the most important geographical terms and feel successful.

Color of Competition

However, revising the globe planning sheet presented an unanticipated problem. Of the three students in the interview group, Daniel had received a white plan sheet, while Nan and Rosa continued with the green plan. Noticing the different colors, Nan said, "Near the end, Mr. Kesler said a few kids aren't really getting this so he made a small sheet that has less things on it."

There was an edge of competition in the words, "a few kids," "aren't getting it," "small sheet," "less things." Trying to steer the conversation into a positive pathway, I asked Daniel to explain how the new sheet helped him. He was very positive as he explained, "Because it's so little and it's much easier to understand what it's trying to say. It just says a couple of things like—did you color your continents? Did you make the equator?"

Nevertheless, Nan pointed out that she was doing the green sheet, *all* of the green sheet, with *all* the little details.

Undeterred, Daniel asked, "Did you make the hills and the rivers?"

"Did you make the South, East, West, North?" countered Nan.

Timing and Appearance

Differentiating curriculum can be a delicate matter. While the competitive conversation between the students was soon resolved, this situation is a reminder that timing and appearance are important in differentiating learning activities. Ted made helpful revisions to the planning sheets to meet the various needs of students in his classroom. It was clear, however, that differentiating the materials early in the project and using the same color of paper would help avoid problems. Fostering an environment in the classroom that helps each student know that the teacher plans specifically for his or her learning helps students understand when differences in instruction occur.

Student Participation in Planning

Participation in the planning helps students feel more invested in their projects. Again, the students demonstrated understanding by recognizing what was missing. The students were well aware that they did not participate in developing the globe plan. Nan, considering the teacher's job, pointed out that Mr. Kesler *had* to make the plan because the students did not know the steps. Yet, they had helped set criteria in planning their work for the heritage collage during the immigration unit.

I asked if they could figure out the steps by observing a globe. Daniel said yes. Nan, however, vetoed the idea because the steps had to be in a special order. I held up an imaginary globe and asked, "What do you see? Pretend you have not made a globe before. What do you see?"

They all joined in, "I see countries. I see continents. Oceans and seas and the equator. I see rivers and mountains. We see names and colors."

Next, I asked them to imagine writing all those ideas onto Post-it notes and then organizing them. Very quickly, Daniel made a discovery. Excitedly, he exclaimed, "You'd make yourself a plan!" He recognized that the geographical terms on the imaginary Post-it notes were those included on the green and white planning sheets. The difference was in how the terms were generated. Ted gave the students the plan for the globes, instead of having the students help construct the plan through their observations.

Learning Analysis

The imaginary globe exercise led Nan to analyze their learning. She could not ignore what she had learned while making the globe. "I actually think we see more because we've made a globe," she explained. She recognized the relationship between doing and learning. Because the students made the globes—using materials, their hands, and their thinking processes—they learned content from the field of geography. After making the globes, the students could make more detailed observations, even in their imaginations, because they now had more background knowledge.

Well-planned, well-structured project work helps students work their way across a bridge of learning that begins with needing knowledge to the end where knowledge has been acquired. The students needed the geographical content knowledge found in their atlases to *make* the globes. At the same time, they acquired knowledge of geography by *making* the globes. As students move across this bridge of gaining content knowledge through project work, they develop self-management, research, and collaboration skills. Additionally, they learn metacognition skills. When project work is of sufficient depth and well structured, students have a lot to say about their learning and the thinking processes they are using.

Understanding Self-Organization outside School

Connecting the concepts of decision making, planning, and self-evaluation used in project work to other contexts outside of school was another indication that students were developing an understanding of self-organization processes. The students based their examples of previous planning on similar as well as disparate experiences. Daniel told how he plans his chores by writing down what he has to do. He also used in-class examples, telling about the plan Ted writes on a white board at the beginning of each day and the plans the students make for writing. Rosa and Nan each told of planning birthday parties. Nan also recalled making decisions during a vacation in Germany.

STUDENT DISCUSSION OF THINKING PROCESSES

The students interviewed in the final assessment were able to discuss their thinking in ways the students the previous year were unable to do and in ways they could not do during the baseline interview. Even though Ted was not as articulate in discussing thinking as he felt he should be, classroom observations and interview conversations showed that the students were able to talk about their thinking and learning.

Comparing Projects

The students compared the immigration project that had occurred earlier in the year with the globe project. The two girls stated how the projects were similar. "We had a lot of help from other people. We got to glue things."

Nan added, "In the immigration project we went to Ellis Island. In the globe project we looked at globes."

It seemed that Nan had misunderstood the question since she gave examples of differences. She saw the puzzled looks and defended her statement, "But they [immigration and the globes] *are* the same. We had to use things to study them [a trip to Ellis Island and observation of maps and globes in the classroom]."

A Deeper Interpretation

Nan's examples addressed *cognition* that includes research and finding information. Seeing well below the surface, Nan saw the similarities in the two very different projects because they both required students to gather content information. Aware of the importance of content in projects, Nan perceptively saw that research is research, regardless of content or by what means the information is obtained. While the geographical research used globes, maps, and atlases, the immigration project involved an excursion outside the school to gather information from the actual place where immigrants arrived.

Visuals and Articulation

The TIEL bulletin board and the TIEL puppets helped the students discuss the thinking and social-emotional processes. Ted's bulletin board was on a wall in the carpeted area where he met with the students for teacher-directed instruction. The bulletin board consisted of five strips of paper in the TIEL colors with charts naming the thinking operations and qualities of character. In addition, Ted invited me to present the TIEL puppets to help his students learn the names of the thinking processes.

Metacognition

One day I did a creativity activity with Ted's class. I found an object in Ted's cupboard that looked like a very large nail attached to an electrical cord. Only Ted knew the actual use of the object. I gave the object to the students and as they passed it around, they gave their ideas about how it might be used. Focusing on divergent production, I wanted them to use their imaginations and become more fluent and flexible in their thinking.

Using TIEL Friends Puppets

Did the students know what thinking processes they had used as they passed the mystery object around the circle? Using the TIEL charts and the puppets to make the discussion of abstract concepts more concrete, I asked, "Which puppets helped us with the thinking we did in the creative thinking activity?"

"All the puppets really," Conrad replied.

Conrad was right. As they passed the object around the circle, the students used the following skills represented by the TIEL puppets. The students made observations (*Connie Cognition*); they found connections to other objects they had seen before (*Molly Memory*); they used imagination to think of possible uses (*Daniel Divergent*); and they analyzed the object by considering the component parts and made decisions about its use (*Ellie and Elmer Evaluation*). Even in this very open-ended activity, there was an element of convergent thinking as each student followed the instructions to take turns and not interrupt each other (*Christopher Convergent*).

"Was there one TIEL friend who was the star of this activity?"

They agreed that it was *Daniel Divergent* with his creative thinking, imagination, and many possible answers.

Connections to Globe Project

I helped the students bridge the discussion of thinking to the globe project. "How does this connect to our globe work?"

The globe project involved two costars of thinking. The students first mentioned the yellow puppet, Christopher, who represented *convergent thinking*. They explained how they had focused on problem solving with right answers when they attached the continents, labeled countries, and named the oceans. One student pointed out another aspect of *convergent thinking* in the globe project, "Basically, all the globes should look the same."

Finally, the students nominated *Connie Cognition*, the pink puppet, as the second star. "Connie," they said, "because we are doing a lot of learning and finding things out."

SUMMARY

As Ted became more conscious of teaching self-organization skills through project work, he made changes in his teaching. He was well aware of the developmental component in learning new teaching strategies. Ted knew he was not yet independent with his new learning and felt that another year would help him gain needed confidence. In subjects and projects with which he was familiar, as the immigration study, Ted planned for students to participate in setting criteria for the projects. For first-time projects like the globes with which he was less familiar, he made the plan for the students. Yet, referring to teaching self-organization skills, he stated emphatically, "But I definitely see the value now."

Ted became a more intentional planner using the TIEL Model to design learning activities that included all the thinking processes in the poetry study, his final unit of the year. Ted also discovered that talking less, but asking more questions increased student thinking in his classroom.

The research year was a challenging year for Ted as he learned new ways of teaching while piloting an inclusion class. Yet, Ted gave himself a positive evaluation for his work in using TIEL to teach self-management skills. He recalled the previous year when several articles were written for the *New York Times* about how he taught reading in his classroom. Ted gave himself a positive evaluation for our research year on teaching self-management skills using TIEL. Repeating himself with escalating emphasis, he said, "I think that I'm a much better teacher now than I was last year when they did all those articles about me. . . . I think I'm better now, than I was then. . . . I think I did a much better job this year."

As Ted altered his teaching, he saw that the students were becoming more conscious of their own learning. Using the TIEL puppets as reference, the class could discuss the thinking processes involved in learning activities. The three students who participated in the interviews often showed understanding of their learning by recognizing what was missing. They recognized when they did not have an opportunity to make decisions in a project. They knew the difference between their participation in planning and being given a checklist created by the teacher.

The students made connections to previous experiences with evaluation. They had mixed feelings about evaluating themselves, but they were able to discuss criteria used to evaluate their projects. The three students showed a deep sensitivity to student differences. Yet, in spite of wide differences in experiences and abilities, the students supported each other in their projects and showed empathy when others had difficulties.

III

COMMUNICATION

com · mu · ni · ca · tion (kə myōō'ni kā'shən), n. 1. the act or process of communicating; 2. the imparting or interchange of thoughts, opinions, or information by speech, writing, or signs.

—Webster's Unabridged Dictionary

Teaching and learning depend on communication between teacher and
learner. Organizing subject content into learning experiences that help students develop understanding is a complex form of communication. Education in the twenty-first century requires not only content knowledge, but the
thinking and social-emotional skills that will prepare students to make informed and ethical decisions, carry out effective planning, and evaluate their
own work and social conduct. Teaching these skills requires new tools of
communication.

CHAPTER 5: COMMUNICATION OF THINKING AND
SOCIAL-EMOTIONAL PROCESSES

How does TIEL facilitate teacher learning and communication with students
about thinking? This chapter follows Erica from her first through her third year
of teaching and tells how TIEL influenced her own learning and helped her
communicate with her students about thinking.

CHAPTER 6: CHALLENGES OF CLASSROOM CONTEXT

How does the context of the classroom affect the teaching of self-organization skills? Erica shares how she coped with challenges of class size, larger and older students, and a crowded classroom during the research year.

CHAPTER 7: TEACHING SELF-ORGANIZATION SKILLS

How does teaching students to make decisions, plan, and self-evaluate their project work look? Erica develops tools to teach her students self-management skills in a study of their own school and in the creation of a state fair.

CHAPTER 8: STUDENTS BECOMING TEACHERS

How do students feel about managing their own learning and discussing their thinking? Empowered and articulate students share the decision making, planning, and self-evaluation skills they learned in the process of preparing to teach at the conclusion of the Mexico study.

5

Communication of Thinking and Social-Emotional Processes

They [the students] also felt really proud of what they'd done and powerful in doing it, no matter what happened in all the stuff. They completed something and they went through all these problems and they changed a lot because of it.

—Erica, fifth grade teacher

The Sonoran Desert of Arizona is an unfamiliar place of great beauty. Having lived in the Pacific Northwest for many years, I can communicate about the conifers, Douglas firs, and the Ponderosa pines. I can talk about the lush maidenhair ferns and the delicate three-petaled trillium found in the rainforest of the Columbia River Gorge. Yet, as I walk through the desert landscape so new to me, I find that I do not have the vocabulary to accurately discuss the plants native to the desert. In order to communicate adequately about this unfamiliar landscape, I need new terminology. Educators are in a similar situation as they struggle to bring teaching and learning into the twenty-first century.

COMMUNICATION FOR TEACHING

Communication about Thinking

Communication is of primary importance to the teacher's job. Teachers communicate about learning and teaching with students, parents, colleagues, administrators, and student teachers. Now in the new landscape of teaching and learning, educators need new vocabulary. Students must learn not only to master subject matter content and the basic skills of reading, writing, and math, but also the intellectual processes of how to find information, solve problems, and think critically and creatively. Students need to learn the self-management skills of setting criteria, making decisions, planning, and self-evaluation. As Friedman (2005) points out, students of today need to learn how to learn.

Communication about Social-Emotional Learning

Teaching and learning in the twenty-first century must include more than academic knowledge and intellectual skills. Teachers need to communicate with students about the social-emotional processes involved in character development, including the capacity to reflect, feel empathy for themselves and others, demonstrate ethical reasoning, manage mastery, and show appreciation for the differences in people, beliefs, cultures, and environments. Teachers need to be able to communicate with their students about thinking and learning through the process of metacognition.

Communication Evolves

Learning to communicate with students about their thinking and social-emotional learning is a process that evolves over time. This section follows Erica through her first three years of teaching as she learns to teach the self-organization processes of decision making, planning, and self-evaluation found in the *evaluation* component of the TIEL Wheel and how to communicate with students about these thinking processes. During the first year, Erica learned to teach self-organization skills without the TIEL Wheel to place these skills within a larger context. Later, in Erica's third year of teaching, she learned how the TIEL Model provides a context for self-organization processes as well as other thinking and social-emotional processes. This section illustrates how using the language of the TIEL framework facilitates communication about thinking and social-emotional learning.

Erica's learning and teaching help address the following questions. Why is a new language of teaching and learning needed? How does learning to discuss thinking and social-emotional processes with students develop over time? How does the TIEL Model provide a valuable tool that helps teachers deepen their understanding of thinking and social-emotional learning and the capacity to communicate about learning processes with students? How does learning to articulate their thinking help empower students to take more responsibility for their own learning?

NEW LANGUAGE

Erica learned to articulately discuss thinking and social-emotional processes with her fourth and fifth grade students during her first three years of teaching. However, she did not learn these communication skills in her teacher preparation program or during student teaching. I met Erica when I was assigned to be her student teaching supervisor. During the weeks I worked with Erica, it became clear that she was acutely aware of her own learning. "I have to know where I'm going," she explained. "I need to see the big picture."

Learning Needs

Erica discovered her learning needs during her undergraduate work in political science. In spite of graduating *magna cum laude* from a noted university, Erica felt she knew nothing about political science. She could see that other people were making connections in her program that she could not seem to make. The disconnected piecemeal methods of teaching in her college classes that focused on facts and recall did not address her way of learning. Groomed for a career in law, she entered law school, but soon left. She realized she wanted to teach and help children learn in ways that would help them understand the thinking that underlies learning. Erica enrolled in a top teacher preparation program and began student teaching.

Student Teaching

Ted was Erica's cooperating teacher. She thrived in Ted's open and intellectually challenging third grade class. Learning from Ted gave Erica many opportunities to build her expertise in conducting reading and writing workshops with the students. She was exposed to teaching the self-organization processes of decision making, planning, and self-evaluation within the context of teaching reading and writing. Yet, she was not learning to make these skills explicit to the students; she did not understand the place of self-organization skills within a wider range of thinking and social-emotional processes, nor did she see the application of these processes to other curricular subjects.

While supervising Erica, I saw the gap in communication. Ted needed vocabulary that would make him aware of the self-organization skills he was teaching and how they transferred across subjects. Erica needed vocabulary that would help her learn the deep structures of learning. I needed a vocabulary to more clearly guide Erica as she planned, presented, and reflected on her lessons. We were all having difficulty communicating with each other with no common theoretical foundation or language on which to base discussions of thinking, learning, and teaching. That would come later.

After supervising Erica during her student teaching, I became more determined to focus my research on ways to help teachers communicate about thinking and learning. I wanted to explore ways that would help teachers develop curriculum that teaches the self-organization skills of decision making, planning, and self-evaluation through project-based curriculum. When I began my research, Erica and Ted agreed to participate.

DEVELOPMENT OVER TIME: LEARNING TO TEACH
SELF-ORGANIZATION SKILLS

Erica began to develop her first project-based social studies unit during the spring of her first year of teaching as part of the pilot project for my research. The study of colonial life in seventeenth- and eighteenth-century America included opportunities for students to set criteria, make decisions, plan their projects, and self-evaluate their work. The unit required students to research, work with a group to create a project, and make a presentation.

The unit clearly contained content, process, and product. Content was the study of seventeenth- and eighteenth-century life in colonial America. Process included teaching the students the self-organization processes of decision making, planning, and self-evaluation within the context of their project work. The product was a poster or mural that depicted colonial life. Erica developed five self-organization tools to guide students through the processes of decision making, planning the project, monitoring their daily work, conferencing with the teacher, and evaluating the presentation.

Learning to teach self-organization processes revealed more about Erica's learning style. She processed information on an as-needed basis, learning when she was ready. Providing Erica with information she did not ask for only overwhelmed her. This was understandable as Erica needed to apply new strategies in order to truly understand them. Bombarding her with too much information did not allow her the time she needed to try out the new learning.

Communication through Asking Questions

Instruction was most effective when Erica asked a specific question. Learning to develop materials to teach students how to use criteria in decision making is an example. As she thought about possible projects the students could do as culminating projects for the colonial life unit, Erica asked, "How do I help my students decide on their projects?" After introducing her to a decision-making grid, Erica made a decision-making tool with the students to help them decide on their projects from several possible options (see figure 5.1). The grid included three components:

- A place to write ideas
- A place to write criteria to be considered in making the decision
- A numerical system for rating the ideas

First, Erica drew a large decision-making grid on a piece of chart paper. She then asked the students questions that led them through each component of the decision-making process.

Name_____ Date_____

CRITERIA FOR DECISION MAKING
Using Criteria to Rate Ideas

State Problem   _____
or Decision   _____
                 _____

List Criteria

List ideas   Score

Scoring: 3 points – very workable
            2 points – somewhat workable
            1 point – not so workable
            0 points – won't work

Figure 5.1.   *Criteria for Decision-Making* worksheet.

- What will you do to show understanding of colonial life in the eighteenth century?
- What are some possible projects that will show your group's understanding of one aspect of colonial life in the eighteenth century?
- What criteria will help you decide on your projects? What will tell us that you did a good job? What will show your understanding of colonial life?
- How can you use the criteria to rate each of the possible projects?

Based on their responses, Erica completed the sample decision-making sheet with her students (see figure 5.2).

Name_____ Date _____

CRITERIA FOR DECISION MAKING
Using Criteria to Rate Ideas

State Problem
or Decision: <u>My group will design a project that tells</u>
                <u>about colonial life in the 18th century</u>

List Criteria:

List Ideas:	Group interest	Availability of research resources	Availability of materials	Visual appeal	Audience understanding	Score
Model of a bank	3	1	1	1	1	7
Diorama comparing urban & rural life	2	2	2	2	2	10
Model of Plymouth Rock Settlement	3	3	3	3	3	15

Scoring: 3 points – very workable
            2 points – somewhat workable
            1 point – not so workable
            0 points – won't work

Figure 5.2.   Example using *Criteria for Decision-Making* worksheet.

• Statement of problem or decision: My group will design a project that tells about colonial life in the eighteenth century.
• Possible projects: model of a bank, diorama comparing urban and rural life, model of Plymouth Rock settlement.
• Criteria for decision making: group interest, availability of research resources, availability of materials, visual appeal, audience understanding.
• Rating: 1 to 3

Rating ideas numerically helps students make decisions about their projects.
    Erica's learning and teaching hinged on questions. Just as her questions facilitated her students' learning, my questions facilitated Erica's learning. When she mentioned that some kind of plan should follow the decision-making

process, I responded with a question. "What components should you include in developing a planning tool for your students?" Erica offered the following:

- Description of the project
- Who the audience is and when it is due
- How the project should look at the end
- Materials that will be needed
- Steps needed to complete the project
- Problems I might have

Erica did not include the last component, *problems I might have*, but it is an important one. As students get older, projects get bigger and the possible problems increase. Students need a place to forecast the challenges they might have in completing their projects. These can include lack of time and materials, insufficient research, procrastination, or difficulty working with the group. This important part of planning makes students aware that most likely there will be problems as they work on their project. It helps students develop their problem-solving skills as they learn to see problems as challenges to be solved, not reasons to give up.

Considering problems as part of the planning helps students to look ahead and take measures to prevent many of the problems that can arise in developing a project with a group. For example, a common problem is procrastination. When students receive a handout with the instructions planned by the teacher for a project to be completed at home or during nonschool hours, it is easy to put off starting the project. To some students it can feel more like the teacher's project than their own and they lack the motivation to begin. Other students procrastinate because they become overwhelmed by the amount of work involved in the project and don't know where to start.

Even with explicit instructions, most students need help in planning how to complete the steps of the project by the due date. On the other hand, when students participate in setting criteria for the project, decide how they will present their research, and plan the work over a set amount of time, the project is theirs. They are more motivated to begin and to finish. The *Basic Planning Sheet* shows how these components can be organized (see figure 5.3).

Designing Self-Management Tools

Application of new ideas was an essential part of Erica's learning. After establishing the components needed in a planning sheet, Erica designed self-management tools that met her needs and those of her students. She learned best when she constructed materials based on her own understanding of what was needed. She often did not want to see an example, preferring to work the ideas out on her own through a process of trial and error.

Name_____ Date_____

BASIC PLANNING

I am going to:

Due Date:
Audience:

I will evaluate my project by:			

The things I will need are:

The steps I will take are:

Problems I might have are:

Figure 5.3.   *Basic Planning Sheet.*

Planning

Erica referred to project work as *inquiry*. She entitled her planning worksheet *Inquiry Group Planning Sheet* to help her students focus on using research to answer questions (see figure 5.4). Erica's *Inquiry Group Planning Sheet* included

- Group name
- Individual name
- Materials needed
- Criteria to be used as guidelines for evaluation
- Steps for division of work among group members
- Problems that may arise

INQUIRY GROUP PLANNING SHEET

Group Name_____ Your Name _____

Describe what your group's final project is
_____
_____

What materials do you need? (BE SPECIFIC)
_____

Who are possible Resource People that you will contact?
_____

CRITERIA TO BE USED AS GUIDELINES FOR EVALUATION
1. Does your project have a written, visual and oral component?
2. Did you choose an appropriate way to share information that you have discovered?
3.
4.
5.

STEPS FOR DIVISION OF WORK AMONG GROUP MEMBERS
1.
2.
3.
4.
5.

PROBLEMS THAT MAY ARISE
1.
2.
3.

Figure 5.4. *Inquiry Group Planning Sheet* for Colonial Life study #1 (pilot).

Erica included most of the eight components found on the basic planning sheet example—description of project, due date, audience, criteria for evaluation, numerical rating, materials needed, steps, and the section for predicting problems. On this first planning sheet, she did not include the due date, the audience, or a numerical rating system for the final evaluation.

Evaluation

If planning logically follows decision making, then evaluation logically follows planning and presenting a project. Erica designed a basic reflection worksheet for peer evaluation to be used after each group completed their colonial life presentation. The *Inquiry Group Evaluation Form* required students to complete three tasks (see figure 5.5).

INQUIRY GROUP EVALUATION FORM

Date _____

Presenting Group's Name _____

Please answer the following questions using a scale of 1–5:
    1 = not at all   4 = very much
    2 = a little   5 = absolutely/totally
    3 = pretty much

****

1. The presentation was clearly organized.   _____
2. I could understand/hear the presenters.   _____
3. I learned something that I did not know before.   _____

****

Please list 2–3 things that you learned from the group's presentation.

What questions do you still have for the group?

Figure 5.5.   *Inquiry Group Evaluation Form* for Colonial Life study
#1 (pilot).

First, she asked the students to answer three questions using a rating scale of 1 to 5.

- Was the presentation clearly organized?
- Could you understand and hear the presenters?
- Did you learn something that you did not know before?

The numbers represented the following: (1) not at all, (2) a little, (3) pretty much, (4) very much, and (5) absolutely/totally.

Second, Erica asked students to write two to three things that they learned from each group's presentation. Erica wanted the students to understand their roles as both teachers and learners. Projects give students an opportunity to develop expertise in a topic and teach what they learned to their audience. Asking students to write what they learned from other presentations helped make sure that they were attentive listeners.

Third, in keeping with Erica's focus on inquiry, the final question on the reflection worksheet was evidence of Erica's passion for developing students' curiosity and her belief that you can always learn more. The last question: "What questions do you still have for the group?"

Self-Monitoring Tools

During the research pilot, Erica was frustrated about the time students wasted in getting started on their colonial life projects. Even with careful planning, students, like many of us, often procrastinate taking those first steps. I suggested that she develop a progress sheet for the students to use at the conclusion and at the beginning of daily work time. She designed a *Daily Group Progress Report* that included the following information (see figure 5.6):

- Date and group name
- Group members and each person's specific job (facilitator, reporter, procurer of materials, debriefer, encourager)
- Today's work
- Tomorrow's plans
- Problems the group is having

Erica also designed a worksheet for her own use. Using the *Inquiry Group Conference Sheet*, she documented the communication she had with each group during conferences (see figure 5.7). On this sheet she recorded the following:

- Date of the conference
- Group with whom she was meeting
- Overall progress of the group since the last conference
- Problems and issues the group was experiencing
- Additional support needed
- Possible mini-lessons

As Erica held conferences with each group, she began to see areas that could be addressed in a short lesson with all of the students. She used this information to plan mini-lessons on such topics as research skills, taking notes, recording group progress, or sequencing the steps necessary to complete the project.

Changes in Teaching and Learning

Erica's teaching changed during the pilot project. After learning to incorporate the teaching of decision making, planning, and self-evaluation into project work, Erica saw changes not only in her teaching but in the students' learning as well.

SELF-DIRECTION AND RESPONSIBILITY

During the short three months of work on developing ways to teach self-organization processes, Erica noticed that the students had become more self-directed and empowered in the classroom. They were taking more control over their work. Erica saw examples of the students taking more responsibility for their work. Most students promptly began their work time where they had left

---

DAILY GROUP PROGRESS REPORT

Group Name_____ Date _____

Was all group homework done?   Yes ☐   No ☐

Group Members: Job
1. _____ _____   F = Facilitator
2. _____ _____   R = Recorder
3. _____ _____   M = Materials
4. _____ _____   D = Debriefer
5. _____ _____   E = Encourager
 * If you have only 4 members, one person may have 2 jobs
 * Change jobs so that it makes sense for your group

Today, we did the following: _____
_____
_____
_____
_____

Tomorrow, we plan to do the following: _____
_____
_____
_____
_____

My group is having problems with the following: _____
_____
_____
_____
_____

Figure 5.6. *Daily Group Progress Report* **for Colonial Life study #1 (pilot).**

INQUIRY GROUP CONFERENCE SHEET

Group Name_____ Date_____

Status: (overall) – Progress . . .

Problems/Issues:

Support Needed: (Materials . . .)

Possible Mini-Lesson:

Figure 5.7. *Inquiry Group Conference Sheet* for Colonial Life study #1 (pilot).

off the previous day. Students asked to work on their projects, some requesting that they be allowed to work during recess time.

Nevertheless, Erica had learned by experience that learning self-management skills through project work does not always go smoothly. Even though both she and the students were at times disappointed when they had difficulties carrying out the processes of self-organization, the students were proud of their increasing self-efficacy. Erica commented, "They [the students] also felt really proud of what they'd done and powerful in doing it, no matter what happened in all the stuff. They completed something and they went through all these problems and they changed a lot because of it."

Social-Emotional Changes

Erica also noticed important social and emotional changes in the students. As students developed a personal sense of owning their learning, their relationships with each other changed as well. They seemed to have more empathy for each other and showed appreciation for each other in new ways. She described what she was seeing: "It [using decision making, planning, and self-evaluation] broadened the [numbers of] people they talked with and learned with. Now I've been trying to figure out where that's coming from because I see it a lot now in the room. People that they'll go and talk to—and it's not necessarily people that were in their groups."

Erica did not attribute the changes that she observed in the students to simply working together in groups. Prior to the pilot study, Erica used cooperative learning in her classroom (Johnson, Johnson, & Holubec, 1994; Kagan, 1994; Slavin, 1995). Now, however, she was seeing a change in the classroom beyond that brought about by group work alone. She felt that the students were "better people" because of the experience of using decision making, planning, and self-evaluation in their project work. When she asked them to turn to somebody next to them and share their thinking, they were now sharing with different combinations of people.

Erica analyzed possible causes for the changes she was seeing in the students. They had struggled with making decisions and planned together. They solved problems together—not always peacefully—and finally, experienced the accomplishment of completing a project together. She felt that in some ways her students had bonded in the way of soldiers sharing battlefield experiences: "They [the students] had to work through those difficult times with people they just wanted to kill. It kind of makes you a different person because of that—and maybe you have a little better coping skills—just a bit—or you can empathize a bit with people's struggles or you can kind of relate a little bit to people because of that."

MORE CHANGES AT END OF SECOND YEAR OF TEACHING

At the end of Erica's second year of teaching, I checked in with her to assess her use of self-organization skills before we began the official year of research work in the fall. As before, this fourth grade class was completing the study of colonial life. Using what she had learned the previous year, Erica had developed self-management tools for Colonial Life study #2. While Erica used some of the same planning and evaluation materials that she had developed the previous year, she made three significant changes. She now added context, detail, and visibility to the project work.

Context

First, Erica gave the students a context for their projects in keeping with Chiarelott's (2006) recommendation that curriculum be developed within a real world context. Erica decided to have the students develop a museum on colonial life to place their projects in more of a real world context. As the students worked, they focused on creating exhibits appropriate for a museum with an accompanying information card that provided background on their project. The general criteria for the end project included these questions:

- Would this belong in a museum?
- Does this project show your information?

Detail

Second, Erica developed the criteria for evaluating the project in more detail. In project-based learning, each project should include a written, visual, and spoken component. Students share their research and answers to their research questions through a written component. Essays, reports of factual information, scripts, stories, or poems are some possible forms the written portion can take. The written component for the *Colonial Life Museum* projects was an information card displayed with the visual project similar to those found with exhibits in actual museums. The visual component shares the research visually. This can include posters, three-dimensional models, dramatizations, and newspapers. In the spoken presentation, students use the visual component of the project to share their research and answer questions from their classmates.

With the students, Erica set criteria for evaluation in each of the three components of the project. She asked questions to help draw possible criteria from the students.

Written Component

What does the information card for your museum exhibit need to include?

- Specific amount of information
- Accurate content
- New information for the audience
- Well-organized details
- Clearly written text

Visual Component

What characteristics will we look for in the visual project that will help us evaluate your work?

- Neat, clear, and easily understood
- Well prepared and sturdy

Speaking Presentation

How will we evaluate the speaking presentation when you share your research and project with all of us?

- Speaking is clear and understandable.
- Presentation made the audience think.
- Audience asked good questions.
- Students can answer questions competently.

Visibility

Third, Erica made the criteria for evaluation for the projects and presentations openly visible in the classroom (see figures 5.8 and 5.9). After developing the criteria with the students, Erica typed up worksheets with the criteria for each component for the students. In addition, she hung large charts displaying the criteria from the classroom "clothesline" to further focus the work and facilitate communication. As the day for the presentations grew nearer, she placed another chart on the clothesline with some additional criteria for the presentations. These criteria were written in the form of questions:

- Is the presentation the right amount of time?
- Did we learn things we didn't know before?
- Could we hear the speakers?
- Was the group well prepared?
- Was the information useful?

Validation and Responsibility

Teachers spend a lot of time providing validation for students. While working on their projects, students frequently came to Erica asking, "Is this good?" Both the worksheets and the criteria displayed in the classroom served as a ready reference to help students answer their own questions. For example, when a student asked Erica about the written portion of the project, she pointed to the criteria chart and redirected the question to the student. She

asked, "Do you have the information that we all agreed to? Do you have information that will be new to your audience?" In this way, Erica continually
encouraged the students to develop more responsibility for their own learning.

Growth over Time: Comparing Colonial Life #1 to Colonial Life #2

Comparing the self-management tools from the first colonial life study to
those in the second one shows Erica's development in learning to communicate project requirements. She used what she had learned in the first study to
guide her planning for the second.

COLONIAL LIFE STUDY #2

Criteria for the Projects

General Criteria
   Would this belong in a museum?
   Does this project show your information?

Written
   Contained specific amount of information
   Contained accurate content
   Content contained new information for the audience
   Was well organized
   Was clearly written

Visual
   Neat, clear and easily understood
   Well-prepared and sturdy

Speaking presentation
   Speaking was clear and understandable
   Presentation made the audience think
   Audience asked good questions
   Students could answer questions competently

Figure 5.8. *Criteria for the Projects* for Colonial Life study #2.

COLONIAL LIFE STUDY #2

Criteria for the Presentation

Is it the right amount of time?

Did we learn things we didn't know before?

Could we hear the speakers?

Was the group well prepared?

Was the information useful?

Figure 5.9. *Criteria for the Presentation* for Colonial Life study #2.

Criteria for Evaluation for Colonial Life Study #1

In the Colonial Life study #1, criteria for evaluation are found in two places. The *Inquiry Group Planning Sheet* (figure 5.4) includes two criteria and blank spaces to add three more:

- Does your project have a written, visual, and oral component?
- Did you choose an appropriate way to share the information that you have discovered?

The written, visual, and oral components are lumped together with no details about what was expected in each one. Students are asked if they chose an appropriate way to share the information. However, in the first study the students had no context to help them decide the best way of sharing their information. The criteria for the presentation are not included on the initial *Inquiry Group Planning Sheet*, only on the *Inquiry Group Evaluation Form*.

Written and Visual Criteria for Colonial Life Study #2

The criteria for the projects in Colonial Life study #2 grew out of Erica's previous experience in teaching self-organization skills. In the second study, Erica realized that she needed to be much more specific about the context as well as about criteria for the written, visual, and spoken components of the projects.

Before Erica set the criteria for projects with her students, she carefully thought through her expectations. She had learned from the previous year that she wanted the students to produce better writing. Therefore, the expectations had to be more clearly stated. She knew that it was important for the visual part of the project, like the writing, to be neat, clear, and easily understood to avoid embarrassing questions such as, "What's that!?" She had also learned that in a busy classroom, projects must be sturdily constructed in order to survive through presentation day.

Criteria for Spoken Presentation in Colonial Life Study #2

The criteria for the spoken presentation in the second study showed Erica's increasing understanding of the importance of communicating with her students about thinking. In the first study, the criteria for the presentation provided a strong guideline for the students.

- The presentation was clearly organized.
- I could understand/hear the presenters.
- I learned something that I did not know before.

Nevertheless, Erica wanted the students to focus on thinking and inquiry as well as clear speaking. Scaffolding the discussion through carefully chosen questions, she developed more complex criteria for the second study that address the role of thinking during the speaking presentation.

Erica: What do we need to include in the criteria for evaluation for the speaking presentation? What should be the quality of the speaking?

Student: The speaking should be clear. We should be able to understand people when they talk.

Erica: What do you want the audience to do as a result of your presentation?

Student: I guess we want them to think about what we are saying.

Erica: How can we tell if the audience is thinking?

Student: Maybe if they ask us questions about something.

Erica: If the audience asks questions what do you, the presenters, need to be able to do?

Student: We should be able to answer the questions.

Erica: Now, what are the criteria we've developed for the speaking presentation?

Based on their responses, Erica wrote a list of criteria for the speaking presentation on a piece of chart paper (see figure 5.10). Before Erica discussed the setting of criteria with her students, she made sure she was clear about the criteria. She reflected on previous experience to determine the self-organization tools that had worked well and where she might make adjustments. The revised criteria for the speaking presentation in the second study emerged from her own learning about how to teach self-organization skills. As she learned more about how to communicate about thinking with her students, she wanted the students to be aware of how their presentations can affect the thinking and learning of the audience.

Communication with Students

The students reflected Erica's growing capacity to discuss self-organization skills. They explained that their projects included a written, visual, and an oral presentation component. One group, with scripts lost and a clay bank that had collapsed, felt their organization could have been better. Nellie, speaking for the hapless group, clearly felt that she had done more than her share of the work by writing the speech for the presentation. Indeed, their group had had difficulties, but they kept trying.

Although the written and visual portions of the project were challenging, the speaking presentations went well. The speaking was clear and understandable, the presentation made the audience think and ask good questions that the students could answer competently. Nevertheless, one student, in all honesty, pointed out, "Yes, but there were a few questions that I wasn't sure about."

Speaking Presentation

- Speaking was clear and understandable
- Presentation made the audience think
- Audience asked good questions
- Students could answer questions competently

Figure 5.10.   Criteria chart for speaking presentations.

In the end the students had an awareness of not only information concerning colonial life, but a better understanding of the processes required to plan, research, and develop a group project. They credited Erica for the successful completion of their projects saying, "Our teacher helped us make decisions, she motivated us to keep going, and she helped us evaluate if our project was good or not so good." They told about a chart that she made with them that helped them decide the best method for doing the projects.

Their teacher motivated them by "expanding and pushing" their thinking. At the end, they assessed the quality of their projects using the evaluation sheets that their teacher designed for them. The evidence at the baseline assessment indicated that Erica had a good grasp of discussing decision making, planning, and self-evaluation with her students. Yet, she knew she needed to know more, but was not at all sure what "more" entailed.

Limited Communication about Thinking and Learning

Erica did not have the knowledge needed to support project work in her classroom before the pilot study. I asked Erica what had prevented her from having students make decisions, plan, and self-evaluate before. She explained that she had not known what to do. "For me it was just being new at it and not really knowing what I wanted to come out of it. When I became more aware of what I really wanted, then I could figure out how to get there."

For all she had learned, at the end of the pilot project Erica still lacked important knowledge. Erica was now able to help students make decisions, plan, and evaluate their work in very purposeful ways. Yet, she still had no framework to help her put those evaluative skills into a wider context of thinking and social-emotional processes.

I did not introduce the TIEL Wheel to Erica during the pilot project. Because of the short time period, I decided to concentrate only on teaching the self-organizational skills of decision making, planning, and self-evaluation. Since she learned to teach self-organization skills in isolation, Erica still lacked a deeper understanding of her new skills. While she noticed significant changes in her teaching and the students' learning, she still lacked the language she needed to more fully communicate the thinking and social-emotional aspects of her teaching and the students' learning.

Erica sensed her learning gaps. Seeing ahead to what she needed to learn, she anticipated the need for a theoretical framework that could help her situate her new knowledge. As we discussed how she talked to her students about thinking, she said, "I know now that different things that we're doing fall into different places, but I don't really have a handle on what those things are. If I did then I would be able to use it better with my kids."

In the following chapters, Erica learns to use the TIEL language and deepens her understanding of how to communicate with her students about thinking and learning.

6

Challenges of Classroom Context

TIEL makes all the difference. You need to have the framework. I need to have it in order to categorize and sort and scaffold and give myself a framework to go back to. I think it's critical.

—Erica, fifth grade teacher

Erica ended her first year of teaching with a growing sense of how to develop a project-based unit of study. She planned for students to participate in making decisions involving their projects; she helped students develop criteria with which to evaluate their projects; and she created planning worksheets that helped students organize their work. Her students responded to her efforts by taking more responsibility for their learning, working in groups more effectively, and showing appreciation for peers with whom they had not previously worked.

Learning to teach students to manage their own learning is challenging. Students need space to work on projects, a certain amount of autonomy, and an understanding of the thinking skills of decision making, planning, and self-evaluation. However, those challenges are made more difficult by both the visible and invisible contexts of the classroom. The visible context of the classroom includes the size of the classroom and the children, the numbers of children in the class, the teaching materials, and student behavior. The invisible context includes available time to teach, social-emotional influences on student behavior, and an understanding of the intellectual processes of teaching and learning new skills. This chapter shares how Erica changed the physical and intellectual space in her classroom to create the time, space, and level of student autonomy needed to teach self-management skills.

VISIBLE CONTEXTUAL FACTORS

Teaching students the self-organization skills of decision making, planning, and self-evaluation occurs within a tangle of physical factors that affect both teaching and learning. Some of the conditions are alterable, but some are not. Factors that Erica could not change included the number of students, the size of her classroom, and the size of her students.

Nonadjustable Factors

The number of students greatly affects the amount of space, time, and attention available for project work. The larger the class size, the less time, attention, and physical space are available. During her first year of teaching, Erica's moderately sized class was helpful as she initially learned how to teach self-management skills. However, during her third year, the research year, Erica had thirty-one students, twenty-one boys and ten girls. In addition to the number of children, the age and size of the students also affects the teaching and learning.

Erica's class was looping, an organizational structure in which a class has the same teacher for two consecutive years. Erica was teaching the same group of students for a second year, but at times she felt that they were strangers. The fourth graders were now fifth graders. They were older, larger, and exhibited social and emotional behaviors announcing their impending entry into middle school.

At other times, she wished they *were* strangers. Erica had only considered the positives of teaching the same students two years in a row. She would know their strengths and weaknesses; she would know the content they had learned, and they would already have experience in planning and evaluating projects. The students would be familiar with her teaching style and expectations.

It seemed to be an ideal situation. Yet, Erica had not anticipated that teaching the same students for the second year would eliminate the honeymoon—that illusionary period of peace that exists in a classroom before the students and the teacher learn to know each other well. The friendships and frictions had long been established. Instead of the excitement of unknown expectations and the nervous restraint common at the beginning of the year, the looser behaviors of familiarity were present as the year started. While the advantages to teaching the same group of students would emerge as the year progressed, rough spots marked the beginning.

Adjusting the Visible Space

Creating an inviting and comfortable learning environment was important to Erica. She wanted the ambiance of a nonclassroom environment with the freedom of movement found in a casual family room. During her first year of teaching, she had a large carpeted meeting area bordered on three sides with benches. In addition, she had three smaller carpeted areas that included book-shelves and pillows in other parts of the room. Rectangular desks were arranged in groupings of four. She also had a large couch and a sizable brown swivel rocker.

Erica's classroom arrangement was crowded. In her second year of teaching, she kept the couch but replaced the desks with round tables. This afforded more space, but produced other drawbacks. The tables were large enough to seat four students, but too small to spread out large amounts of work. How-ever, she retained the carpeted meeting area and the smaller carpeted spaces with bookshelves and pillows.

Students Increase in Number and Size

In the third year, the fifth graders entered a classroom organized much as they had left it as fourth graders. They were basically the same students, yet now there were more of them and they were larger. With the new move-ins, the numbers had grown to thirty-one students. The arrangement of the physi-cal space was especially cumbersome when the students returned after their summer growth spurt. Upon entering the classroom in the fall, they had out-grown the already limited space. Beyond the individual crates for storing sup-plies, the students did not have a space to call their own.

There were too few tables for all thirty-one students to sit at the same time. Therefore, during small group work, two groups were required to sit on the couch or in the carpeted meeting area.

Fortunately, there were tables in the hallway that could accommodate work that overflowed the classroom. When students worked on large projects, they used the hallway tables or the floor. Full-class discussions of thinking and learning, as well as mini-lessons for teaching decision making, planning, or evaluation skills, still took place in the carpeted meeting area.

Adjustments in Autonomy

Students had a great deal of autonomy in Erica's classroom. During her first and second years of teaching, there were no assigned seats at either the tables or on the carpet. The students were free to work at any table or on any of the several carpeted areas in the room and had self-monitored bathroom privi-leges. As she began her third year, she established the same organizational structures that allowed a high degree of freedom. However, she quickly recog-nized that this arrangement was no longer working.

As the students' behavior began to deteriorate early in the school year, Erica recognized that they had too many choices and too much autonomy. She be-gan to restore order by removing certain privileges: names were attached to ta-bles and bathroom privileges were limited. She established stricter routines for movement within and without the classroom. When this was not enough, she realized that she needed to reevaluate the overall organization of the physical space.

Erica's battle for workspace continued throughout the year. Although she had tried to solve the space problem by adjusting and readjusting the furniture, the decision to make substantive changes was traumatic, forcing her to compromise some of her deepest philosophical beliefs about classrooms. She began by removing two of the carpeted areas, but left the large meeting area and one small reading area at the back corner of the room. She removed the oversized comfortable couch and spread out the tables, opening more space for movement.

Frustrated and disappointed, this was a difficult time for Erica. She thought that having the same students for a second year would shorten the months of learning how the classroom worked, if not eliminating it altogether. She expected that the students would climb up on the platform established the previous year and dive into learning. Instead, she found herself needing to make changes that were antagonistic to her teaching philosophy in order to find the right level of autonomy for the students.

THE INVISIBLE CONTEXTUAL FACTORS

The invisible factors of classroom context also present problems that affect the teaching of thinking and social-emotional processes. The problems of time, processes of learning, and how to teach so students can understand the social-emotional dimension of their learning must also be solved. While student behavior improved with changes in the physical environment, Erica wondered how she could increase instructional time. She also wondered how to communicate the abstract skills of decision making, planning, and self-evaluation more effectively to her students.

Time

Time is an important factor when teaching in ways that promote thinking and social-emotional development. It takes time to let students participate in setting criteria and then use that criteria in making decisions about the topics they will research or the method they will use to construct their projects. Teaching students to carefully plan project work is time intensive. It requires careful time management to help students use the original criteria from their plan sheets to evaluate their projects and those of their peers. Teaching self-organization skills requires carefully planned blocks of time, while the amount of time available in the school day remains immutable.

Erica expressed a feeling common to teachers, "Lots of stuff to cover, lots of stuff to do, and I want to get in as much stuff as I can." Yet, because she saw the teaching of self-organization skills as a priority, she made a conscious decision to allow the time needed. She explained her thinking, "I'm better at using time in general because I'm more experienced as a teacher. But I'm giving it [teaching self-organization processes] the time even if it means I need to cut time from other places. I'm seeing it more as a *worthwhile* use of time."

Alternating Content

One way Erica created more time involved the teaching of content. Science and social studies are both rich in possibilities for project-based learning and both provide opportunities for teaching self-organization skills. However, teaching two units simultaneously that involve planning, researching, and constructing a project can be overwhelming for the teacher as well as the students. Therefore, Erica alternated the teaching of science and social studies so that each could be done in more depth and with more hands-on learning. Each unit was planned for approximately four weeks. As a social studies unit ended, the students would begin a study in science.

Integrating Subjects

Another way that Erica carved out more time for teaching self-management skills involved literacy skills in the content areas of social studies and science. Erica maintained separate reading and writing blocks that focused on the skills and strategies involved in literacy. However, she often identified particular skills and strategies that applied to both literacy and the studies in social studies or science. She then decided if she would teach the skills in social studies first or in the writing block first. For example, in the social studies unit called the School Study, which will be discussed in detail in the next chapter, Erica taught the students how to conduct an interview and how to take notes. Later, the students used that information to learn informational writing in both the School Study unit and in the writer's workshop. While the School Study was going on, Erica maintained a complete writer's workshop unit of study.

A Teacher's Learning Process

The teaching and learning process itself kept Erica from progressing as fast as she would have liked in developing these new pedagogical skills. Yet, teachers, like everyone, need time to develop new learning. She could see the possibilities in teaching thinking processes, but she was not yet able to consistently turn the possibilities into reality. She explained, "As I become more comfortable with it [teaching thinking processes] and know more, I feel that I can tap into stuff that's going on in the room that could probably build right into this. I don't necessarily pick up on it right away. Like stuff that you'll see and you'll be able to plug it right in. I'm better at it, the more I use it."

Reflection versus Self-Flagellation

For many new teachers, reflection often turns into self-flagellation. Erica felt that if she had worked more, completed more projects, or pushed herself harder, her teaching and the students' learning would be better. Developing the complex teaching skills required to focus on higher-level thinking and student understanding cannot be rushed. Darling-Hammond (1997) states that the complex teaching skills that are important in progressive teaching methods have not been maintained because of the "the extensive skill needed to teach both subjects and students well" (p. 12). Feeling the stretch as she developed these skills, Erica struggled to explain her feelings, "I feel like it's all swimming around in my head a little bit. I don't have a really strong understanding. . . . I need to remind myself of what it is . . . I get the what-I'm-trying-to-do in the end, but how I am really doing what I want to be doing throughout the whole work. And also I just want to . . . know more."

Erica needed help in organizing the new learning that was "swimming around in her head." She understood the end result of teaching self-management skills— students would be able to make decisions, plan, and, at the end, evaluate their projects. However, she needed to understand what she was "really" doing on a deeper level as she incorporated the teaching of self-management skills into her instruction.

At the beginning of her third year of teaching, Erica was deliberate about teaching the self-organization skills of decision making, planning, and self-evaluation. In an effort to increase her students' understanding, she made every effort to make the abstract concepts visible to her students. For example, as she had learned in Ted's classroom, Erica displayed lists of criteria for projects on clotheslines. These guidelines that emerged from classroom discussions spanned the classroom.

Needing More Knowledge

Yet, Erica knew there was more to be done. She wanted to give the students more responsibility for their own learning, while, at the same time, she wanted to help them become more aware of the thinking processes they were using to carry out that responsibility. She wanted to be able to readily recognize the opportunities for teaching thinking skills that were within the curriculum. And, she wanted to communicate with her students about the thinking skills they were using in their learning activities. She asked, "Where [in the curriculum] are the thinking skills that I'm going to be explicitly teaching? What are the research skills that I'm going to be teaching and naming things under?"

Erica was ready to be introduced to the TIEL Model. It would help her organize much of what was "swimming around in her head" and provide a tool to help her turn her intentions into reality. Erica was ready to make another physical change in her classroom that would make the TIEL framework visible and provide language for communication that supported her learning as well as that of the students.

THE TIEL MODEL:
MAKING THE INTELLECTUAL CONTEXT VISIBLE

A Chinese proverb attributed to Confucius states, "I hear and I forget. I see and I remember. I do and I understand." Words alone are quickly forgotten, but when words are combined with an image, a memory is more easily constructed and understanding takes place.

TIEL Bulletin Board

In the middle of the year, Erica created a TIEL bulletin board (see figure 2.3) in her classroom to support the discussion of thinking by making it visual, as discussed in chapter 2. The bulletin board, in the five TIEL colors, included charts that explained the thinking operation and quality of character represented by each color.

Erica referred to the TIEL bulletin board as she taught the students how to do research, set criteria, make decisions, plan, and evaluate. The TIEL bulletin board helped make visible the processes involved in developing projects. Erica displayed examples of student work that focused on a particular type of thinking that she was teaching. The students hung lists of student-generated research questions and idea webs on the pink (*cognition*) section of the bulletin board. On the blue (*memory*) portion, students placed written examples of previous knowledge they brought to a new study. Published memoirs were also placed on the blue *memory* section.

The green *evaluation* section was especially important in helping the students understand self-organization skills. Students mounted examples of their planning and evaluation sheets on the green center panel (*evaluation*) of the bulletin board. The project proposals that Erica required from the students stating their decisions about projects also had a place on the evaluation section of the bulletin board.

The yellow section, *convergent production*, included samples of the outlines for student projects. Sometimes this section included index cards with facts from the students' research. At other times, especially good examples of math assignments were placed on the yellow convergent section.

The orange section, *divergent production*, provided a place to show creative works. The students attached their art work to the bulletin board, and when space allowed, examples of their final creative projects. At other times, Erica placed brainstormed lists of possible topics or projects on the orange section to help students understand that divergent thinking involves generating many options.

Relationships between Thinking Operations and Qualities of Character

Erica's focus was on teaching her students the thinking operations. The TIEL bulletin board, however, clarified the relationships between the thinking operations and the qualities of character. Asking students to wonder and ask questions following a presentation was an example of the relationship between cognition and reflection that Dewey (1964) pointed out. The blue *memory* and *empathy* sections helped students understand that helping someone in need can start a chain reaction of empathy for others.

As students worked in groups, Erica used the green *evaluation* and *ethical reasoning* sections to remind the students that their decisions needed to show fairness and respect. The yellow sections representing *mastery* and *convergent production* was a reminder of the feelings involved in meeting expectations set by others and yourself. When Erica's students began talking and working with students with whom they had not previously associated, it was an example of the relationship between taking risks, an element of *divergent thinking* and *appreciation* of others.

Metacognition

Erica used the bulletin board to support metacognition. According to Hansen and Feldhusen (1994), "*metacognition* is the process of developing awareness of one's own thinking and techniques for controlling and improving thinking activities" (p. 320). Using the TIEL bulletin board to communicate about thinking helped the students become aware of their thinking and how they were learning. After helping students complete a planning sheet, Erica encouraged metacognition by asking, "How can we use the TIEL bulletin board to show the kind of thinking that you used to complete your planning sheet? While we used all the thinking processes to come up with our plans, which one did we particularly focus on?" (*evaluation*).

As the students became more aware of their own thinking, they began to take more responsibility for their own learning. One fifth grader shared her sense of awareness of her own thinking as she told how decision making and planning helped her with her projects.

> I think it helped me a lot. First of all, starting with the planning part, decision making [helps] me realize—OK—I've decided to do this certain thing so I'm focusing on what I'm doing. . . . The decision-making part tells me to get ready—like OK—I want to plan this out. Then actually doing it . . . the decision and planning part helped me do it and then the evaluation part made me think about what kind of good work I did.

TIEL Curriculum Design Wheel

The TIEL Curriculum Design Wheel also facilitated metacognition. Erica placed a large poster of the TIEL Wheel on the wall in the carpeted area at the front of the classroom where she gathered the students for mini-lessons, introducing new concepts, and class discussions. This TIEL Wheel was labeled simply with the five thinking operations on the bottom—*cognition, memory, evaluation, convergent production,* and *divergent production* and the five qualities of character on the top—*appreciation, mastery, ethical reasoning, empathy,* and *reflection.*

Erica referred to the large TIEL Wheel while leading discussions about research, setting criteria, making decisions, planning, or preparing to evaluate projects. The large TIEL Wheel poster did not include the discreet skills within each thinking operation or quality of character, but it was laminated so that Erica could add words with a marker or Post-its. While the bulletin board provided a place for visual examples of thinking processes, Erica used the TIEL Wheel poster to build a vocabulary of thinking with the students.

A conversation about *cognition* is an example. As students gave ideas about how to find information, Erica wrote them on Post-it notes and attached them to the pink *cognition* section of the TIEL Wheel.

Erica: What are the ways that you get information?

Student #1: Reading. (Erica writes *reading* on Post-it.)

Student #2: Looking at something. Watching something.

Erica: Observation, OK. (Writes *observation* on Post-it.)

Student #3: How about the Internet? Finding information on the computer.

Erica: Internet research. That's a good example of getting information.

Student #4: Sometimes you just find things out by accident.

Erica: Do you mean by discovering something? Sometimes you might be looking for something else, and you find out something completely unexpected. That happens to scientists. (Writes *discovery* on Post-it.)

Student #4: That happened when I was looking for information about Mexico.

Erica: What thinking process are we developing as we find information? Where do these thinking words belong on the TIEL Wheel? *(cognition;* see figure 6.1)

Erica clearly communicated that thinking was important. Using the TIEL bulletin board and the large laminated TIEL Wheel helped Erica change the intellectual environment in the class. Thinking was no longer abstract, invisible, and easily forgotten in the rush of the day. The students knew their thinking was respected. They understood that they were becoming better thinkers just as they were improving their skills in reading, writing, and math. Just as they

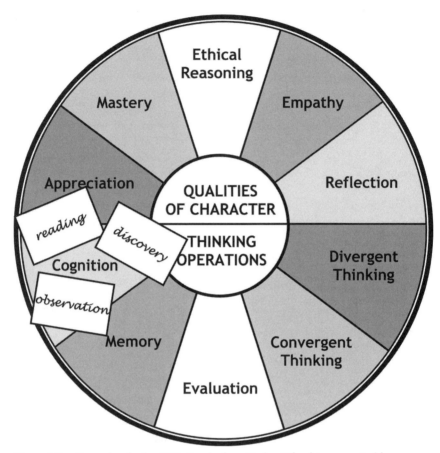

Figure 6.1. Example of using TIEL Curriculum Design Wheel to generate ideas.

were gaining knowledge in social studies and science, they were developing a deeper understanding of themselves as learners.

Balance

In addition to providing a language of thinking and feeling, the TIEL Model gave Erica a way to bring more balance to her curriculum. When she saw how the self-organization skills of decision making fit into a larger context, she began planning how to consciously include other thinking processes into her curriculum and make these visible to her students as well. Now that she had a way to communicate about thinking, she needed to make sure the students had opportunities to develop their thinking in all the areas of the TIEL framework.

Erica used the TIEL categories as an assessment tool to determine if she had planned sufficient activities in each of the five areas of thinking. As she developed curriculum during the research year, she asked herself the following questions:

- Cognition: What research skills do I want the students to learn?
- Memory: How can I help the students make connections from the thinking processes they are using in the current unit to thinking processes they used in the previous unit?
- Evaluation: How can I teach students the evaluation skills of decision making, planning, and self-evaluation in this unit?
- Convergent Production: Am I including activities that require logical, factual, convergent thinking?
- Divergent Production: What activity can I plan that will give students the opportunity to develop their creative, divergent thinking?

TIEL LINKS IN THE COMMUNICATION CHAIN

The TIEL framework supplies important links in the communication chain from teacher educator to teacher to students in a classroom.

Teacher Educator to Teacher

Using the TIEL Model made my teaching and Erica's learning much easier. The TIEL Model provided a context for self-management skills that helped Erica understand where she was in her learning. It also formed a scaffold that helped Erica reach the next steps. She commented, "TIEL makes all the difference. You need to have the framework. I need to have it in order to categorize and sort and scaffold and give myself a framework to go back to. I think it's critical."

TIEL Helps the Teacher

Erica cited several TIEL characteristics that she found especially helpful to her as a teacher. These included the common language, the visual concreteness, the flexibility of the framework in addressing various levels of learning, and the way it helped her and the students make generalizations.

First, Erica appreciated the common language that the TIEL Model provided for her and the students. Seymour Sarason (1982), who visited many classrooms throughout his long career as an educator, wrote about the lack of discussion of thinking and learning he observed. If he visited Erica's classroom, he would see a teacher and students articulately discussing thinking processes involved in learning activities and project work. He would hear the teacher ask students what kind of thinking they used in preparing their projects. He would hear students clearly discuss the planning and decision making that had gone into their work.

Second, Erica liked the visual concreteness of the colors that represented the framework. Placing examples of the students' work on the TIEL bulletin board helped the students "see" their thinking in a concrete way.

Third, the flexibility of the TIEL framework met the needs of learners at many levels. Whatever one's understanding of the framework, beginning level or more advanced, the TIEL framework helped deepen that individual's understanding of his or her learning. While the TIEL bulletin board helped some students "take baby steps" in learning about thinking, other students were able to see patterns. One student makes a "noticing" decision about thinking processes by placing a planning sheet on the green evaluation section of the bulletin board. At the same time, another student notices a pattern emerging over several projects that supports the generalization that planning is an important part of every project.

Fourth, as seen in the previous example, the TIEL framework facilitates the formation of generalizations. Learning becomes more manageable when generalizations are made through linking experiences, ideas, or information. Erica formed generalizations by making connections among the thinking processes. Displaying the names of the thinking processes on the bulletin board and laminated TIEL Wheel made the concepts of thinking less abstract. As Erica pointed out, "From seeing those small isolated things, you can take that next big step of forming generalizations."

The TIEL structure helped clarify both big and small learnings. An example of a "small learning" was a chart stating the criteria for evaluation for one project. Erica placed these group-constructed charts on the *evaluation* portion of the bulletin board. Later, she used the criteria for evaluation to construct the final evaluation rubric for the project. As she discussed the rubric with the students, she asked, "What similarities and differences do you notice about the criteria for evaluation that we set at the beginning of the project and the criteria included in the final evaluation rubric?"

Erica helped the students notice that these same or very similar criteria reappeared at the end of the project to assess their learning. After discussing the rubric with the students, she placed the rubric that she had designed from the original criteria on the bulletin board under evaluation.

Erica connected these small observations to form a larger generalization. After a number of small observations were made and became visible on the bulletin board, Erica made the generalization that the criteria set in the beginning was a very good guideline for students to follow while working on a project. As Erica became aware of the connections that existed from the beginning, through the middle, and to the end of a project, she was able to help her students see that pattern in their project work. At that point, it became clear how criteria for evaluation are a monitoring tools for students to use as they work on their projects.

TIEL Helps the Students

Students saw patterns and generalizations that emerged throughout their project work. They noticed that Erica had them alternately work individually or in groups to research information and complete their projects. The students mentioned several generalizations as we discussed similarities between projects:

- Studies begin with criteria setting.
- Setting criteria helps students make decisions about projects as well as understand the expectations for the end product.
- More detailed planning follows the setting of criteria for evaluation.
- Projects culminate with a presentation.
- Criteria for evaluation of a project are based on criteria developed at the beginning of the study.
- Criteria for evaluation guides work on the project.

Communicating about their thinking and learning helped the students develop a deeper understanding of self-organization skills. As the students became more adept at making decisions, planning, and self-evaluating their work, the classroom contexts and structures changed. The students' behavior and ability to work cooperatively improved. The students responded to the expanded number of hands-on projects with more effort, a greater sense of responsibility, and increased creativity.

SUMMARY

Communication is important in teaching the self-management skills of decision making, planning, and self-evaluation. Both the visible and invisible contexts of the classroom affect the teaching of self-management skills. Erica learned to adjust the physical space in the classroom so that her students would have more private space as well as room to work on projects in groups. As the students' behaviors improved, the opportunity for communicating about thinking and learning increased.

The TIEL Model helped Erica modify the less visible intellectual space in her classroom to facilitate communication of thinking and learning. She used the TIEL Wheel to design learning experiences that required a wide range of thinking. The TIEL bulletin board provided a place for students to display work that focused on a particular thinking operation. A large laminated TIEL Wheel was a useful tool for learning vocabulary that described thinking skills. As Erica guided the students in metacognitive discussions, they placed Post-it notes with thinking words in the appropriate sections of the TIEL Wheel. The TIEL language helped the students explain the thinking processes they used in developing their projects.

7

Teaching Self-Organization Skills

I planned so I wouldn't run out of time. I evaluated after each section. I used judgment to help me along.

—Nan, fifth grade student

Communicating about thinking and learning helped Erica's students develop a deeper understanding of self-organization skills. As the students became more adept at making decisions, planning, and self-evaluating their work, the context of the classroom changed. The students' behavior and ability to work cooperatively improved. They responded to the expanded number of hands-on projects with more effort, a greater sense of responsibility, and increased creativity. There were now periods of time when students worked with such focus on their projects that Erica needed to respond only when they had a question or asked for help. However, the peaceful moments during which students managed their own learning had not come easily. It began with Erica's consciousness of her own thinking processes.

PERSONAL DECISION MAKING, PLANNING, AND EVALUATION

Erica had a strong grasp of the processes she wished to teach. She considered decision making, planning, and self-evaluation as a package that was the same for her as for the students, using these skills in her professional life, her school life, and her personal life. She outlined her use of the processes in four simple steps: decision making, goal setting, steps to accomplishment, and self-evaluation. She explained,

> It would start with setting a goal, what is it you want to do, and then setting criteria for what it is that you want to find out, how are you going to know when you have achieved what it is you want to find out. How are you going to evaluate that? Planning—laying out the big things that you want to do and then the baby steps to get there. And ways to self-evaluate while you're doing that. Like checkpoints for yourself. Is this where I want to be going? Making choices and decisions along with that. And then at the end hopefully reaching your goal and then going back to those criteria from where you started—and evaluating that way.

This personal understanding of decision making, planning, and self-evaluation needed to be transformed into learning activities for children. Erica knew that she needed consistent practice in planning units that included the teaching of self-organization skills and that students needed many opportunities to practice these skills in their project work. At the same time, both she and the students needed continual practice in communicating about thinking and learning.

COMMUNICATION ABOUT THINKING THROUGH THREE PROJECT-BASED UNITS

Erica planned several project-based units that included the explicit teaching of self-organization skills. She had planned only one such social studies unit before, which she had taught in both her first and second year of teaching. Now, as she began her third year of teaching, she set the goal of planning three project-based units. As she taught the units over the course of the school year, Erica's planning skills improved; the students became more skilled at organizing their learning; and communication about thinking and learning increased.

This chapter includes examples from two of the three project-based social studies units, a school study of the students' own elementary school and a study of the United States. A study on Mexico is found in chapter 8. Each example shows how Erica and her students developed the capacity to more clearly communicate about thinking skills.

The purpose of the School study was to review self-organization skills and prepare the students for choosing a middle school. More about middle school choice will be discussed in the School study section. The other two studies addressed the New York State Core Curriculum for fifth grade social studies. All three studies included culminating projects at the end of each unit. Each study included decision-making, planning, and self-evaluation tools that Erica designed to teach the students how to organize their project work. Figure 7.1 shows the self-organization skills developed within each unit of study for the year.

SELF-ORGANIZATION PROCESSES	SCHOOL STUDY	STATE STUDY	MEXICO STUDY
DECISION MAKING	Set criteria for deciding on research tool with large group		Set criteria to decide presentation visual aid with the whole class
SETTING CRITERIA FOR EVALUATION	Set as group	Set as group	Developed criteria for evaluation with the whole class
PLANNING	Presentation notes that outlined the project	Description of project Requirements of State Fair booth Due date State study proposal State study planning sheet (unused)	Description of project and audience List of research questions No formal planning for individual visual
SELF-EVALUATION	Group and individual reflection sheets that each included: 1. Group set criteria with yes or no response 2. Reflection questions	Self-evaluation using a numerical rating based on three sets of criteria developed with whole class in beginning of project. Individual analysis of thinking processes involved in the projects.	Peer evaluation of projects. Individual evaluations based on original criteria.

Figure 7.1. Analysis of self-organization skills in Erica's units of study.

SCHOOL STUDY

The School study grew out of real-life need. New York City schools offer a wide range of school options. While elementary students generally attend a school within their neighborhood, there is a wide range of choices available at the middle and high school levels. Therefore, learning what to look for in making a decision about a school is an important skill for a New York City fifth grader.

Students and their families may choose from among many middle schools. There are large traditional schools as well as smaller schools with themes: Academic and Athletic Excellence, Dual Language, Community Action School,

Computer School, or The Museum School. There are also schools for academically advanced students who meet the selection criteria.

During the fifth grade, students apply to middle schools. Teachers, in a precursor to the college application process, write recommendations for their students. This search begins in earnest in the early days of fifth grade, and often sooner, for many students and their parents. For those who want to attend a middle school that begins at the fifth grade level, the search for a school begins in fourth grade. Erica wanted her students to practice their self-organization skills on this real-life decision.

Goals of the School Study

Parents and students visit middle schools before they apply. Therefore, Erica planned the School study with specific goals in mind to prepare the students to know what to look for in a school. First, she wanted her students to *develop an understanding* of the choices they would be making and the information they would need to make those choices. Second, she wanted students to learn how to *critically read* advertising by creating similar kinds of information to that found in middle school brochures. Analyzing the positives and negatives of their own school would help students recognize what to look for in middle school advertising. Finally, the School study provided an opportunity for students to review self-organization processes and learn new thinking processes.

Overview of the School Study

Erica began the study by explaining to the students that they were going to make brochures about their own school in order to learn what to look for as they make their decisions about middle schools. She asked the students to identify aspects of a school they might want to know about. For example, if a parent was considering sending a kindergarten child to their school, E. S. #1, what might they want to know? With Erica's help, the students developed a list of questions.

- How do current students feel about the school?
- How do parents with children in E. S. #1 feel about the school?
- What does the school believe about teaching and learning?
- Who works in the school?
- What do the teachers teach?
- What's special about the school?
- Does the school have a gym?
- Do the students go on field trips?

Next, the students organized the research questions into categories that included school philosophy, support staff, special features, and curriculum. Erica placed the students into small groups and assigned each group a category. The students researched their topic through interviews and by listening to guest speakers. To help all the students become familiar with how to look at physical space, each group made a blueprint of the school. Using the information gathered from interviews, guests, and the blueprints, the students designed brochures that explained various aspects of their own school to parents of incoming kindergartners and transfer students.

Real-World Problem, Choices, and High Motivation

The School study began with high motivation. Erica immediately began by introducing the students to a thinking process other than the self-organization skills found in the *evaluation* component of the TIEL Curriculum Design Wheel. She introduced the students to the new word *cognition*, the pink thinking, explaining that it referred to gathering information. She asked, "How will we get information about our own school?" Jack suggested interviewing parents at the upcoming PTA meeting. When Erica asked him to go to the office and find out when the meeting would be held, Victor enthusiastically jumped up, went to a bulletin board in the classroom, and found the schedule. Erica remarked, "That the study matters and is leading to making a real-life decision has created high motivation, high interest. The kids demand to work on it every day."

Communicating about Criteria

In spite of the high level of enthusiasm for the School study, problems developed that had their roots in communication about the criteria that would guide the project. A common communication problem in project-based curriculum development is mixing product criteria with content criteria. For example, the School study required setting both kinds of criteria. Product criteria states how the finished product will be evaluated, while content criteria is used to decide on the most important information to include in the brochure.

Setting *criteria for evaluation* of the product establishes the qualities the project will have when it is successfully completed. It is through these qualities, or criteria, that the project is evaluated. The criteria for evaluation of a brochure might include that it has pictures and words, it is colorful and artistic, it contains the necessary information, and correct spelling and grammar are used.

Deciding on information to include is one of the most challenging aspects of project work. Setting criteria for *deciding* on the content provides students with points to consider as they select the content for the project. Some content criteria that students need to consider are the purpose of the information, the audience who will receive the information, and the quality of the information.

As Erica began discussing the criteria that would help students select information, she asked, "How do we select 'the good stuff' to go into the brochure?" She showed them some sample brochures to help them see what a brochure looks like and what kind of information a brochure contains (*cognition*). The discussion about how to select the information continued.

Erica: Who's the audience for your brochure?

Students: The parents.

Erica: What's the purpose of our brochures?

Students: To sell the school.

At this point, Erica asked a question that changed the course of the discussion. "What are the criteria that can guide us in *making our brochures?*" At this point the focus changed from selection of information to the making of the product. Instead of a discussion about how to select information, the conversation turned to making the brochures. After the students showed that they understood the purpose of making the brochures, Erica needed to continue guiding the students in thinking about what to consider in choosing information to put in the brochure. A question that maintains focus on information is, "What kinds of information are included in a brochure?"

Content First, Then Product

Discussing content criteria and product criteria simultaneously results in a common problem in project-based learning. The problem is similar to a horse that jumps over the starting gate instead of waiting for the proper signal. Students become excited about the hands-on final product and are anxious to begin. Most students prefer getting out the markers and poster board to the more difficult work of finding the information they need and deciding what information to use in their projects. The hard work of research, selecting, and organizing content information then receives minimal attention.

An initial description of the product is necessary in order to give meaning to the research. The students needed to know that they were creating brochures about the school to help prepare them to visit middle schools. Yet, if the product becomes the focus too early in the project, both content and process often become shortchanged. Not enough time is spent on the content involved in research and writing. Teaching self-management processes becomes more difficult because the attention of the students is on the physical aspect of making the product.

Students will complete the final project. However, the project may lack much of the intended information and students will miss learning important thinking skills. Setting criteria for the product and the selection of information separately helps alleviate the confusion and maintains focus on both the product and the processes involved in the project. At the end of the project, criteria from both can be combined for the final evaluation.

Solving the Criteria Confusion Problem

Erica recognized the problem. When she realized that the students were focusing on *making* the brochures instead of on *researching* the information that the brochures were to share, she came up with a plan to solve the problem. She explained to the students that there was some confusion about the criteria for their project and they needed to talk about it again.

Two blank chart papers helped solve the problem. In order to show the students that they needed to consider *information* for the brochures before they actually *made* the brochures, Erica placed the two chart papers side by side on the board. She labeled one *Criteria for Choosing Information* and the other *Criteria for Brochure Production*. Before beginning the discussion, she reviewed the goal for making the brochures.

Revisiting the purpose of the project, she asked, "What is the purpose of making school brochures?"

The students replied, "To share information about our school with parents so that we will understand what to look for when we visit middle schools."

Erica and the students were back on track. Pointing to the chart labeled *Criteria for Choosing Information*, she asked, "What criteria can help us select information?" Refocused on the importance of research, the students responded with the following suggestions (see figure 7.2):

- We have to think about what the audience needs to know.
- The information tells our audience something important.
- We should be positive about our school.
- We should include things that make people want to come here.
- The information should be true.

She wrote the students' suggestions on the chart paper in the form of questions. "What information do the parents need to know? Is this information telling our audience something important? Is the information positive? Does the information sell E.S. #1? Is the information accurate or true? The chart was posted in the classroom as a guide for the students to use as they considered various pieces of information to include in the brochures.

Next, Erica turned to the second blank chart labeled *Criteria for Brochure Production* (see figure 7.3). She asked the students, "How do we evaluate our finished brochure? What criteria will tell us that the brochure meets our goal of sharing information about our school?"

- The brochures teach the parents something about the school.
- The brochures answer questions parents might have.
- The brochure is attractive so you want to read it.
- The brochure is well planned.
- The writing is edited and revised.

CRITERIA FOR CHOOSING INFORMATION

**How do we choose the information
to include in the brochure?**

- What information might the parents want to know?

- Is this information that will inform the audience?

- Is the information positive?

- Does the information sell E.S. #1?

- Is the information accurate or true?

Figure 7.2. *Criteria for Choosing Information,* **School study brochure.**

- It looks like a brochure.
- The language sounds like brochure language.

After setting the criteria for evaluating the finished brochures, Erica completed the chart in the form of questions.

The charts helped Erica direct the students in answering their own questions and solving their own problems. When students asked, "Should I put this information in my brochure?" Erica pointed to the chart and asked the students to make their own decision based on the agreed-upon criteria. As they worked on their brochures, the students frequently asked, "Does this look good? Is the writing OK?" Referring to the chart, Erica gently directed them to evaluate their own writing using the questions they had developed together.

CRITERIA FOR BROCHURE PRODUCTION

How will we evaluate the finished brochures?

- Does the brochure teach parents?

- Does the brochure answer questions parents might have?

- Does the brochure show the research you have done?

- Is the brochure attractive?

- Is the brochure well-planned?

- Is the writing edited and revised?

- Does it go beyond the basics?

- Does it look like a brochure?

- Does the language sound like brochure language?

Figure 7.3. *Criteria for Brochure Production,* School study brochure.

Solving Communication Problems

Communication between teacher and students and among the students is facilitated by setting clear criteria for the decisions that need to be made in the course of a project. Erica and the students identified four categories of information that they thought were important to include in the brochures. These included school philosophy, support staff, curriculum, and special features. These categories answered the following questions. What were the beliefs of the school? Who helped the principal and teachers to keep the school running smoothly? What was the curriculum of E. S. #1? What were special features of E. S. #1? For example, the school housed special services for children with physical disabilities and was equipped with elevators, special equipment, and a staff of specialists and assistants who worked with the children.

Group Problems

Each group of children made one brochure that contained information in each of the four categories. Once the categories of information were selected, the students had to decide within their groups who would do the research on each category. Some groups had difficulty deciding who would do the research on a given category. The following incident was an example.

Nan, Patrick, Yamin, and Michael were doing special features that included special education, sports, and the library. Yamin insisted on researching the special education feature, because, "I'm the only one [in this group] who's been in special ed." That Yamin felt comfortable discussing his special needs was evidence of Erica's efforts to create a classroom environment of openness and safety.

Choosing the other topics was not so clear-cut. The other three began to argue over who would research sports and who would research the library. Inevitably, sexism came up in the conversation.

Patrick: Michael and I are going to do sports.

Nan: Why do boys get to do sports while I have to find out about the library?

Michael: Why does every thing have to be your way?

Nan: Then I'm not going to do anything.

Patrick threw down his pencil and stomped out the door. Nan started to cry.

As in life, working with others can be difficult. This incident illustrates one of the challenges inherent in project work and brings up the following questions to be considered:

- How does information get selected?
- Who decides on jobs within the group?
- How are conflicts to be resolved?
- How much does a teacher intervene?
- How much do you help the students?

Possible Solutions

Since decisions about information are often the most difficult in project work, spending increased time setting criteria for selection and distribution of the work can prevent some of the conflicts that require teacher intervention. After the teacher and students establish the information to be included in the project, a short discussion of how the research tasks will be distributed among group members provides students with a structure for making these decisions. For example, criteria for choosing a topic can include

- I am interested in this topic.
- I have experience with this topic.
- I can find the information and resources on this topic.
- I would like to interview the people involved with this topic.

When students still have difficulty, the teacher can provide further help. If two students want the same topic, the teacher can suggest that they work on the topic together. Sometimes several students want one topic, but other topics must be researched as happened in the School study. The teacher can allow the students to share in the research of the favorite topic, but help them use the established criteria to each choose one of the less popular, yet necessary, topics. Where there are fewer students, as in the case of Patrick, Michael, and Nan, the teacher can suggest that they all share responsibilities in researching sports and the library.

Self-Evaluation

In addition to planning ways to teach decision making and planning, Erica wanted the students to evaluate their work in the group as well as their individual work. She combined the criteria that had been set at the beginning of the unit—*Criteria for Choosing Information* and *Criteria for Brochure Production*—into a chart stating the final criteria (see figure 7.4). Using some of the final criteria, Erica designed two self-evaluation tools for the students to use in evaluating their brochures.

Group Evaluation

The first evaluation worksheet, *School Study Group Reflection*, focused on the thinking aspects of the project (see figure 7.5). The purpose of the group evaluation was to evaluate the students' research and writing. The group evaluation had several blank lines for the students to choose additional criteria from the list of final criteria. This allowed the students to indicate parts of the project where they did especially well. The *School Study Group Reflection* sheet included open-ended questions that asked the students about problems they had in their group in the process of making the brochure and how they would do a similar project differently. Erica also asked if there was anything else she should know about the work of their group.

Individual Evaluation

The second evaluation tool, *School Study Individual Reflection*, focused on the social-emotional aspect of the project (see figure 7.6). It asked the students to focus on how they felt about both their individual work and their work as a group. The first six questions focused on social-emotional development of the

FINAL CRITERIA FOR BROCHURES

- Is this information that will inform the audience?

- Is the information positive?

- Does the information sell E.S. #1?

- Is the information accurate or true?

- Is the brochure well-planned?

- Is the writing edited and revised?

- Does the brochure show the work you have done?

- Does it go beyond the basics?

- Does it look like a brochure?

- Does the language sound like brochure language?

Figure 7.4. Final criteria for brochures, School study.

Group Name _____

Members _____

SCHOOL STUDY GROUP REFLECTION

1. CRITERIA EVALUATION

   Is the information accurate?   Y   N

   Does the brochure inform the audience about   Y   N
   your focus area?

   Is the writing revised and edited?   Y   N
   (fill in your group's other criteria from your
   planning sheet)

   _____   Y   N
   _____   Y   N
   _____   Y   N
   _____   Y   N

2. What problems did your group have?

3. If you were to do this project again (or one similar), what would
   you do differently? *BE SPECIFIC.*

4. What else do you think that I should know?

Figure 7.5. *School Study Group Reflection.*

individual and asked for a simple yes or no response from the students. Three questions focused on the *ethical reasoning* component of the TIEL Wheel asking students to give a fair and honest evaluation of their work within the group.

- I feel that I did my share of the work in my group.
- I feel that I was able to contribute to the work of the group.
- I feel that I did my own best work in the group.

Name _____

Group _____

SCHOOL STUDY INDIVIDUAL REFLECTION

1. I feel that I did my share of the work in my group.   Y   N
2. I feel that I was able to contribute to the work of   Y   N
   the group.
3. I feel that I did my own best work in the group.   Y   N
4. I feel proud of the work that my group did.   Y   N
5. I feel that I learned more than I knew before about   Y   N
   my topic.
6. I feel that I learned more than I knew before about   Y   N
   making a brochure.
7. THE PROCESS THAT WE WENT THROUGH IN OUR
   SCHOOL STUDY WAS: (Describe or list or show the entire
   process, starting with naming what we know about P.S. 199 all
   the way through republishing the brochures.)

8. Our school study will affect my Middle School choice because:
   (What will you now look for or think about that you wouldn't
   have before the study?)

9. What would have made this study better?

Figure 7.6. *School Study Individual Reflection.*

The next three questions focused on the *mastery* component of the TIEL Wheel. These questions asked students to reflect on the quality of their work and the new skills they had learned.

- I feel proud of the work that my group did.
- I feel that I learned more than I knew before about my topic.
- I feel that I learned more than I knew before about making a brochure.

Metacognition

Each of the final questions focused on metacognition, asking students to reflect on their thinking and learning during the School study in more depth. The seventh question assessed the students' awareness of the processes they had used in creating the brochures.

- Describe, list, or show the entire process we went through in our School study, starting with naming what we know about our school all the way through to publishing our brochures.

Increased knowledge leads to better decision making. Erica wanted to know if this real-world study would have any effect on the students' middle school decisions. The eighth question asks each student to think about their decision making.

- Our School study will affect my middle school choice because. . . . What will you now look for or think about that you wouldn't have before the study?

The final question has two purposes. It allows the students to reflect on what they might have done to make the study better, as well as giving them a place to give suggestions on how the teacher could improve the unit.

- What would have made this study better is if . . .

Lessons about Communication

Erica and her students learned important lessons about communication from the School study including time management, setting clear criteria, and solving group problems. Erica now had a better idea about the time required for project work. The study had extended for several weeks beyond the original three weeks that were planned and she knew that in future studies she needed to communicate the time parameters more clearly.

The School study gave Erica the opportunity to work out the kinks in setting criteria for projects. She now saw the importance of clearly establishing both content and product criteria. Recognizing the confusion at the beginning of the study, she taught the setting of criteria again. By separately setting criteria for selecting information and setting criteria for final evaluation of the finished product, Erica refocused the students on the research and writing before constructing the final product.

The students learned more about how to work in groups. They saw that problems occur when you work with others, but that those problems can be solved. In beginning to think about the processes involved in creating a project, the students were developing a foundation that would support them in project work throughout the year.

UNITED STATES STUDY

The State study showed Erica's increased sophistication in communicating expectations. This unit culminated with an ambitious state fair. The final product had three parts: a booth, a brochure, and a project. Each student chose a U.S. state to research and created a "fair booth" that displayed maps, artifacts, and information about their state. To use the skills the students had developed during the School study, each student made a brochure that included information about geography, history, business, and trade, as well as special features about their state.

The students also created a project that was part of their presentation. Some made models representing important monuments or buildings found in their states; others made posters that shared information. One girl made a timeline and prepared a simulation of panning for gold to teach the history of California. Visitors dipped a pie pan in water mixed with sand and gold flecks. The creator of the Vermont booth handed out samples of Ben and Jerry's ice cream. On the day of the fair, the students arranged the desks so that everyone had space for their displays. Classes in the school signed up for a time to visit the fair, see the students' work, and sample a bite of special food.

Planning Packet for Clear Communication

Such a large undertaking requires clear communication about expectations. Using what she had learned from the previous unit, Erica created a planning packet for the students to use in managing the components of the state fair projects. This packet included several components.

- *State Study Proposal* sheet (7.7)
- *State Study Planning* sheet (7.8)
- *Criteria for evaluation* for each component of the project (7.9)
- *Thinking Analysis* worksheet (7.10)

For this study, Erica designed an evaluation tool based on the thinking operations of the TIEL Wheel to assess the students' understanding of the thinking processes used in their projects.

Proposal

Erica wanted the students to think ahead about the special project that would be part of the display booth. The *State Study Proposal* provided space for the students to describe, state the purpose, and tell what information they would include in their project (see figure 7.7). Since beginning is often the hardest part of a project, the proposal helped the students get started. It also gave Erica information about each student's initial plan and made sure he or she had one.

Name _____ Nan _____ State _____ California _____

STATE STUDY PROPOSAL

Write one to two paragraphs explaining what your other project will be and what information you will include in it. Please make sure to include what the purpose of the project will be (what will people learn?)

For my project, I plan on doing 2 things--
1. A time line of California's history
2. A mini gold rush.
The time line will teach people who people that played.

___√___ Approved _____ Not Approved

Comments:

Nan,
This sounds great. The time line will also help people better understand the GOLD rush. Maybe you also want to include books in your booth.

Figure 7.7. *State Study Proposal* sheet.

Detailed Planning

The *State Study Planning* sheet asked students to plan their project in more detail (see figure 7.8). Students needed to outline the steps they would take to complete their project, give information about the supplies, and think ahead to possible problems they might have.

Setting Project Criteria in Three Areas

This project required setting criteria in three areas. Erica set criteria with the students to evaluate the brochure, the project, and the state fair booth. Using the criteria they had developed together, Erica typed up the *State Study Criteria* form and assigned numerical values for each criterion (see figure 7.9). When

---

Name _____   State _____

STATE STUDY PLANNING SHEET

What steps do you need to go through from start to finish when making your project? (be as specific as you can)

1.
2.
3.
4.
5.
6.
7.
8.
9.
10.

What supplies will you need? Where will you get them?

What problems may come up?

1.
2.
3.
4.

Figure 7.8. *State Study Planning* sheet.

Name _____ Nan _____ State _____ California _____

BROCHURE CRITERIA
Does my brochure contain all that information that I need to?

General state information (2 points)	2
State geography (2 points)	2
State history (2 points)	1
State special features (2 points)	2
Business and trade (2 points)	2
Is my brochure easy on the eyes? (3 points)	3
Is my brochure perfectly edited? (3 points)	3
Total Points	15

PROJECT CRITERIA

Does my project have a written part? (2 points)	2
Is my writing edited perfectly? (2 points)	2
Does my project have a visual part? (2 points)	2
Is my project neat and professional? (2 points)	2
Reflects that I challenged myself? (3 points)	3
Teaches at least three important things. (3 points)	3
Is the audience attracted to my project? (2 points)	2
Total Points	16

STATE FAIR BOOTH CRITERIA

Does my booth have a state sign? (1 point)	1
Does my booth contain my brochure? (2 points)	2
Does my booth contain my project? (2 points)	2
Does my booth contain a state map? (1 point)	1
Reflects that I challenged myself? (3 points)	3
Shows what life is like compared to New York? (5 points)	5
Total Points	14
Bibliography (4 points)	4
TOTAL POINTS	49
TOTAL POSSIBLE POINTS	50

Figure 7.9.   *State Study Criteria* form.

the state fair was completed, Erica used this evaluation tool to assess the students' work.

Each set of criteria included content criteria used to judge the information and product criteria used to judge the visual portions of each project. Following what Erica had learned in the School study about prioritizing the content, she placed the content criteria first for both the brochure and the project. Since the fair booth was the collection point for all the materials involved in the state fair project, the criteria focused on what would be included in the individual display booth. One of the last two questions in this section asked students to reflect on their efforts. The other asked students to show how life in their researched state compared to New York.

Metacognition

Erica created a new evaluation tool for the State study. She used the TIEL language to assess the students' understanding of the thinking skills used in creating their projects. This assessment tool included each thinking operation with space for the students to write how they used the thinking operation in the State study

---

Name _____ Nan _____   State _____ California _____

THINKING ANALYSIS

Do you know your Thinking Operations?
Think of the activities you have completed in the unit.
List the activities which go with each puppet's thinking operation.

Cognition   I named the states and my state's big cities. I
              discovered things about my state. I researched
              when I took notes.

Memory   I remembered everything I knew about the
              U.S.A.

Evaluation   I planned so I wouldn't run out of time. I
              evaluated after each section. I used judgment

Convergent   I narrowed down info from each resource
Production   until I got 1 correct answer.

Divergent   I took risks when I tried a new way of researching.
Production   I opened up my mind and thought of all the
              different things I could do.

Figure 7.10.   Thinking analysis for State study, student.

(see figure 7.10). For *cognition* a student wrote, "I named the states and my state's big cities. I discovered things about my state. I researched when I took notes." In the space for *evaluation* she showed her understanding of the self-management skills that Erica was teaching. "I planned so I wouldn't run out of time. I evaluated after each section. I used judgment to help me along."

TIEL Visuals

Erica moved her teaching to the next level in more explicitly discussing thinking and learning with her students. Although I used the TIEL language and visuals as I worked with the teachers, they put the TIEL visuals in their classrooms when they felt they were ready to discuss thinking more explicitly with their students. As the State study was beginning, Erica put up the TIEL bulletin board in her classroom. The brightly colored charts with the thinking operations and qualities of character were now part of the bulletin board that occupied one wall of Erica's classroom. The bulletin board was a new tool giving the class an easy reference for the discussion of thinking.

Mapping Thinking

In order for Erica to help her students understand the thinking processes they had used in their projects, she needed to be clear about the kind of thinking activities she was planning. To help her do this, she developed a kind of curriculum map that focused on the thinking processes involved in each of the learning activities of the State study (see figure 7.11). The thinking map helped Erica create a more balanced curriculum. It helped her assess her own planning and assured that students had an opportunity to develop a wide range of thinking skills throughout the course of the study.

STATE STUDY				
COGNITION	MEMORY	EVALUATION	CONVERGENT PRODUCTION	DIVERGENT PRODUCTION
Research: • Books • CDROM, web • Resource experts • Letters	• Helping students connect newly researched information to old learning • Recall when presenting to visitors to the State Fair	• Critical questioning— What factors make the state what it is? • Deciding how to make the display • Planning, setting criteria for evaluating • Self-evaluation	• Following directions • One right answer • Facts • Factual reporting (expository writing) • Corral the information	• State fair • Brochure • Relief map (convergent and divergent)

Figure 7.11. Erica's curriculum map analysis of thinking operations for State study.

SUMMARY

Communicating about thinking processes helped Erica's students develop a deeper understanding of the self-management skills of decision making, planning, and self-evaluation. As the students used these skills, they worked together more cooperatively, showed more effort and creativity, and developed a deeper sense of responsibility for their work. Erica understood the importance of practice for herself and her students in learning new skills. Therefore, she planned three hands-on, project-based units using the TIEL framework a guide. Two of these units, the School study and the State study are described in this chapter.

The School study focused on the real-life problem for New York City fifth graders of selecting a middle school. In this unit, which required students to create brochures advertising their school, Erica learned the importance of setting clear criteria for the content of a project first. When she noticed the confusion between setting criteria for the *information* to include in their brochures and setting criteria for *making* the brochures, she restructured her lesson to more clearly set the criteria for the project with her students.

The State study was more extensive than the School study with multiple facets to the project. Using what they had learned in the School study, each student designed brochures that advertised their chosen state, a visual product that shared a major factor about the state, and a State Fair booth that brought together a wide range of materials about the state. The planning was also more sophisticated. Erica guided the students in setting criteria for the written, visual, and speaking components of the project. They presented their learning by inviting other classes to come into their classroom to visit the State Fair. In addition to planning and evaluation sheets, Erica designed a worksheet based on the thinking operations of the TIEL Curriculum Design Wheel for the students to use in analyzing the thinking processes they used in developing and presenting their projects.

8

Students Becoming Teachers

> I think it helped me a lot . . . the decision and planning part helped me do
> it and then the evaluation part made me think about what kind of good
> work I did.
>
> —Beatrice, fifth grade student

The students became teachers in the study of Mexico. The culminating project involved a formal teaching presentation that included visuals and written information used to share their research about Mexico. In this study, Erica capitalized on her increasing ability to plan and communicate self-management skills to her students. They, in turn, took the opportunity to demonstrate their ability to organize themselves and to produce their most scholarly work of the year.

THREE-PART PROJECT

The projects for the Mexico study had a written, a visual, and a formal speaking component. Each group project in the Mexico study involved researching one of seven categories that addressed content knowledge about Mexico. Each group was required to use two visual aids in the speaking presentation. These could include posters, overhead transparencies, or displays. Although each student in the group was not required to make a visual aid, each student was required to speak during the presentation.

Speaking in a formal presentation was a new skill for the students to learn. Along with reading and writing, the New York State English Language Arts standards include speaking and listening. The students had talked about their published writing, shared previous projects, and spoken with the visitors who toured the state fair, yet, in the Mexico study, they were expected to teach the rest of the class important content more formally.

Planning for Clear Communication

Careful planning contributed to the most well-prepared projects Erica's students had produced up to that time. One of the two objectives focused on content and the other on research skills. She wanted the students to gain an overall understanding of Mexico and then conduct research on a particular aspect of Mexico. She meticulously documented her thinking for the Mexico study, asking herself at the beginning, "What do I want the students to know and be able to do?"

In project-based teaching, the teacher and the students share responsibilities for learning and teaching. Erica's planning reflects consideration of questions that address the responsibilities of both. What concepts and skills do the students need to learn? How will the students gain information about the content? How will they learn the skills needed to do the research, organize the information, and prepare the presentation? What content and skills will be presented in formal, teacher-directed lessons? What content will be taught by the students who will research an aspect of the unit's topic?

Planning the Skills to Teach

There were several skills that Erica wanted the students to learn. These included learning to outline the chapters and take notes, read the textbook to gather information, use note cards for their presentations, and create a bibliography.

Erica carefully divided the work over a four-week period that included both teacher and student work (see figure 8.1a). During week one, Erica planned to teach a lesson on how to use the textbook to gather information. Her planning shows that she also thought about using a video as another avenue for finding information about Mexico. Weeks two and three featured teacher-directed lessons on outlining and creating a bibliography. By week four, Erica focused on the outline that the students needed to prepare for the presentations.

During the four weeks, the students gathered information about Mexico, made outlines, built bibliographies, and created the visuals for the presentation. During the final week, they prepared their speaking parts for the presentation and made the timeline.

Planning the Content

Erica carefully outlined the content of the Mexico study (8.1b). The Mexico study was based on the New York State social studies standards and core

MEXICO STUDY (APRIL)

What do I want to do?

I want them to get an overall understanding of Mexico and then find out more information about a particular thing.

I want kids to learn how to outline the chapters and take notes off of them.
reading textbook to gather general information
outlining as a way of note taking
writing notes and note cards for presentation
bibliography

WEEK 1: Reading textbook and gathering general information about Mexico (video?)
How do you read the text? Using bold print, etc., to support that
Introducing outlining in another context to get general structure
Textbook reading for homework
Topics for study for groups
Give calendars of study out
OVER VACATION: gather sources for study

WEEK 2
Outlining (collecting outlines—will be marked)
Gathering information for groups

WEEK 3
Bibliography
getting visual aids ready

WEEK 4
Presentations: each person's part needs to be written as an outline to support their talk
each person's outline will be marked
each person's group work
each person's participation in presentation
Create a timeline of Mexico (lay it next to the other two timelines)

Figure 8.1a.   Teacher planning for Mexico study (front).

The research groups will research the following subjects and give oral presentations with visual aids to the class—posters, overheads, display

Everyone must create a timeline to go with historical information so that we can create one large timeline for the entire study.

Native settlers and their influence

I do the first group
600 BC Olmecs 1200–300 BC
200 BC–600 AD Teotihuacan

1. 250–900 AD Life during the Maya

2. 1100–1500 AD Life during Aztec rule

3. 1500 AD Life during Spanish conquering and rule (Cortez) (takeover by a people of another people)

4. 1810–1821 The War of Independence and Life after Independence

5. Present Day Life: problems and concerns

6. City life vs. country life (present day)

7. Culture (food, dress, dance, religion)

8. Climate/Geography/Resources (how it affects life, etc.)

Figure 8.1b. Teacher planning for Mexico study (back).

curriculum for fifth grade. She used these resources and her own research to decide what content she wanted the students to learn during the unit. The content of the study of Mexico was divided into two large categories—historical and present day. Each of these categories included four topics. Topics in the history category included the Mayans, the Aztecs, Spanish conquest, and the 1810 revolution against Spain. Present day topics included life today, city life versus country life, culture, and geography.

Each of these eight topics was further divided within the groups giving each person a content piece to research and present. For example, the Mayan group (Juris, Melik, Dona, and Emily) researched war, daily life, gods and religion, and games. To place their information within a historical context, each group designed a timeline depicting events pertaining to their topic. They pieced all the timelines together to form one large timeline for the entire study.

PLANNING PACKET: MANAGING THE PROJECT AND TIME

At the time of the Mexico study, the processes of self-organization no longer had the appearance of an added layer, but were fully integrated into all of the project work in the classroom. Equally important, Erica could clearly communicate what the students were doing.

> *They* choose the subtopics within the country. *They* choose what they will focus on. Then *they* research, connect to what they have already known. Then *they* choose how to present the information. *They* plan how to complete the project. *They* understand how their divergent thinking is being developed and how they use the convergent skills of presenting established facts, outlining, and logically organizing the work.

The students were developing those skills due to careful teacher planning. The five self-management tools that Erica designed for the Mexico study included a description of the project, planning page, planning calendar, peer evaluation for presentations, and an individual evaluation.

Since managing the time spent on project work had been a problem, she distributed planning calendars to the students marked with important due dates.

Description of Project Criteria

The description sheet, *Our Study of Mexico*, described the overall project and stated the requirements for the presentation, the written materials, and the final due date (see figure 8.2). During the presentation each group member must speak, the presentation must cover all the research questions, at least two

OUR STUDY OF MEXICO

Requirements:
FINAL PROJECT (Due Friday May 15th)

Each group must make a **10–15 minute presentation** during which you "teach" the rest of the class about the topic that you were studying (times to be determined by the class).

To be handed in by *each and every individual:* (the day of the presentation)

> an outline of what your part of the presentation will be (with correct outline form)—each person writes his/her own after group research and discussion.

> a bibliography of the resources that you used (as an individual and as a group)

> an individual reflection

During the presentation:

> each group member must speak

> the presentation must cover all of the group's research questions

> there must be visual aids used (overheads, maps, charts, graphs, etc.) *each person does not have to do one, but there must be at least two made and used by the group*

> each group must prepare a tool of assessment (some way to get feedback from the rest of the class about the group presentation)—*will be discussed in class*

Figure 8.2. *Our Study of Mexico*, description of project requirements.

visual aids must be used, and each group must prepare an assessment tool for receiving feedback from the audience about their presentation. In addition, each student was required to submit an outline, a bibliography, and an individual reflection sheet.

Two Planning Tools

The *Planning Page* helped the students organize the content of their topic and the distribution of the work (see figure 8.3). What are our research

Name _____ Group _____

PLANNING PAGE

What are our research questions?

_____
_____
_____

How will we begin our work?

_____
_____
_____

Where will we gather information?

_____
_____
_____

How will we divide our work?

_____
_____
_____

How will we create deadlines and due dates?

_____
_____
_____

When will our due dates be? (Use planning calendar)

Figure 8.3. Student *Planning Page* for Mexico study.

questions? How will we begin our work? Where will we gather information? How will we divide our work? How will we create deadlines and due dates? When are our due dates? Determined to improve time management, Erica designed the *Planning Calendar,* which helped the students monitor their progress according to the work schedule (see figure 8.4).

Peer Evaluation Tool

The *Mexico Study Presentation Feedback Sheet* emerged from the individual feedback sheets each group prepared for their presentation (see figure 8.5). When the class discussed how to assess a presentation, several criteria were repeatedly suggested. Erica used five of these common questions to develop a

May				
Monday	Tuesday	Wednesday	Thursday	Friday
			Get into groups and decide topic	**1** Group homework
4	**5** Go over requirements and deadlines	**6** Work time	**7** Work time	**8** Work time
11 Work time	**12** Work time	**13** Group assessment tool due for copying	**14** Individual bibliography due	**15** Group presentations Outline/ Reflections
18	**19**	**20**	**21**	**22**
25	**26**	**27**	**28**	**29**

Figure 8.4.   Student *Planning Calendar* for Mexico study.

My Name _____Nan_____

MEXICO STUDY PRESENTATION FEEDBACK SHEET

Group	Were they well prepared?	Did they share important information?	Was the presentation interesting?	One important thing I learned	One question I now have (after the presentation)
Mayas	3	3	3	They played a game and hit a rock with hands	What kind of battles did they have?
Aztecs					
Spanish Conquering and the Revolution	2+	3	3	Cortez didn't like Aztecs	What happened in Spain with Cortez?
Life Today	2-	3	2+	?	Do they still mention the Aztecs?
City vs. Country	1	1½	0	There's more stores in the city	Is it colder in winter in city or country?
Culture	2	3-	3	Was there a certain sign for the culture?	What do they believe about culture?
Geography	2½	3-	3+	The hottest month is July!	What is the population?

Scale: 3 – Yes, completely   2 – Basically   1 – A little   0 – Not at all

Figure 8.5. *Mexico Study Presentation Feedback Sheet.*

group assessment. Using a 5 × 7 grid, she placed the five questions or statements across the top of the grid.

- Was the group well prepared?
- Did the group share important information?

- Was the presentation interesting?
- One important thing I learned.
- One question I now have.

The seven research topics—Mayans, Aztecs, Spanish conquest and the revolution, life today, city life versus country life, culture, and geography—were in

---

Name _____Nan_____

Group _____Aztecs_____

MEXICO STUDY RUBRIC
Criteria for Evaluation

Individual Work/Research	Self	Teacher
Outline of my presentation in correct outline format?	3	2
Bibliography of my sources in the correct format?	3	3
Consistently contribute to the work of my group?	3	3
Did I do my best work?	2	3

Presentation	Self	Teacher
Did my visual aids teach something?	3	2
Did our presentation last 10–15 minutes?	3	3
Did we have at least two appropriate visual aids?	3	3
Did we discuss all of our research questions?	3	3
Were we practiced and ready?	3	3
Presentation included research from our group?	3	3
TOTAL	29	28

Scale:

3 – a lot of evidence   Student Signature ___Nan_____

2 – some evidence   Teacher Signature ___Erica Leif____

1 – a little evidence   Nice job! Outlines don't have

0 – no evidence   so much writing. In future presentations,
                                  don't write as much on overhead.

Figure 8.6. *Mexico Study Rubric.*

the left column. Using the questions across the top, the students evaluated each group following their presentation.

Individual Evaluation Tool

The *Mexico Study Rubric* listed the criteria for evaluation and served as the tool for both student self-evaluation and teacher evaluation (see figure 8.6). The rubric was divided into two sections, *Individual Work/Research* and *Presentation*. A pair of short lines to the right of each criterion provided a place for both the student and the teacher to write a numerical evaluation.

The first section of the rubric, *Individual Work/Research*, included four questions. Did I make an outline of my presentation in correct outline format? Did I complete a bibliography of my sources in the correct format? Did I consistently contribute to the work of my group? Did I do my best work?

The second section, *Presentation*, included six questions. Did my visual aids teach something? Did our presentation last ten to fifteen minutes? Did we have at least two appropriate visual aids? Did we discuss all of our research questions? Were we practiced and ready? Did our presentation include research from our group?

MEXICO PRESENTATIONS

The Mexico presentations showed the students' increased creativity, autonomy, and the underlying thinking work that went into their projects. Their growing self-management skills were evident. The presentations were well organized and well rehearsed, and they met the criteria for final evaluation that Erica had set with the students at the beginning of the project. As Erica observed her progress and that of her students, she saw the importance of teaching thinking consistently. She commented,

> As my understanding of it [facilitating decision-making, planning, and self-evaluation processes] has deepened and the kids' understanding has deepened, I see how much more important it is to be ongoing. To get what I want to happen, it has to be an ongoing thing for the year.

Yet, how had Erica's hard work influenced her students' learning of content, creativity, and self-management skills? Were they able to communicate about their thinking? Could they articulate how they made decisions, how they planned, and how they evaluated their own work at the end? Could they discuss the criteria they used in creating their projects?

Creativity

One of the great benefits of project work is fostering creativity. While research skills and the more convergent work of organizing the findings into written work are being learned, the opportunity to create a visual product encourages divergent thinking. The Mayan presentation featured a poster of Mexican art, pictures, and a model of an Aztec temple. Michael had made a replica of Utah's Salt Lake Temple during the State study. As he researched the Aztec temples, he realized the connection between the two religious buildings and decided to construct a model of an Aztec temple. He used it to explain how it was built in concentric squares, resembling a city swallowing itself.

Others showed their creativity through resourcefulness. The four boys in Victor's group presented a comparison of city and country life in Mexico. What Victor's group lacked in research and planning skills, they made up for in their ability to make connections to previous projects. The group decided to use Victor's project from the State study that compared urban and rural areas of his state. Their planning consisted of adding a few plastic figures to the diorama created of wood, bark dust, and Legos.

Teaching Presentations

Project work offers an opportunity for students to teach an audience in a formal setting. The presentations brought out hidden teaching talent in many of the students. Rashawn, Michael, and Victor each felt comfortable in front of the audience showing their ability to present information and answer questions. Rashawn, a leader in the group studying the Spanish conquest, referred to a map of Mexico while lecturing clearly and eloquently. In his presentation he made two comparisons—the Mexican revolution to the American Revolution, and Father Adalfo to George Washington.

Michael was part of the group that studied life today in Mexico. He had a remarkable teaching presence for a fifth grader. I wrote, "Michael is very sensitive with a wonderful teaching presence; I was listening so intently I forgot to take notes. I was so busy watching him that I missed hearing what he said."

Victor was perhaps the most surprising of those showing exceptional stage presence. An average student, Victor was part of the city life versus country life group whose members displayed minimal content knowledge of their topic. Nevertheless, Victor enthusiastically engaged his audience using his recycled visual aid from the state project to explain differences that existed between city and country life in Mexico.

Beatrice was particularly meticulous about filing her self-organization papers. In the interview, when asked to explain her conscientiousness, she said,

> I felt that since I spent a lot of time on all this planning and everything, I thought I'd keep it and my project part on the overhead [transparencies] because like sometimes Miss Leif takes our stuff and shows it to other teachers to show people's work (in the writing project). And I just think that's a good tool to have with you since you spent so much time and work on it. It will help your thinking for the next study.

Students Communicate about Thinking

At the final assessment, the students showed increased understanding of all the thinking processes. Erica reported hearing the students refer to the kinds of thinking in different ways throughout the day. "That's cognition, that's pink," was one example. At another time, while discussing pictures they had drawn, Paul said, "Our pictures can be both convergent and divergent."

Yet, it was in the discussion of the self-management skills that the students were most articulate. Erica saw that the students were empowered by the opportunity to make decisions, plan, and use criteria to evaluate their own projects. She noticed that the students now used the criteria set at the beginning of the project to monitor their work throughout the course of the project. Earlier in the year they would have set the criteria, moved on with the project, and never looked back.

EMPOWERMENT THROUGH SELF-MANAGEMENT SKILLS

The students were excited to explain how they had planned and evaluated their projects. I sat with three students who shared how they used the planning sheet to explain their project ideas to their teacher, used the calendar to help manage their time, and evaluated their projects at the end.

Planning

Sasha began with a broad, general statement, "We plan our stuff out first of all."

Moving straight to the details, Victor added, "We get our information. We had a calendar and we check off stuff and if we want to have something done before it's even supposed to be done [we can]." Victor, with the recycled city and country life project, was confident that the calendar could solve his work issues.

Sasha, skipping right past the planning, the research, and even creating the project, went straight to the presentation. "Get all our props ready. Pick our spots."

The planning calendar that Erica designed for the Mexico study was a big hit. They were so enthusiastic about this planning tool that they all began speaking at once. Sasha's voice broke through. "I really, really liked the calendar!" Verbally jumping over each other, they all shared their opinions about how the calendar gave them more control over their work.

Victor said, "The calendar *really* helped us!"

"It helped us divide up our time and work," Beatrice replied.

Sasha, ever practical and to the point added, "We couldn't memorize all our due dates, like March 16."

Reflecting on previous projects, Beatrice said wistfully, "We could have done the same thing with the State study and the Colonial Times study [from the previous year] I think. We had special due dates and like in our colonial times—oh, my god—our group was so confused."

"Yeah," Victor added, "without that calendar we would have never been done with the Mexico project. We would have been, 'When's the due date again? When's the due date again?' We had the state project for two months and on the second month we said, 'Miss Leif, Miss Leif, this is confusing,' and she got us the calendar."

Decision Making

Criteria were used at the beginning of the project to help the students plan their work. The same criteria reappeared in the evaluation at the end of the project. However, students also used criteria as they evaluated options involved in decisions about their projects. Beatrice shared how she arrived at her decision to use overhead transparencies for the visuals in her presentation. What would be the best way to share her information visually? She thought about how her information would look on a chart or portrayed through a model. After much consideration, she decided on the overhead.

> Because I thought [about] all my thinking and what I want to talk about—Who were the Aztecs? And the food—it wouldn't look good on charts really. Because I wasn't sure how it would be on charts, I pictured a chart and then all my thinking—but how would my thinking be on the chart? So then I said, "A model of food?" But then I said, "No. Because I don't want to do the entire project on food." And then I said the overhead because I could put all my thinking down instead of like making lists and lists. And everyone could see it still. And it would be a good way to cover my thinking (see figures 8.7, 8.8, and 8.9).

Different students used different criteria to make decisions. Whereas a significant quantity of information was a major consideration for Beatrice, it was a lack of information that guided Victor's decisions. He explained, "From the information that I had, I saw that it wouldn't be good to do it on the overhead. I didn't have enough [information] to put on the overhead. But I had enough to make a model." Actually, Victor had enough information to revise a model.

Evaluation

Understanding criteria for evaluation, the heart of critical thinking, is often difficult for adults. Yet, the students were able to easily discuss how they used criteria to evaluate their projects. The students recalled the State study and shared three of the criteria they used to evaluate their brochures. Were our brochures in the State study noticeable? Did they grab the audience's attention? Was our spelling accurate?

Beatrice

PRESENTATION!

HI! I'm here today to talk and make you understand more about "who were" the Aztecs, and what kind of food did the Aztecs eat. So let's get started!

"Who were the Aztecs?"

"What kind of food did the Aztecs eat?"

Now here is Sharon with her Aztec <u>family information!</u>

Figure 8.7. Presentation outline notes for Beatrice's presentation on Aztec daily life.

WHO WERE THE AZTECS?

The Aztecs lived in Mexico, a harsh, mountain land in North America. The Aztecs state flourished from about 1345-1521—while they were in power, the Aztecs ruled rich territories, fought countless battles, created exquisite works of art, and built one of the largest and most beautiful cities in the late world.

The Aztec power began in about 30,000 yrs ago, (Before the Mayas power began)

During the Aztecs power, a lot of things were going on—like: the Aztecs started growing their own crops, and started trading their live animals what they killed for gold & money, and by the time they reached Central America, many tribes had become farmers—they didn't have to keep moving and could stay in one place.

All this stuff what the Aztecs did helped Mexico more!

Figure 8.8.   *Who Were the Aztecs?* overhead for Beatrice's presentation on Aztec daily life.

AZTEC FOOD!

The Aztecs ate 2 meals a day.
(Morning & night)

In the morning the Aztecs ate mostly fruit and vegetables, and chocolate. (What only the rich people could afford.)

At night the Aztecs ate: deer, rabbits, corn, dogs, sweet & hot peppers, beans, green & red tomatoes, potatoes, avocadoes, fish and shellfish, tropical fruits and a lot of others.

Aztec Food!!	N.Y. Food!!
dog, deer, fish & shellfish, guinea pig, squash, rabbit, cactus leaves, llama, ETC.	hamburgers, French fries, hot dogs, pizza, chicken, MC-nuggets, rice, fish, ETC.

There is a big difference in food!

Figure 8.9. *Aztec Food* overhead for Beatrice's presentation on Aztec daily life.

Understanding the criteria for evaluation affects how students work. Sasha talked about how the criteria for evaluating the Mexico project influenced her work and how she assessed her project.

> I thought very hard of what I would do so that my criteria and evaluation would come out good. When we evaluated we got all the questions and everything to do our scores. And I just kind of like looked at my project and everything for some of the questions and I really thought back about the work that I did. And I think it helped me to know the stuff that I really didn't do well.

Objective—Assessment Connection

Often, students demonstrated extraordinarily sophisticated thinking about evaluation. Beatrice showed a deep understanding of the connection that exists between objectives and assessments, a concept every teacher must know. She recognized how the proposal explains the objectives of the project and how the evaluation at the end of the project assesses whether you met the objectives. She explained, "In the proposal planning you explain to Miss Leif how you want your project to be so she can really get a sense of how everybody's project is going to be. The end of the project is really similar because we evaluate . . . like . . . Was our presentation done well? Was it in the right form?

Cognition—Evaluation—Doing

One day, as Erica was discussing the TIEL Curriculum Design Wheel with the students, Nan made an insightful connection. She explained, "Evaluation is a bridge between cognition and doing." Nan recognized that *evaluation* includes the processes of decision making and planning that make it possible to transform information into a tangible product that can be shared.

Nan recognized that in project work, students use the thinking operation, *cognition,* to research and gather information about a topic—in their case, the school, the states, and Mexico. Students use the thinking operation *evaluation* to make decisions and plan their projects. Using their plans, the students do hands-on work to create the product. The expository writing, involved in the projects is an example of *convergent production.* Creating the visual part of the projects is an example of *divergent production.* After the presentation is complete, students use evaluation skills to evaluate their project.

Levels of Metacognition

While some students communicated remarkably sophisticated thinking, others communicated their thinking more modestly. Erica, however, appreciated that all kinds of learners could benefit from learning self-management skills and using the TIEL Model. Teaching students thinking skills had allowed the students to work and express themselves at their various levels of ability.

Beatrice summarized how learning to make decisions, plan, and evaluate helped her as a learner,

> I think it helped me a lot. First of all starting with the planning part, decision making [helps] me realize—OK—I've decided to do this certain thing so I'm *focusing* on what I'm doing. And the planning part helped me . . . the decision-making part tells me to *get ready*—like OK—I want to plan this out. Then actually *doing it* . . . the decision and planning part helped me do it and then the evaluation part made me think about *what kind of good work I did.*

As Victor discussed the rubrics for evaluating the Mexico project, he stated simply, "We wanted to do our best." Pointing from the criteria to the list of possible scores, he added, "And that's how we got to do our best. We have to do this [use criteria], if we want to get to that [a high score]."

SOCIAL-EMOTIONAL LEARNING

The focus of Erica's work was on learning to teach thinking operations represented by the TIEL Wheel. Yet, when students have the opportunity to develop thinking skills that empower them as learners, qualities of character emerge and social-emotional learning occurs. Throughout the year, students had many opportunities to develop reflection skills as they worked on their projects. They also learned to have appreciation for each other, show empathy for a student who was struggling, and demonstrate leadership in making ethical decisions within their group. They acquired confidence as they gained mastery in the skills needed to develop their projects.

Grouping to Meet Learning and Social-Emotional Needs

Projects offer an opportunity to group students in different configurations to address learning needs. However, this can yield social-emotional dividends as well. In seeking ways to meet individual learning needs, Erica decided to place four struggling students together to see if each of them would have more opportunities to contribute when grouped with peers of similar abilities. She was pleased with the outcome of this group studying the culture of Mexico.

Emilio, a student from Mexico in his third year with Erica, emerged as a very competent leader. Erica had been his teacher as a third grader, a fourth grader, and now as a fifth grader. As part of the group researching the culture of Mexico, Emilio took a leadership role in two ways. He helped his group members select traditions about his country to share in the presentation and he became a mentor to one of the students in his group.

Juris was from Latvia. He had entered the class in September speaking no English. At the time of the Mexico project, Juris's English was emerging but he was still struggling. During work time on the Mexico project, Emilio helped Juris with the required reading. When it came time for the presentation, Emilio stood firmly by Juris's side and helped him with his first speaking presentation in English.

Erica wisely provided him with a chance to develop his leadership skills. Emilio had his own language and learning problems, as well as a walking disability caused by a spinal condition. Operations for the spinal condition resulted in Emilio missing many days of school throughout his education. In group work, he often struggled to keep up. Yet, when given the opportunity, he showed skills that no one knew he had.

Social Awareness

The Mexico study gave students an opportunity to develop social awareness that extended beyond the classroom. A question and answer period followed each presentation. The students who had studied Life in Mexico Today discovered that Mexico is a struggling democracy. They pointed out that the country is very divided between the rich and the poor, which contributes to high rates of immigration to the United States. Oil is a key business, while industry consists of manufacturing for Nike and other U.S. companies.

The Life in Mexico Today group elicited thoughtful questions that focused on many of the qualities of character described in the TIEL Wheel. The students who listened to the presentation asked reflective questions that indicated an awareness of ethical issues and showed empathy for the people of Mexico. Some of their questions were,

- What would you do if you were president of Mexico?
- Is there child labor?
- Are any countries stepping in at all?
- What is the biggest problem?
- Is there overcrowding in Mexico?

TRANSPARENT TEACHING

The TIEL Model helps make teaching transparent and transparency fosters understanding. In using the TIEL Model to teach and discuss thinking skills, the students were able to articulately discuss their own thinking as well as analyze their teacher's thinking. They saw a pattern in how Erica planned for their work. Victor explained matter-of-factly, "It's a pattern. Because when we did the School study it was in a group. Then we did the State study which was individual and then we're doing Mexico which is group so it's a pattern. Groups for the School study and then individual for the State study and Mexico, group."

Victor seemed clear on the purposes behind Erica's planning, "She wants us to get a sense of each other, get along with each other, and share our work with other people. She wants us to do some of our own work."

While the state and Mexico projects differed in the way the work was done, in both the state and Mexico studies the students had to gather certain kinds of information, such as geography and history. Beatrice took note of the similarities and differences and how the work in one project helped them with the next project: "I think the Mexico study project was a lot like the State study . . . because we each got to do a different project. In the Mexico study we did it as a group. It's similar because we're dealing with states [geography] . . . from the work we did in State study, it helped us get ready for the Mexico study."

When students begin to understand their learning, they begin to appreciate teaching. The students thought Erica should teach her next class in the same ways she had taught them. They had learned about Mexico, the states that make up the United States, and how to observe a school for their middle school decision. They had learned processes of self-organization and how to present projects that represented their learning. Equally important, the students had learned about good teaching by having opportunities to teach and also learn from their classmates.

Their suggestions to Erica indicated a clear awareness that *they* learned because of good teaching. As they thought about Erica's next class, all three students suggested that Erica "keep on doing what you're doing. Plan and stuff—teach." Beatrice recommended that Erica continue to use the planning calendar and keep the TIEL charts on the wall. A summary of successful teaching was tightly packed in Victor's simple advice, "Be a teacher."

SUMMARY

The Mexico study gave students the opportunity to prepare a teaching presentation. The content of the study of Mexico was divided into two large categories—historical and present day. Using New York State social studies standards and core curriculum, Erica carefully selected the content and skills she wanted the students to learn in this unit. Erica used what she had learned in the previous units to more clearly communicate time parameters for this unit.

Communication about thinking and learning was deeply woven into the fabric of this unit. The ability of the students to communicate about their thinking was evidence of increased communication about thinking in the classroom. Students excitedly explained how they used the planning calendar to plan their Mexico projects. They told how they made decisions about the making the visual part of their projects. Students clearly articulated how they used evaluation to assess their own projects.

IV

CURRICULUM

cur · ric · u · lum (kə rik'yə ləm), *n*. 1. the aggregate of courses of study given in a school, college, university, etc. 2. the regular or a particular course of study in a school, college, etc.

—Webster's Unabridged Dictionary

curriculum. 1824, modern coinage from L. curriculum "a running, course, career," from currere. Used as a L. word since 1633 at Scottish universities.

—Online Etymology Dictionary

Curriculum, what teachers teach and what students learn, is usually focused on subject content and the teaching of basic skills, of reading and writing, that allow students to communicate what they learn and enable them to learn more. Today, however, the concept of curriculum needs to expand to include the explicit teaching of the intellectual and social-emotional skills described in the TIEL Curriculum Design Model. Instead of the preprocessed curriculum that too often lacks the intellectual nutrients needed for complex learning, students need curriculum that demands their thinking, requires them to problem solve together, encourages them to persevere, and teaches them the skills to organize and evaluate their learning.

CHAPTER 9: COURAGE TO TEACH
SELF-ORGANIZATION SKILLS

How does a teacher with a traditional approach to teaching add complex teaching and learning to her practice? This chapter shares how Stacy made changes in her thinking that allowed her students to do more of the thinking in her classroom.

CHAPTER 10: FREEDOM FROM THE FEAR FACTOR

Stacy overcomes her fear of large projects and student anarchy and begins to plan project-based learning for her fourth grade students. With careful planning, she teaches her students to made decisions, plan, and self-organize their project work.

CHAPTER 11: CREATING COMPLEX PROJECTS

In the study of African American heroes, Stacy demonstrates how to plan curriculum where students develop complex thinking skills, social-emotional characteristics, and basic skills through an important part of the New York State social studies curriculum.

CHAPTER 12: TRANSFORMATIONS IN THINKING

How does the teaching of self-organization skills transform teachers and students? Stacy appreciated the changes she saw in herself and her students. Empowered, confident, and articulate about their thinking and learning, Stacy's students share their learning experiences.

9

Courage to Teach
Self-Organization Skills

It feels so much more natural and wholesome in a way. The kids can be swept up in it. . . . I'm not always dragging them on this heavy sled.

—Stacy, fourth grade teacher

Designing curriculum is a fundamental part of teaching and learning. During the course of the research, Stacy moved through three different approaches to designing curriculum. A traditional curriculum is generally found in a teacher-directed classroom where students follow instructions and have minimal choices in their work. Textbooks, workbooks, and professionally published worksheets have a central role in a traditional classroom.

Student-centered classrooms focus on student interests, feature more choices, and include a variety of hands-on project work. In a traditional classroom, the focus is on learning content and basic skills. In a student-centered classroom, content and basic skills are also a priority, but they are taught in ways that take into account student interest, choice, creativity, and a wider range of learning processes (Blumenfeld et al, 1991; Darling-Hammond, 1997; Dewey, 1964; Folsom, 2005; Thomas, 2000).

Classrooms where complex teaching and learning take place have all the features of a child-centered classroom and a focus on basic skills. In addition to this balance, teachers consciously plan the curriculum to include the explicit teaching of thinking and social-emotional processes integrated with content (Folsom, 2005). In these classrooms, teaching students to set criteria that guide decision making, planning projects, cooperatively solving problems, and self-evaluation are also basic skills.

STACY

In many ways, Stacy was the most traditional teacher of the four. She had had a traditional Catholic school education. On the surface Stacy often appeared to fit Hollingsworth's (1989) description of a teacher whose traditional ideas were little affected by her teacher preparation program. She tended to teach as she had been taught, holding the reigns of the classroom tightly in her control.

At the same time, Stacy was unusually aware of the social and emotional needs of her students. If she was traditional in her approach to teaching content, she was remarkably open and perceptive in her understanding of the deep emotional issues that often interfere with a student's learning. Stacy seemed to have a natural mastery of the emotional components of the upper half of the TIEL Curriculum Design Wheel as she designed learning activities that focused on reflection, empathy, and ethical reasoning. Stacy helped her students reflect on and question the information they studied. She was unfailingly empathetic to the children, breaking many tense situations with humor and kindness. She often used history as a forum to discuss the place of empathy and ethics in the events of the past.

There were few student projects in Stacy's classroom prior to the year of research. The projects at that time were teacher-directed and did not include any materials for teaching the students how to make decisions, plan, or self-evaluate their work. Stacy understood the value of having students take more responsibility for directing their own learning; however, she did not know how to teach these skills to students.

The next three chapters tell how Stacy significantly transformed her thinking and changed her practice from a tightly controlled approach to curriculum to teaching self-organization skills through project work that opened her students to a world of thinking and creativity. This chapter explains how Stacy thought about developing curriculum before the research. The following chapters share changes in her thinking and include examples of how she planned project-based curriculum that included the teaching of thinking as well as content.

Challenges to Project Work and Teaching Self-Organization Skills

Learning new ways of doing what has become familiar can cause anxiety. Teachers put structures in place in their classrooms that help maintain the management necessary to support students' academic progress. They are not eager to upset the delicate balance. Therefore, it is especially difficult for teachers to alter a proven routine that has been successful.

Learning something worthwhile is seldom a smooth or easy road. The piano needs to be practiced. The soccer ball needs to be kicked and occasionally headed. A new computer program needs to be mastered. Yet, most of the time we are able to work through new learning in relative solitude. Teachers do not have that luxury. During the process of learning new teaching strategies, a teacher has an impatient audience of thirty depending on him or her to make things clear as the students encounter their own struggles with learning.

Stacy clearly associated learning and teaching self-organization processes with project-based learning and she saw the implications for disorder. She was fully aware that the difficulty in carrying out project work is directly proportional to the number of students in the classroom. At the baseline assessment, Stacy had twenty-three students in her third grade class, a good number for doing projects. However, she was feeling anxious about the next year when she would teach a fourth grade class with ten additional children. She saw the implications and shared her anxiety,

> Too many kids in the classroom. Though that is not a problem this year, it will be next year when I have ten more students than I have now. I had two kids absent and I had twenty-one kids in my room. We could do art projects, make clay, [and] of course I could have three kids sit under my desk. We had so much extra space, it was lovely. They could all be talking to their partners and still hear my voice. Thirty-one kids . . . I think if I can keep them all sitting for the first month, I'll be so happy.

Project work with such a large class seemed risky to Stacy, for purely physical reasons. Yet, she also thought that involving student thinking in project work threatened classroom order even further, creating an additional risk. She wondered how she would manage when students had more choices. Stacy hesitantly thought that perhaps she could do just one project during the research year. She tentatively offered this possibility, "Maybe I can be brave enough to try a project. But it feels risky for me. The deep recess of my mind just wants my day to be smooth. Once everybody starts thinking, it's going to get rough."

Teacher Preparation

Teaching self-organization skills made sense to Stacy. While class size presented definite problems, her main challenge in teaching thinking skills was that she did not know how. She wondered why she had not learned this in her teacher preparation programs. The subject of thinking in the context of project work had not been addressed in any of the college programs that had prepared her for teaching: "It [thinking] certainly never came up . . . the whole idea that kids would make decisions. In fact it never came up that *teachers* would make decisions."

Piaget's (1948) theory of cognitive development was the closest any of Stacy's education classes came to the subject of thinking. However, she found that Piaget's orderly, linear way of looking at human development offended her sense of individuality and diversity. Adamantly, she said, "I firmly hate that whole . . . way of seeing people as stages and they always go in order and it's very linear. We know what normalcy looks like. We can tell when people are abnormal. That whole philosophy of humanity makes me so nauseous. It never seemed appropriate to me." Stacy did not feel she had received adequate instruction that connected concepts of thinking to practical teaching in the classroom. Neither did she agree with or find helpful the small amount of instruction she had received.

Structure of Stacy's Education

Stacy attended a university for her undergraduate work where she could design her own major in international relations. She was frustrated by the separation that existed among the departments and created her own program. After receiving her bachelor's degree, Stacy attended another university to obtain her teaching license. A master's degree required forty-five credits and was too expensive to pursue at the time, so she left with only her teaching credential.

After teaching for two years in a middle school with overwhelming challenges, she enrolled in a prestigious teacher preparation program to obtain her master's degree. She was not required to take methods courses or to student teach because she held a teaching certificate and had previous teaching experience. Since Stacy had already taken courses in teaching reading, math, and other subjects in her previous certification program, she enrolled as a full-time inservice master's candidate.

Nevertheless, Stacy wanted more than theory courses. She had come from a difficult experience teaching in an inner city middle school, and she wanted courses that addressed the social-emotional aspect of teaching. Stacy met with an advisor and tried to differentiate between intellectual needs and emotional needs based on her recent teaching experiences. She recalled the conversation as they discussed possible classes:

> The problems I had teaching had nothing to do with my ability to teach reading. The problems that I had were overcrowded classes, lack of confidence, and I was being emotionally battered, and I was distraught and I had no support, and I didn't know how to network. Nothing anybody's teaching me is attending to any of those needs. You can take eight classes on math, but guess what? The problem was, I was depressed and I was in a destructive environment. And [it seemed that] people were doing everything they could to make sure I didn't feel better. Somebody's got to attend to the fact that teachers deal with more than academics and nobody seemed to have that [class for me].

Educational Gaps

After attending three colleges, two specifically focused on learning to teach, Stacy still had large gaps in her teacher education. She felt that she had learned little quality practical information. She knew little about teaching classroom content, nothing about teaching decision making to students (or how to make decisions as a teacher), and she was frustrated by the lack of attention given to social-emotional issues. She had received no instruction in project-based learning and no instruction in teaching thinking processes. She could see the possibilities of student thinking within the context of project work, but the development and management of project-based learning had never been mentioned in her teacher education classes.

Stacy's teacher education programs had been part of the problem rather than part of the solution in preparing her to teach self-organization skills. Stacy explained the effect of not knowing, of not understanding, of being overwhelmed, "Well, not knowing. That's been a big roadblock. Not knowing how [to facilitate self-organization processes within the context of project-based learning], or not knowing what to do to make it that way, and feeling like for me to make it up would be way more energy than I could invest in it."

In spite of extensive teacher preparation, high grades, and requisite degrees and licenses, Stacy still lacked the knowledge required to successfully carry out the fundamental teaching practices that underlie Dewey's description of education based on experience and self-organization (Dewey, 1938, 1964; Kliebard, 1995).

CURRICULUM DEVELOPMENT

After receiving her master's degree, Stacy began teaching third grade in New York City. Stacy had a difficult time planning curriculum during the year of teaching third grade. Although she had taught previously in a middle school, she had not taught in a self-contained classroom. This was her first experience with third grade and she was unfamiliar with the curriculum. She shared the challenges that this presented,

> I have a really hard time with curriculum planning because this is my first year with a regular classroom and it's in a different grade. So I feel very sort of stymied . . . because I don't know what the curriculum is. So I'm stuck with how creative I can be. I don't have a couple years of resources in my room that I can pull out and use in a different way. I have to kind of do it all over for the first time again . . . which is going to be hard for me in some ways.

In terms of curriculum, Stacy had experienced three first years of teaching. She had taught preschool, middle school, and now third grade in an elementary school. The following year, the research year, would mean another first year with fourth grade curriculum.

Understanding of Curriculum

Stacy saw curriculum in dialectical terms, consistently seeing two sides of each curricular issue. On the one hand, she saw that designing traditional curriculum that depended on worksheets required less demanding planning skills. On the other, she saw the rewards of the more complex project planning.

Trying a Project

During the final month of her third grade year, I suggested that Stacy try more projects. She planned a study of growth using lima beans that included making bean sculptures. She liked the results. While her bean project did not involve teaching self-management skills, it got her thinking more deeply about curriculum planning. Stacy explained how she felt about the paradox of curriculum planning,

> What feels like the least demanding way to plan is always the most staid. You know, if I just go by the workbook, I can see where everybody is and it is very easy on some level. Doing complicated planning, workshops and the like . . . I think, how can I get into it? Yet, when I am into it, it is so rewarding and in some ways there is such a clear agenda. In a way, it's like announcing, "We're going to be great now. How do we make the room a place where we can be great?" It feels so much more natural and wholesome in a way. The kids can be swept up in it . . . I'm not always dragging them on this heavy sled.

It was hard to think about giving up the ease of a more traditional approach to curriculum planning. Yet, Stacy recognized the advantages of project work as she watched her students. Even though the projects were predominantly teacher directed at this time, the students were clearly invested in their work.

Experience and Creativity

Stacy linked knowing and experience with the creativity she could bring to curriculum planning. Sternberg (1985) makes a similar connection. Within his triarchic theory of intelligence, Sternberg explains that creativity is a function of experience. Stacy felt that planning and self-evaluation "hold hands" and together are important factors in building experience. The teacher plans, teaches, and then evaluates the results of her teaching. After many repetitions of this cycle, the teacher gains the experience that allows her to be more creative within the curriculum.

Stacy was frustrated by not having the experience she needed for the creative planning she expected of herself in the third grade classroom. She recognized that complex teaching leads to complex learning and to more motivated and engaged students. However, she also realized that she did not have a structure that could guide more ambitious planning. Stacy's struggle between the safety and ease of traditional teaching and the more complex experiential teaching intensified her need for a structure that could help her with more intensive planning.

Curricular Decisions

Stacy's decisions about curriculum were not based on any theoretical models. Even after her coursework in two teacher education programs, she did not refer to any theories that influenced her as she developed curriculum. Instead, echoing Daniel Lindley (1993), who authored *This Rough Magic*, Stacy described the challenge of preparing learning activities for the students as an "act of magic" that involved the consideration of two "agendas."

Content

The first agenda concerned the content that the students need to understand. Stacy explained what went into her curriculum decisions,

> One of [the agendas] is that there is a certain amount of content that needs to be understood. And that is partly just a race against the clock and partly . . . it's like I feel like it takes every fiber of my intellect and insight to try to think of ways to make sure that the kids are really learning, given what I know about their personalities and about the time structure that we have together. Making that happen is like a magic act.

She selected content based on the New York State core curriculum, the state learning standards for fourth grade, and curriculum materials purchased by the school. When planning, Stacy considered the time available for teaching the content and also the personalities of the students in her class. The result of carefully interweaving content with time constraints and consideration for individual students was what Stacy referred to as "magic."

Emotional Well-Being

The second agenda item that influenced curriculum development was Stacy's concern for the emotional well-being of her students. Recognizing a "very direct" interconnection between the academic and the emotional components within curriculum, Stacy took pains to create an emotionally safe environment for her students. She explained,

> You just can't do your best thinking when you're upset and you can't put yourself on the line to be creative or do any kind of bold thinking, especially not to express it, if people around you are going to tease you for it. Especially not if you're eight [years old].

Stacy understood that thinking and project work involve risk. In an environment where there is empathy for those who are vulnerable as they try something new, students are more likely to take those risks. According to Stacy, the magic act of teaching depended on a special relationship between the actions of the students and the curriculum that occurs when each student takes responsibility to show empathy for his classmates. In the course of a day "somebody's going to have a really strong need somewhere" and Stacy wanted to make sure that someone would be there to notice. She added,

> A big part of that magic act for me is making sure it [teaching and learning] happens in an extremely supportive and comfortable environment. It's painful for me to think of one of my kids going home feeling really crummy about their day. I don't care that they feel crummy because they fooled around all day and I yelled at them . . . they need to feel crummy about that . . . but to feel unloved . . . For me to let them go through the door not thinking, "Well, Miss Silver loves me," or "I had a good idea today," or something good about themselves, or any other act of self-esteem issue, would be just criminal.

STRUCTURES THAT SUPPORT SELF-ORGANIZED LEARNING

At the time of the baseline assessment, Stacy had several classroom structures in place to support self-organized learning. These structures included small projects, methods of evaluation, ways of communicating, and the warm, caring, emotionally safe atmosphere mentioned earlier. In addition, she had a strong internal belief that teaching thinking is important and she had a strong desire to learn. All of these factors supported Stacy as she changed how she developed curriculum in order to explicitly teach self-organization skills.

Project Work

Stacy had not let the lack of understanding how to teach students decision making, planning, and self-evaluation prevent her from undertaking project work. By the end of the year, the third graders had completed three simple hands-on projects. They made masks, grew plants, and created sculptures of beans in various stages of development. In addition, they wrote memoirs that were presented at a publishing party. At this point there were no planning tools to help students organize their projects. There were no self-evaluation tools to help them assess their work. Each project was teacher-directed with Stacy planning the work and the students following her instructions.

Isolated Projects

During the preresearch year, the landscape of Stacy's teaching varied minimally. The creative projects seemed to erupt on this smooth geographical terrain much like unconnected monoliths rising from a desert floor. Each seemed to be an isolated project. The students enjoyed their work and were proud of their products, but there was little connection from one learning activity to another. The feeling of intellectual connection that can permeate the atmosphere of a classroom would come later.

Student Behavior

The level of student behavior in Stacy's third grade classroom at baseline supported the project work they were doing at the time. The class of twenty-three students were respectful to their teacher and to each other. Classroom management was based on mutual teacher–student respect that Stacy consciously and continuously worked to develop. The students were good listeners and conscientiously followed instructions. They did not, however, show the high level of autonomy in their work that Stacy's fourth grade class would demonstrate the following year. At the end of third grade, these students were accustomed to a relaxed, respectful, but, nonetheless, teacher-directed classroom. It did not feel like the students were driving their own learning.

Methods of Evaluation

The beginnings of teaching self-organization skills were present in Stacy's classroom. Although students were not self-evaluating their work and Stacy was not using specific thinking vocabulary, there was evidence that she was making the children aware of expectations for their assignments.

Teacher Understanding

Stacy did not use the term *criteria* that would help students see the pattern of evaluation across assignments and subject areas. The students, however, knew that the memoirs had to include a written, visual, and spoken component. Like Ted and Erica, Stacy made the expectations in the writing workshop visible to the students. A checklist stating what constituted a good story was posted in the classroom. The students analyzed their handwriting and developed a list that described what good cursive handwriting looks like.

Fact-Fiction Story
- Beautiful writing
- Clearly organized
- Blends fiction and fact in a natural way

Good Handwriting
- Letters are correctly shaped
- Letters are connected smoothly together
- Writing is large enough to read easily
- Writing is on the line

While substantial in quantity, the discussions about thinking lacked the quality that comes with a deeper understanding of the processes and a common language with which to discuss them. There was much discussion surrounding the concepts of decision making, planning, and self-evaluation, but the conversations lacked vocabulary that would label the concepts and make them explicit. Other operations of thinking were also inexplicit. Stacy often used the word *creativity* when describing student work, but she had difficulty in differentiating between creative thinking and other kinds of thinking.

Student Understanding

Stacy felt that the students understood a certain amount of the thinking involved in self-organization skills, yet they were not necessarily aware of the thinking processes in which they were engaged. She realized that they needed a language to gain understanding and awareness. Stacy explained the ubiquitous nature of decision making and planning and how the students understood these processes: "Part of getting through the day is making decisions. And in terms of their work, I think that they know when they're doing it, but I don't think they can name it. So it's not a 100 percent there for them. Unless we share it with them they don't have the language, to say, 'I'm going to make a plan about something or other.'"

Decisions in School

The students did have various levels of understanding of the processes involved in creating a project. As we talked, they recognized experiences in making decisions, plans, and evaluations in projects from earlier grades.

Vonda shared her memory of project work, "We made pillows in second grade. I remember I wrote down something about planning my pillow."

Danette was more specific, "I made a play in second grade. I had to sketch bodies to design the costumes."

"I worked with a kindergarten buddy, but I didn't plan at all," John reported.

Noticing what is missing is sometimes as important as seeing what is there. John took this approach, as he shared his work helping his kindergarten buddy read a book and draw a picture.

I then asked them about evaluating their projects. John immediately gave a numerical rating to his work with his reading buddy. Danette assigned her costume project a number. Vonda seemed unclear about the question and did not assign her pillow a number. However, she evaluated it in another way, describing the pillow as special. While they could all evaluate their work in retrospect, none of them had actually evaluated their work at the time they concluded the projects. Nevertheless, each of them thought self-evaluation was a good idea.

Danette, looking into her future as a teacher, said, "Yes, I think it would be a grown-up thing to do—like grading other people's papers."

Vonda agreed, adding, "But I don't know why."

Seeing self-evaluation in terms of motivation, John explained, "It would be good to know how you're doing. It would rev you up to do more."

Decisions Outside of School

The three students in the interview group each had variable amounts of understanding about the processes of decision making, planning, and self-evaluation. As the students talked about their perceptions of decision making, planning, and self-evaluation within school, they appeared to have a similar knowledge base. Yet, when asked about their experience with self-organization skills outside of school, it became apparent that their experiences were not equal.

There were clear differences in their experiences outside of school. Culture and background appeared to affect the opportunity for choice and the recognition of those choices that students brought to the classroom. Danette, from a well-educated, middle- to upper middle–class family, pinpointed clearly where she made decisions, formulated plans, and participated in self-evaluation outside of school. She had these opportunities in her religious classes, her drama class, and in playing different positions on the soccer team. John, growing up in similar middle-class circumstances, stated that he made decisions about going outside and playing with his friends. Vonda, from a less educated family of more modest means who lived in a nearby public housing project, had nothing to share about making decisions outside of school.

Ways of Communicating

Stacy had several methods of communication that would support the explicit teaching of thinking. Socratic discussion, peer conferencing, using resources to spur conversation, and problem posing were all used in the classroom.

Socratic Discussion

Stacy engaged the students in a Socratic form of discussion in which she "teased out" the concept she was teaching. When teaching a vocabulary word, she might ask, "Have you seen that word before? Where have you heard that word used? Can you break the word apart? Are there any parts of the word that are familiar to you? Is there anything about the word that gives you a hint to its meaning? How can we use the word in a sentence to help us figure out the meaning?"

The ability to draw information from the children is important in teaching self-organization skills. Helping students participate in setting criteria and making their own plans requires a different kind of conversation than simply giving instructions.

Peer Conferencing

Planning a group project requires that students share information. Stacy had in place opportunities for the students to confer with each other. She explained to the students that just as she conferred with other teachers about classroom work, she wanted them to learn to turn to each other for help. In reading, students read with partners so that they could discuss their books. In writing, students read each others' stories and offered suggestions. If a student was having difficulty spelling a word, he or she was to confer with a neighbor on possible spellings and then turn to the dictionary before bringing the word to the teacher.

Using Resources

Visual resources can start the conversation about criteria setting. Before having the terminology to describe criteria for evaluation, Stacy used resources to help establish guidelines with students in reading and writing. Stacy used a resource to provide a catalyst for the discussion that led to the chart describing *Fact-Fiction Stories*. Early in the year the class wrote stories about animals that combined facts with fiction. Stacy needed to help the students understand how to write such a story. Using the classic, *The Trumpet of the Swan*, she asked the students to analyze the qualities that make the book great. From the checklist that emerged—beautiful writing, clearly organized, blends fiction and fact in a natural way—they established criteria for their own stories.

Emotional Safety

The caring, emotionally safe environment for learning would provide the proper atmosphere for students to make choices, plan, and create. Stacy's approach to classroom management was supportive and affirming. Her flexibility and ability to see the humor in almost every situation prevented the escalation of many of the myriad problems that arise in a classroom. The emotional environment of the classroom was further sustained by Stacy's sense of risk-taking—an important quality when undertaking large and messy projects. She had no fear of letting the students help mix salt and flour to make the bean sculptures. This emotional foundation would support the kinds of work that she would be doing during the year of research.

Classroom Community

The concept of community was important in Stacy's classroom. The underlying philosophy of community provided the basis for most problem solving. For example, over a period of days during the beginning weeks of teaching third grade, items were taken from Stacy's desk. Since her desk had no lock, everything was subject to theft—chalk, stickers, office supplies, and candy she kept for rewards or special treats. She began by saying to the students, "This is our classroom . . . this is our space."

Stacy then took three actions. First, she informed them that she would no longer bring candy, as she could not afford to lose it, and she no longer felt good about buying candy that was going to be stolen. Second, she explained to them the necessity of having a safe place to call their home during the day: "This can't be a place where I come in the room and feel unsafe. I walk into this room and I already feel like I need to lock my stuff up. What an awful feeling to have in your own home. This is my home all day. This is my room. We can't do that to each other."

Stacy's third action was to establish a policy of communal property. This meant that the students were not allowed to have their own rulers, pencils, crayons, calculators, or paper. All supplies would be put in a common place where the students would have equal access to all materials. Stacy gave them a clear reason, "It's simply not acceptable for you to have fifteen pencils and the person next to you has to ask you for one if theirs breaks. That's not nice. It doesn't feel good to be protecting your stuff from your neighbors all the time. We don't need to have that kind of community. We're eight years old. We will all share the paper."

Stacy turned an unpleasant experience into a learning experience that helped the students appreciate how to share materials. While the Era of Common Property did not last the entire year, it helped students understand consequences.

Respect for Personal Differences

Stacy championed the emotional well-being of the children in her class. She was uncompromising about the importance of personal difference and was unfailingly accepting of the differences of others. She saw each child as a normal individual regardless of difference and was determined that no one would feel alienated. Danitza, slightly overweight and physically uncoordinated, was often teased by the other students. Instead of simply telling the students not to tease Danitza, Stacy helped them understand Danitza's situation. She spoke with them clearly and calmly,

Stacy: Every one of us has something specific we need help with. What is something you need help with?

Kayla: I have a hard time with my swimming lessons.

Robert: I need help with my handwriting.

Timothy: I wear glasses because I need help seeing things that are far away.

Stacy: How would you feel if someone teased you because you wear glasses or that you can't run as fast as someone else? I've heard some people teasing Danitza. I think there are some things that can help us understand more about Danitza just like we're learning to understand more about each one of us. Sometimes you get special help at school with the things that are difficult. She goes to occupational therapy for help with her special needs. Danitza has feelings just like all of you. How might you feel if you were her?

Seating Arrangement

The seating arrangement in the classroom also existed because of Stacy's deep commitment to emotional safety. The desks were arranged in groups of four to promote cooperative learning, an arrangement favored by most of the teachers in the building. The students' work, however, was predominantly individual, so I wondered why Stacy chose to have the students seated in this way. She recalled her experience as a student in a Catholic school sitting lined up in desks unable to see anyone's face. With the empathy that often emerges from unpleasant experiences, Stacy explained, "They [the students] need to see a friendly face across from them, someone to support them."

Internal Structures

Stacy had a web of internal structures that would help in developing curriculum that supported the teaching of thinking skills. She valued the teaching of thinking, she was able to be flexible with her thinking, and she was motivated to learn new ways of teaching.

Values

Stacy strongly valued the teaching of thinking. She was aware of the differences between her current practice and what could be possible in her teaching. She recognized the difference between talking about thinking and doing the work of helping students become conscious of their thinking. Insightfully, Stacy said, "if we're working on a project, of course, we'll talk about how we make decisions and how are we going to plan it . . . how do you *make* a plan? That's a whole separate issue and that's much harder for me."

Recognizing that talking about making a decision or plan is not the same as explicitly teaching the processes of decision making or planning is the first step in transforming thinking and changing teaching practices. At baseline, Stacy had this understanding in place. She was ready to learn how to go beyond merely talking to students about deciding, planning, and evaluating their projects to teaching her students the skills to organize their own learning.

Self-Evaluation and Feelings

Values often clash, requiring flexibility in thinking. Stacy valued the teaching of thinking; however, her strong values about the emotional aspect of teaching caused her to hesitate when it came to teaching self-evaluation skills. Since she personally found that writing an evaluation of herself was difficult, she found the idea of teaching self-evaluation to students especially challenging. She explained,

> I tend to be very emotional about self-evaluation. If I don't think I did well, then I get really upset with myself and everyone can tell I didn't do well. When I feel really good about what I did . . . I feel proud of it. . . . I'm not very good about going through the process of writing about how I did or filling out a form on self-evaluation. So what seems to work for me personally is to figure out why I didn't feel good. Then I try to do it differently and that's where I have to leave it.

Stacy perceived the conflict that could exist between evaluation and feelings. Because of her experiences, she was highly aware of striking a balance between self-evaluation and self-esteem. Profoundly concerned with the social-emotional issues of teaching, she wanted the students to trust their instincts, yet learn to evaluate their work more thoroughly.

How do you manage a discrepancy between the students' evaluation of their work and the teacher's evaluation? Wrestling with the conflict between evaluation and self-esteem, Stacy began to think of evaluation in a new way. Instead of an onerous drudgery, she saw that the setting of criteria can serve as a tool for negotiating between teacher assessment and student assessment.

For example, when there is disagreement on the evaluation, Stacy might say, "You [the student] feel like this piece is done, and I [the teacher] don't. So we need to go through some criteria for what would make it feel complete, or best work. And, on the other hand, you need to feel proud about good work. You have to let yourself say, 'I'm working hard.' And it feels good to be doing that. There has to be a balance."

The concept of balance is an important one in developing curriculum. John, a third grade student, presciently pointed out that evaluating oneself could "rev you up." Yet, for self-evaluation to be motivating, two conditions must be in place. First, students need to know the criteria for evaluation of an assignment and how to use it to judge their work. Second, they need to feel good about the effort required to continue working until the learning objective is accomplished.

Motivation

Teaching students in a way that helps them become more responsible and self-aware learners required new skills. Stacy was motivated to learn this "whole other bag of tricks" that would help her teach her students to be more responsible for their decisions and their learning. She knew their opportunity to learn decision-making skills depended on the curricular decisions she made. "Decision making seems so unavoidable and fundamental. I try to be conscious of the decisions I make so the kids do not end up doing things by default but by design. I need to evaluate my work with the students more and then do more of what works well."

Stacy saw decision making as critical for students. She felt that the following-directions aspect of school was excessive and far too little time was spent helping students gain "insight into what would make sense for them to do academically." Instead, students too often hear, "Now open up your workbook. We're going to be doing sentence structure."

Students are accustomed to going through school and doing what they're told. Stacy recalled making a decision about a homework assignment that gave the students options and an opportunity to develop criteria for their choices. After explaining that they would be doing reading and writing during the day, she allowed them to choose which they would like to do for a half-hour at home. They had to have a reason for their choice, as well as a plan for completing the homework. At first they were hesitant, but then they experienced the powerful feeling of being in charge of a decision. She explained, "When I opened that door [of self-awareness] a crack, they [the students] were afraid to step over the threshold, but once they did, they felt totally empowered by it."

Unsurprised when the students completed their homework assignments competently, she commented, "I never really felt that a student who had planned his own work did a bad job of it. They have a pretty good sense of what they're doing."

SUMMARY

Before we began the professional learning process, Stacy had several structures in place in her classroom that would support her in learning to use the TIEL Model to teach self-organization skills to her students. These included a small number of projects, evidence of setting criteria in the areas of reading and writing, and an emotionally supportive manner of communicating with the students. Several internal structures would also support Stacy in learning to teach thinking skills. She believed in the importance of teaching thinking to students; she was flexible in her thinking; and she was motivated to learn new ways of motivating her students.

Stacy needed to learn how to develop curriculum in ways that would consciously promote the teaching of thinking. While she understood the importance of the balance between the intellectual and emotional aspects of learning, her curriculum needed more balance among the thinking operations required in the teaching of basic skills and the divergent thinking involved in creative projects.

Stacy made sure that students experienced a balance between the cognitive and the affective in their work. As she learned to develop curriculum that included the teaching of self-organization skills, she was careful to design materials that addressed all of the thinking operations and both sides of the TIEL Wheel. The next chapter includes examples of how Stacy learned to perform this tightwire act.

10

Freedom from the Fear Factor

> I feel a whole lot more comfortable asking them to be involved [in their decision making, planning, and evaluation]. I now feel a very strong sense of responsibility to involve them. Now I'd feel like I'd almost be cheating them out of something if I didn't involve them.
>
> —Stacy, fourth grade teacher

Ralph Waldo Emerson said that knowledge is the antidote to fear. As Stacy finished teaching third grade, she was fearful of trying project-based curriculum with the following year's class of thirty-one fourth graders. During the baseline assessment, she commented, "Maybe I can be brave enough to try a project. But it feels risky for me." Gaining knowledge about how to teach self-organization skills significantly reduced Stacy's feeling of risk. When she learned how to teach the students the skills they needed to manage their own projects, the nagging feeling that the class might slip into chaos dissipated. Much relieved, she explained, "I feel a whole lot more comfortable asking them to be involved. I now feel a very strong sense of responsibility to involve them. Now I'd feel like I'd almost be cheating them out of something if I *didn't* involve them."

During the research year, Stacy planned four project-based units. These included studies of explorers, African American heroes, the states, and the history timeline project. The self-organization tools for the first three projects were teacher developed. The fourth unit was designed as an assessment of the students' ability to independently apply self-organization processes. Students chose a period of history from their classroom timeline to research in more depth, create a project, and make a presentation to the class. This was the general pattern followed in all of the units except for one major difference. In the history timeline project, the students developed their own planning tools to use in organizing their project work. The details of these units will be shared later in the chapter.

THE TIEL CURRICULUM DESIGN MODEL

Using the TIEL Model helped Stacy transform how she designed project-based curriculum. At the final assessment, she had significantly changed her thinking about how to include the strategies of decision making, planning, and self-evaluation into her planning. Where there had been little balance, there was now a rainbow of learning experiences filled with opportunities for thinking. Earlier, she had felt that she did not plan well because she had no theoretical structure to guide her. Now she had a helpful structure, but she did not see it as a theory.

She had so integrated the thinking and social-emotional processes into her curriculum that the TIEL Curriculum Design Wheel, regardless of its theoretical origins, was a practical tool. She explained, "I think that I'm seeing it [decision making, planning, and self-evaluation] as a more integral part of learning than I did at the outset." While Stacy was not offended by rote textbook work and she liked order in the classroom, but she was not likely to give up a more balanced approach to developing curriculum. "I'm comfortable having all the power in the room. Well . . . not anymore actually. Maybe *that* I couldn't go back to. Not at the expense of this type of thinking work. That I ever taught the other way was more a matter of necessity than conviction."

Learning Can Be Uncomfortable

At times, Stacy felt her teaching of self-organization skills was inadequate. Nevertheless, she was committed to learning the new skills. Yet, teaching the students how to set criteria to evaluate their projects felt unnatural, especially at the beginning. "It would just feel uncomfortable. I would spend the night thinking about what should the criteria be? How many [criteria] do we need? It just needs to feel more natural."

Stacy wanted the planning process to be more graceful as well. The students needed to develop a sense of time, a sense of getting things done, and a sense of responsibility about having something important to do. She decided to require that the fourth graders buy schedule books or week-at-a-glance calendars to use as assignment books. She began the year with a workshop about scheduling homework to teach students possible planning scenarios.

Responding to the questions, the students used their calendar books to determine how project work should be distributed over a period of time. "How long will the project take? How many days do we have left of school? We're starting a project but we're having a vacation in a week, so when do you need to finish most of your work?"

Practice helped Stacy develop the naturalness she expected in her teaching. While learning new skills was at times uncomfortable, Stacy recognized how the TIEL Model expanded her teaching and the students' learning. With each unit, teaching the processes of setting criteria and planning became easier. The following sections share some of the ways she found the TIEL Model valuable to her teaching.

Self-Organization Skills in Context

Stacy found the TIEL Model helpful in placing the self-organization skills that she was learning to teach in a context of other thinking and social-emotional processes. She clearly understood the difficulty of learning a concept in isolation versus learning that same concept within a relevant context. For example, the pilot project for the research, discussed in chapter 5, showed that teaching self-organization skills does not require that teachers have knowledge of other thinking operations or qualities of character. During the pilot, Erica learned how to teach decision making, planning, and self-evaluation skills with no reference to other thinking or social-emotional processes. However, she found that teaching self-organization skills became much easier after she was introduced to the TIEL Wheel.

Stacy also felt that seeing the bigger picture gave her a more solid foundation for designing curriculum. Through naming other thinking and social-emotional processes, the TIEL Wheel places self-organization skills within a broader context.

Seeing the whole circle validates your work with me. I think with just that one piece [evaluation], it would seem too bookish. If ethical reasoning weren't named as part of the project, it would be a missing factor, and I would assume your work was missing that factor. I certainly wouldn't assume that you were concerned about caring in the classroom community. We don't talk about it as part of our academic decision making. Having it [caring, ethical reasoning] there makes the work more valid and more respectable to me.

The TIEL Model is not an isolated strategy added to the layers of teaching. Demonstrating her feelings about directives, she said, "Here's something you have to do. Here's another strategy—teach the students how to plan." She felt that professional development is often presented with little or no historical, intellectual, or emotional context. Teachers are expected to learn how to practice new strategies or methods without understanding why. For Stacy, the TIEL framework provided a more "complete picture" that helped her understand why new ways to develop curriculum are needed.

Support for Social-Emotional Learning

The social-emotional aspects of teaching continued to be central in Stacy's teaching. She firmly believed that while specifically addressing thinking is "painfully overlooked in teaching as a whole," the social-emotional components of teaching and learning are no less ignored. "You make connections using your memory in order to be a caring, ethical person. I think we need to do more focusing on these kinds of thinking [referring to the social-emotional components of the circle] in social skills. Decision making standing alone is pretty pointless."

The TIEL framework clarified the discussions of character as well as thinking that she knew were important to have with her students. These discussions included being fair to others, demonstrating ethical behavior, or showing appreciation. "Those conversations can be very easily framed within the context of the circle. It becomes clear what those conversations need to be."

The African American heroes study provided an opportunity for just such a conversation about ethical decision making. As the class began their research, students had difficulty finding sufficient information about some of the African Americans they were researching. This lack of information brought up some interesting questions. Who decided what information would be included in books? How were those decisions made? After discussing these questions with the students, Stacy wrote a letter to the parents so that they could help with additional research: "We are discovering that many of our history, reference, and even special interest books simply do not offer information on some of these heroes. This fact has already led us into some interesting critical thinking discussions, as we ask 'Why not?'"

Teachers need to lead students to consider reasons for why things are as they are. Stacy did not allow the students to simply say they did not have enough information and allow them to choose another person. Instead, she invited them to explore the decisions that led to the absence of information. In doing this, she helped the students see that, historically, the lack of appreciation for the contributions of African Americans has resulted in their exclusion from some books. Pursuing this discussion helped the students learn that ethical decisions involve empathy and consideration for others.

Facilitating Student Thinking

The TIEL framework helped Stacy analyze students' thinking. "We want to be able to break down our thinking so we can see where we stumble," she explained. For example, Elaine, a bright and talented fourth grader, had difficulty organizing her research note cards during the African American heroes unit. Each student needed to research the person assigned and organize the information into an outline. Unable to see the connections lying just below the surface of her information, Elaine could not develop an outline. Stacy used the TIEL bulletin board to help Elaine see that organizing note cards involved analyzing the information and setting criteria. As Elaine discovered each criterion that would help her make decisions about organizing the information, she wrote it on a note card and added it to the green evaluation section of the bulletin board.

Stacy: What kind of thinking will help you organize these note cards? We need to analyze the information you wrote on the cards. Let's pull the information apart and look at it closely? Do some cards have similar information?

Elaine: These two are about her childhood—oh, and this one is about going to school. Here's another one about school. These are about her work.

Stacy: OK. What categories do we have now?

Elaine: Childhood, school . . .

Stacy: Or education . . .

Elaine: And the work she did.

Stacy: Yes, what she's known for. (Elaine used three cards to write *childhood, education,* and *work.*) Anything else?

Elaine: On this card I wrote about problems she had when she tried to get a job. (On a fourth note card, Elaine wrote *problems.*)

Stacy: So we've discovered four criteria to help you make decisions as you organize the cards and then write the outline. What are they?

Elaine: Childhood, education, work, and problems she had.

Elaine read each note card carefully and decided the category in which to place each card. She then sequenced the cards within each category and began writing her outline.

Balancing Curriculum

The TIEL Wheel helped Stacy balance her curriculum. Stacy, like the other teachers, tried to achieve balance between the processes described in the TIEL Wheel and the content being taught, balance between thinking and social-emotional processes, and balance among the thinking operations. She used the TIEL bulletin board that included subskills within each component as a reference when she planned learning activities. She explained, "If I'm planning a project, I want to make sure it's not all convergent. I think it's useful every so often to see what colors are underrepresented." I shared with Stacy my observation of how her present teaching differed from the year before. I recalled,

Remember the first year, in third grade? Your room was bathed in yellow thinking [convergent] and when there were opportunities for green [decision making, planning, and self-evaluation]—as in the bean project—direct instruction substituted for joint criteria-building. The students were very dependent on you to tell them what to do every minute. Do you remember? Your teaching was enormously different. There was so much more convergent-type teaching that first year. This—is very balanced.

Using Content to Learn Language of Thinking

In order to facilitate students' thinking and create balanced curriculum, Stacy needed more familiarity with the components of the TIEL Wheel. She was determined to learn the TIEL vocabulary so that she could speak easily with her students about thinking and social-emotional learning. She wanted them to be familiar with the thinking operations, but she believed strongly that thinking does not stand alone. She was adamant that learning, thinking, and risk-taking cannot happen in a nonsupportive or uncaring environment.

Thanksgiving presented an opportunity to teach thinking skills as well as address social-emotional learning. Stacy decided to work on the TIEL vocabulary within the context of the Pilgrims' first year in America. Beginning their new lives involved a wide range of thinking as well as significant social-emotional learning. She chose to introduce the students to each of the five thinking operations—*cognition, memory, evaluation, convergent thinking,* and *divergent thinking*. She chose *caring* from the empathy section of the TIEL Wheel to include in the discussion of thinking operations.

For homework, the students found possible meanings for *divergent, convergent,* and *caring*. They could use the dictionary, the Internet, or ask their parents or older siblings for ideas. The next day in class the students referred to their homework to compile lists on chart paper of possible definitions of each word (see figure 10.1). The students understood how caring felt—both to care and be cared for. They were able to complete the *caring* chart on their own. However, understanding the thinking processes required more discussion.

The class discussed the words *divergent* and *convergent* in terms of thinking. "How would you describe divergent thinking?" Stacy asked. The students considered the words that describe divergent thinking. Showing this kind of thinking with arms raised high and spread wide, Stacy helped the students understand that divergent thinking is creative thinking, "stretched out thinking," thinking with no limits. "When you come up with lots of ideas or take a risk to try something new, you are thinking divergently," she told the students.

How would you describe convergent thinking? Again, the students used their arms to show the definition of convergent thinking. Bringing their arms from the divergent position wide above their heads, they brought their hands

Divergent	Convergent	Caring
Lots	Meet in one place	Respect
Stretch out	Come together	Helping
Adapting	Common result	Empathy
Try something new		Commitment
No finite limits		Being kind
		Liking something

Figure 10.1. Student definitions of *divergent, convergent,* and *caring.*

down to meet at a point. Instead of lots of possibilities, convergent thinking refers to thinking with one right answer or solving a problem with one solution. Convergent thinking is also organized, logical, step-by-step thinking.

When the students felt comfortable with the terminology, they identified the ways the Pilgrims may have used the various kinds of thinking (see figures 10.2, 10.3, and 10.4). The Pilgrims adapted to their new surroundings, learned to eat new foods, and even came up with creative sleeping arrangements. They had to learn, experiment, and integrate practices from the Native Americans, such as growing and eating corn, into their own daily lives. When the students mentioned crafts and candle making, Stacy helped them think critically by asking, "What is the relationship between creativity and necessity?" Candle making would be a creative activity for the students, but it was a necessary, well-practiced skill for the Pilgrims. However, while making candles may not be a creative activity for the Pilgrims, perhaps they used creative thinking to figure out new ways to make candles with the materials available.

DIVERGENT PRODUCTION	
creativity, stretching out, lots, adapting, risk-taking	
PILGRIMS	**US**
Using herbs to ward off nightmares	Stretch our ideas
Crafts and candles (But for them was it creative? What is the relationship between creativity and necessity?)	Creative with our writing
Adapt to surroundings	Adapting to a new social arrangement
Learn to eat new foods	Adapt to a new place (new class, moving)
Creative living arrangements— sleeping on the table	Reading strategies
Creative to learn, experiment	
Integrate ideas from the Indians, and come up with something better	

Figure 10.2. *Divergent Production* chart in Pilgrims unit.

CONVERGENT PRODUCTION	
Organizing, facts, one right answer, solutions	
PILGRIMS	**US**
Organized themselves	Organize the room and the books
When they made a decision, they all had to do it	Ms. Silver makes a decision and we have to do it
Rules	Made rules the first week of school
Mayflower compact (rules)	
Coming together on a project, decision	Decided to write a note to the office secretary
Solutions (how dinners would be prepared)	Solved how the homework should be passed out
Arriving at a solution or a belief	Solved the coat problem

Figure 10.3.   *Convergent Production* chart in Pilgrims unit.

CARING	
Respect, helping, empathy, commitment	
PILGRIMS	**US**
Sharing	Share pencils and paper
Made friends with Samoset	
Collected food	Collected food for the food drive
Community cooking	
Cooperation	Cooperate when we work on projects
Took care of each other	Helped Shauna when her leg was broken
Respect	We show respect to each other
Understood that people need to have their own feelings	When someone is unhappy we offer to help but they have their feelings

Figure 10.4.   *Caring* chart in Pilgrims unit.

The students had little trouble seeing ways that they used divergent thinking. They had firsthand experience stretching their ideas each time Stacy asked them to think of another way to solve a math problem or come up with some ways to get to the lunchroom more quietly. They were creative when they wrote stories, adding elaborate details. When they entered a new classroom each fall, they experienced adapting to a new place.

CURRICULUM TRANSFORMATIONS: FOURTH GRADE UNITS OF STUDY

Stacy developed the capacity to plan for two. Planning for two means designing units of study that include opportunities for the students to experience the same planning processes used by the teacher. Teachers use criteria to make decisions about the content they will teach and the pedagogical strategies they will use. They plan the steps involved in lessons and evaluate student learning. These are common tasks of a teacher's job.

Planning for two, however, requires another level of planning. Teachers must very consciously planned opportunities for the students to learn the same skills of decision making, planning, and self-evaluation within their project work that the teacher uses in her planning. She designed worksheets that helped the students consider criteria for guiding their decisions. She designed planning sheets to help the students organize their work and evaluation sheets to help the students assess their own projects.

This chapter includes materials from the Explorers and the United States units. The following chapter includes the African American Heroes and the History Timeline projects. These units show how Stacy's planning became more sophisticated throughout the year.

Explorers Unit

Stacy began the year with a study of explorers that focused on the basic skills of research, using a textbook, and writing a factual report. With the students she developed charts that guided the students through their writing project. First, the students focused on what they wanted to know. Using the basic question words of who, what, when, why, where, and how, Stacy asked the students to develop questions about their explorer (see figure 10.5).

- Who was Cortes?
- What exploration was he known for?
- When did he explore?
- Why did he explore?
- Where did he explore?
- How did he carry out his explorations?

Research: Asking Questions	
Who	What
When	Why
Where	How

Figure 10.5. *Research: Asking Questions* worksheet in Explorers unit.

Second, the students listed possible places where they could find information. Some of the suggestions were the library, asking their parents at home, the Internet, and materials in the classroom. Stacy summarized the information on the chart *Information Sources* (see figure 10.6).

Third, the students explored their social studies textbooks as they responded to the following questions (see figure 10.7):

- What can the cover tell you about social studies?
- Does the cover tell you anything about explorers?

Information Sources	
Library	Class
Home	Books
Computer	People and Places

Figure 10.6. *Information Sources* worksheet in Explorers unit.

- How is the textbook organized to help you find information?
- How do the table of contents and index help you find information?
- How do the chapter headings and boldface type help you?
- What kinds of pictures, illustrations, and maps are included?
- What can you find in the glossary?

Fourth, the students applied the strategies of reading nonfiction that they learned in the reading workshop to their social studies textbook. The students

Using a Textbook

1. Look at the <u>cover and the title</u>.

   Is this book about my topic? Or does this book contain my topic?

2. <u>Table of Contents</u> (at the very beginning of the book)

   List the topics that are in this book

   List the chapters

   List subject headings

   Show topics and pages #s in the order they appear in the book

3. Index

4. Chapter Headings: general titles for each chapter

5. Bold-face type: "titles" for each section

6. Pictures, illustrations, maps

7. Glossary (at the end of the book)

   Lists important words from the text alphabetically

   Gives definitions

   Shows pronunciation

Figure 10.7. *Using a Textbook* chart in Explorers unit.

Textbook Strategies

I. Start looking for key words in the index

2. Start looking in the table of contents.

3. On found page SKIM for a key word.

4. Use pictures, maps, charts (and their headings or captions) to figure out what information specifically would be found in the page.

Figure 10.8. *Textbook Strategies* chart in Explorers unit.

used the index, table of contents, key words, and the graphics found in the book (see figure 10.8).

Finally, Stacy made a simple plan with the students that outlined the steps of the nonfiction writing process. The students gathered information, put their notes in order, and began writing, editing, and revising until it was ready for publication (see figure 10.9).

In this first study of the year, Stacy began where she was comfortable. She chose to focus on writing and did not include a visual. The research paper integrated the skills she was teaching in the reading and writing workshops. Writing a research paper prepared the students for the writing that would be required in the remaining projects.

States Unit

As part of their geography instruction, Stacy wanted the students to have an introduction to the individual states that make up the United States of America. She decided on a short individual project that the students could work on at home. The students each chose a state that they wanted to learn more about. The culminating project was a collage poster that shared each student's research.

Writing Reports

[Expository and Persuasive Writing]

Step 1: Gather important information

Step 2: Put notes into reasonable order

Step 3: Connect your information and ideas in logical sentences and paragraphs

Step 4: Revise

Step 5: Edit (self, friend, then teacher)

Step 6: Final draft

Step 7: Publish

Figure 10.9. *Writing Reports* chart in Explorers unit.

Stacy created a planning packet for the States unit that included four worksheets to facilitate the teaching of self-organization skills. To further reinforce the thinking processes that the students had learned in their discussion of the Pilgrims, she used colored paper for three of the worksheets that corresponded to the thinking process required by the worksheet.

Green Collage Planning Sheet

The first of these, the green collage planning sheet, included a grid that listed criteria for evaluation and boxes to mark ✔−, ✔, or ✔+ (see figure 10.10). The green planning sheet corresponded to the *evaluation* component of the TIEL Wheel. It was important that the students set criteria for evaluating their projects. Stacy explained, "I think that many of them produce better work when they have the criteria laid out for them. They produce better work when they know what they are supposed to be creating. And I hope that the criteria also seem reasonable to them, because they helped set it up."

The green planning sheet provided space for students to list the materials and resources that they would use in the development of their projects. These could include print, human, and technology resources. Stacy included a space for the students to describe the steps involved in the projects, as well as a place for them to write any problems they anticipated as they began their work.

Work Record

Next, the students recorded their daily progress and homework assignment on a white worksheet, the *Work Record* (see figure 10.11). Students wrote the date, what work they had accomplished on that day, and the homework they would do for the project on their work record.

Pink Information Guidelines

The third worksheet, *Information Guidelines*, listed six categories of information to research with a seventh space for open choice (see figure 10.12). Corresponding to the *cognition* component of the TIEL Wheel, the pink *Information Guidelines* sheet was used for gathering information about the state. The worksheet was divided into two columns with space to write *what* the students discovered in each area of research and *how* they would show that on their poster. Would they use a picture, a flag, a map, or a document?

Green Final Evaluation

Fourth, the green *Final Evaluation* sheet contained three sections that were drawn from the previous worksheets (see figure 10.13). Two of these sections, general criteria and information guidelines, recapped the thinking processes

Name _____ State _____

COLLAGE PLANNING SHEET

Criteria for evaluation	√ -	√	√ +
Teaches >7 important facts			
Shows creativity (colorful, original, lots of ideas)			
Includes writing (neat, thorough, edited)			
Information is accurate			
Interesting and catchy presentation			
Done on time			

I will need:

MATERIALS	RESOURCES

What I need to do to make a collage about my state:

_____
_____
_____
_____
_____

Problems I might have

_____
_____
_____
_____
_____

Figure 10.10. *Collage Planning Sheet* in States unit, green (*evaluation*).

Name _____ State _____

WORK RECORD

Date   Today I did (in school): _____

          For homework tonight I will: _____

          _____ Check when complete [   ]

Date   Today I did (in school): _____

          For homework tonight I will: _____

          _____ Check when complete [   ]

Date   Today I did (in school): _____

          For homework tonight I will: _____

          _____ Check when complete [   ]

Date   Today I did (in school): _____

          For homework tonight I will: _____

          _____ Check when complete [   ]

Date   Today I did (in school): _____

          For homework tonight I will: _____

          _____ Check when complete [   ]

Figure 10.11.   *Work Record* in States unit.

Name _____ State _____

INFORMATION GUIDELINES

For each type of information, tell specifically what you will show. In the second column tell how you will show it. Check it off in the box when you have finished adding the information to your collage.

	WHAT	HOW
☐	1. Geography	
☐	2. History	
☐	3. Business and Trade	
☐	4. State Map	
☐	5. Daily Life (as compared to NYC)	
☐	6. Symbols (bird, flower, seal, etc.)	
☐	7. _____	

Figure 10.12. *Information Guidelines* worksheet in States unit, pink (*cognition*).

Name _____ State _____

FINAL EVALUATION – State Collage Project

	√- 0	√ 1	√+ 2	Teacher evaluation
General Criteria				_____
Teaches 7–10 important facts				_____
Shows creativity				_____
Includes writing				_____
Information is accurate				_____
Includes a graph I made				_____
The presentation is catchy				_____
Information Guidelines				_____
Teaches about geography				_____
Teaches about history				_____
Teaches about business and trade				_____
Teaches about daily life				_____
Includes a state map				_____
Shows state symbols				_____
		Total		_____

Reflection Questions

Was your research effective (did it succeed)? Why or why not? Name any problems you had and tell what you did to overcome them.

What did you do **to plan** or **to create** your collage that you will do again next time? Why?

What will you do differently next time? Why?

Figure 10.13.   *Final Evaluation* worksheet for States unit, green (*evaluation*).

that the students used throughout the projects. In the third section, reflection questions, Stacy asked the students to describe the effectiveness of their research and to consider changes they might make in a future project.

Student Learning

Students approached planning differently. Raya focused her decision making on how to effectively lay out the facts and symbols on her poster. She considered these criteria as she made her decisions:

• Is it easy on the eyes?
• Is it catchy?
• Is this good?
• Is this best?
• Does it do what I want?

Harry wanted to make sure his information was visible on his poster. He explained his choices: "See the red. The red was red because it's like facts. It has to be like a color that's bright so it will show up. You don't want to make everything white because if somebody doesn't have time to look over everything [they will miss it]."

At the same time, Vonda, who often had difficulty completing work, was mired in the problem of scheduling her time. Her decisions were not so much about the color or placement on the poster, but more about deciding "what I was going to do and which day I was going to do something." She had so much difficulty organizing her work that Stacy asked me to help her with her planning. As we worked one-on-one, Vonda was able to establish order and make a plan for her project. She made her poster but did not complete it on time. While it took her a few more days past the due date, she experienced organizing and completing her work. These emerging skills in planning would help her in future projects.

SUMMARY

Stacy overcame her fear of project-based teaching. The TIEL model helped her transform her teaching to include the students in the decision making, planning, and self-evaluation involved in their projects. TIEL also helped her understand why developing curriculum that helps students learn about their thinking as well as social emotional processes is important. Passionate about the affective aspects of teaching and learning, Stacy appreciated that the TIEL model placed the self-organization skills within a larger context that included social emotional characteristics we want students to develop. Stacy developed lessons to explicitly teach the students the TIEL language. As she used the terminology to discuss thinking with her students, she became more comfortable in leading these discussions. She created four project-based units throughout the year that show increasingly sophisticated planning. Stacy mastered the art of planning for two where the teacher makes decisions, plans, and evaluates in the process of designing a unit of study, but also designs opportunities and materials to explicitly teach students these same self-organization processes.

11

Creating Complex Projects

I need to be better at writing conclusions that are really explained. I need to be better at writing anecdotes so next time I'm going to make observations and turn them into anecdotes.

—A fourth grader's self-evaluation

The African American Heroes study exceeded Stacy's expectations. The exploration of great African Americans was an elaborate project that included research, written biographies, timelines, and dramatic presentations. It was precisely the kind of project Stacy had feared. Nevertheless, she demonstrated her ability to take risks, adjust her planning, and design materials to fit the project. Stacy proved to herself that with careful curriculum planning the students could create a truly memorable learning experience, and at the same time, learn the underlying skills of self-management that helped make the memories possible.

TWO CULMINATING PROJECTS

The African American Heroes study included two culminating projects. Each fourth grader was assigned a person who has made a contribution to society from a list that Stacy compiled (see figure 11.1). The students did research and wrote a biography that included a timeline of the person's life. *The Life of Myrlie Evers-Williams* is one example of a biography (see figure 11.2) and timeline (see figure 11.3) created by a student. The final biographies were put together to create a class book entitled *Anthology of African Americans Heroes*. The final presentation was a *Famous Friends Conference* where each student dramatized a hero's life.

AFRICAN AMERICAN HEROES: AN ABBREVIATED LIST

Note: names marked with an * are currently selected for study.

* Muhammed Ali
  Crispus Atticus
* Maya Angelou
  James Baldwin
* Benjamin Banneker
* Mary McLeod Bethune
* Ruby Bridges
* John Brown (hero to
    African Americans)
* George Washington Bush
* George Washington
    Carver
* Shirley Chisholm
  Roberto Clemente
* Frederick Douglass
* W.E.B. DuBois
* Marian Wright Edelman
* Duke Ellington
  Medgar Evers
* Merlie Evers
  Lena Horne
* Langston Hughes
  Zora Neale Hurston

  Jesse Jackson
* Mae Jemison
  Jacob Lawrence
* Martin Luther King Jr.
* Audre Lorde
  Wynton Marsalis
* Toni Morrison
* Horace Pippin
* Adam Clayton Powell
* Rosa Parks
* Jackie Robinson
* Betty Shabazz
* Harriet Tubman
* Sojourner Truth
* Booker T. Washington
* Alice Walker
* Cornell West
  Phyllis Wheatley
* Stevie Wonder
  Tiger Woods
  Richard Wright
* Malcolm X

Figure 11.1.   African American Heroes selection chart.

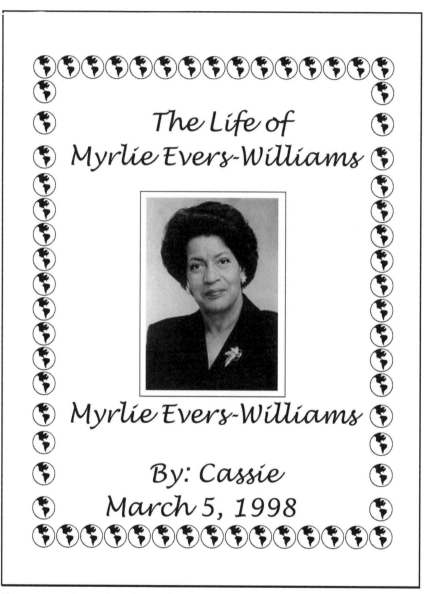

The Life of
Myrlie Evers-Williams

Myrlie Evers-Williams

By: Cassie
March 5, 1998

Figure 11.2.   Cover sheet for Myrlie Evers-Williams biography.

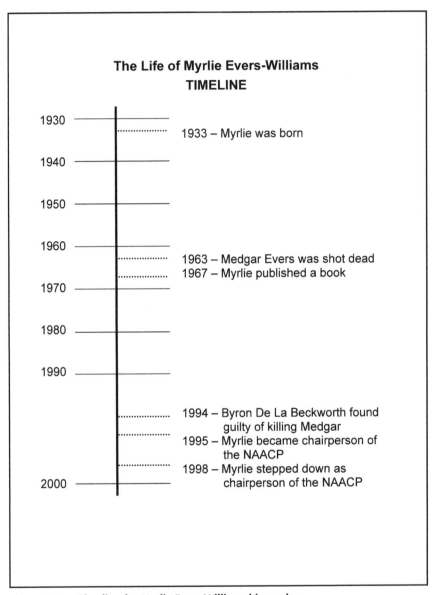

Figure 11.3.   Timeline for Myrlie Evers-Williams biography.

In this project, some choices were eliminated. Stacy made a conscious decision to make assignments in order to broaden the students' interests beyond favorite athletes and singers who would be natural choices for fourth graders. She developed a list of people who represented a wide span of American history from a variety of fields including many individuals with whom the students were unfamiliar (see figure 11.1).

Carefully considering her students' needs and personalities, she matched each student to an African American who had characteristics or interests that would, in some way, be beneficial to the learning of that student. What characteristics could Davon learn from Adam Clayton Powell's life? How could Raylene explore her interest in science through studying Mae Jemison? Would getting to know Jacob Lawrence help Henry recognize his artistic talents? What would Maya learn about her leadership abilities from studying Shirley Chisholm?

The *Famous Friends Conference* provided a place for the students to share what they had learned as they studied their hero. Just as in conferences in the real world, the students chose which presentations to hear. The students were divided into three groups. Students from one group spaced themselves around the room. In small groups of two or three, the other students gathered around a presenter as each one told about whom he or she had researched. The students continued to move in small groups from presenter to presenter until they had heard three or four presentations. After twenty minutes of sharing, another group of students took their places as presenters.

Stacy wanted the students to focus, listen, and learn from each other. To facilitate their learning, she designed a "listening" tool worksheet, *African American Heroes Conference: Celebrating African American Heroes throughout History* (see figure 11.4). There was space for each student to write about seven famous people. If the students were able to listen to more presentations, they could use another listening worksheet. As the students moved from presenter to presenter, they recorded information about the African American heroes:

- Who I learned about
- When they lived
- What they are known for
- Something interesting I learned about them

Planning Calendar

The planning materials for the African American Heroes study reflected the complexity and the limited time of the project. Stacy chose not to use a planning worksheet that included a description of the project, criteria for evaluation, steps, and space to foresee possible problems. Instead, she made a calendar that included February and the first week of March, covering the time allotted for the project (see figure 11.5).

Your [real] name __Cassie__   Date ___March 6th___

AFRICAN AMERICAN HEROES CONFERENCE
Celebrating African American Heroes Throughout History

Listen to presenters carefully, then write down what you learned.
You did a good job if you got to at least four people.

1. Who I learned about: _____Langston Hughes_____

    When they lived: _____1902-1967_____

    What they're known for: ___He's known for his writing___

    _____but mostly poems_____

    Something interesting I learned about them: _____He met a___

    _____famous poet when he was 21 years old_____

2. Who I learned about: _____W.E.B. DuBois_____

    When they lived: _____1868-1963_____

    What they're known for:_____Was a writer and a leader__

    _____

    Something interesting I learned about them: _____

    _____Wrote over 20 books._____

3. Who I learned about:_____Alice Walker_____

    When they lived: _____1944-still alive_____

    What they're known for: _____A wonderful writer._____

    _____

    Something interesting I learned about them: _____

    _____Her eye was damaged_____

Figure 11.4.   Student completed worksheet for *African American Heroes Conference*.

AFRICAN AMERICAN HERO BIOGRAPHY WORK CALENDAR				
Monday	Tuesday	Wednesday	Thursday	Friday
February 2	3 "How do you know a biography when you see one?" lesson	4	5 Begin biography project. Get assignments	6 How to use index cards to take notes lesson. ●
February 9 Work on note taking.	10 Outlining lesson. *	11	12 Outline due. *	13
February 16 MID-WINTER RECESS VACATION 2/16 – 2/20	17 NO SCHOOL keep working on notes!!	18 NO SCHOOL notes!! Adjust or grow outline?	19 NO SCHOOL keep working on notes!!	20 NO SCHOOL keep working on notes!!
February 23 All note cards due. ●	24 Topic sentence lesson. O	25	26	27 Bibliography lesson. ◆
March 2 Finished bibliography DUE. ^	3	4 Famous Friends conference.	5	6 Self evaluation.

Figure 11.5.   Calendar for African American Heroes biography project.

Using an overhead transparency of the calendar, she and the students to-gether filled in the deadlines, assignments, and lesson topics that would give structure to the biography project. They carefully indicated the days of winter vacation, including reminders to continue working on their notes while out of school. Stacy specified the days on which key lessons about biographies, topic sentences, outlining, and bibliographies were scheduled. Using the calendar, the students were able to see how much time elapsed between the due dates.

The biography was due first, followed by the *Famous Friends Conference*. A day was scheduled to complete the self-evaluation of all components of the project. Using the transparency as a rough draft, Stacy made a master copy of the completed calendar for the students. *Biography Calendar Notes* were printed on the back of the calendar, clarifying the details represented by the dates on the calendar (see figure 11.6). The *Notes* gave the students information about

BIOGRAPHY CALENDAR NOTES

● Each INDEX CARD has:
- A complete citation.
- Page number.
- One note or idea in a complete sentence.

* You know your OUTLINE is good if:
- It shows your three topic areas and tells what each area will include in 3 or 4 sentences.
- It is written in the correct format.
- It is neat, etc.

O A TOPIC SENTENCE begins any well-written paragraph. It is a "transition sentence" connecting the last section or idea to the new one. This sentence lets the reader know what the next paragraph will be all about (like a little introduction).

◆ Every biography (in fact, all research papers) must have a BIBLIOGRAPHY. This is a list of all sources used. Check your notes from this lesson to be sure your bibliography includes ALL NECESSARY INFORMATION and is written in CORRECT FORM.

^ FINISHED BIOGRAPHY criteria to be further developed in class.
This will include:
- Using two or more sources.
- Is well-written, including being well organized, having topic sentences, good word choice.
- Gives a thorough life story and a sense of the person.
- Includes a time line.
- Conventions of writing, including spelling, editing.
- Is nicely presented (cover, net, etc.)

Figure 11.6.   Calendar notes for African American Heroes biography project.

how to make an index card, what an outline should include, a description of a topic sentence, parameters of a bibliography, and the criteria for the finished biography.

Self-Evaluation Materials

Such a large project required multiple assessment tools. The students' self-evaluations for the African American Heroes study included one assessment for the research and biography and another for the dramatic performance. In addition, a metacognition worksheet based on the TIEL components helped the students reflect on the thinking processes they had used as they worked on their projects.

Biography Evaluation Tool

The first assessment tool for research and writing evaluation included five short-answer questions about student work and a place to evaluate the criteria for the biography using checks, pluses, and minuses ($\checkmark-$, $\checkmark$, $\checkmark+$). Criteria for the research and writing of the biography set at the beginning of the African American Heroes unit were used in the final evaluation (see figure 11.7).

- Includes all pieces (cover, text, timeline, biography)
- Gives a complete view of my hero's life with facts
- Includes anecdotes to let reader "get to know" this person
- Has clear, well-organized writing
- Follows the conventions of writing (spelling and so on)

The five questions included in the biography self-evaluation addressed learning skills, content, and the social-emotional learning involved in getting to know a famous person through research. The first questions asked the students to evaluate themselves in terms of the skills they learned during the African American Heroes study. After reminding them of the skills—using note cards, outlining, making timelines, using topic sentences, writing introductions, writing conclusions, writing anecdotes, and making bibliographies—she asked the students to evaluate their learning.

- Which two of these skills were very helpful to you, and why?
- What two skills do you need to get better at and what will you do to improve these skills next time?

Next, Stacy asked the students to evaluate their research.

- Was your research effective (feel successful)? Why or why not?
- Did you put the information you found into your own words?

Name _____ *Cassie* _____ Date _____ *March 9th, '98* _____

AFRICAN AMERICAN HEROES STUDY
Self-Evaluation #1
Biography

Research Criteria:
Mark the correct box to show how well it was met

	√ -	√	√ +
Includes all pieces (cover, text, timeline, biography)			√
It gives a complete view of my hero's life with facts			√
Includes anecdotes to let reader "get to know" them		√	
It has clear, well-organized writing			√
It follows the conventions of writing (spelling, etc.)			√

1. We learned how to do many new things during this study, including: using note cards, outlining, making timelines, using topic sentences, writing introductions, writing conclusions, writing anecdotes, and making bibliographies.
   <u>Tell two</u> of these things that were very helpful to you, and why.
   Using topic sentences was helpful because the wording sounded better. I also found using note cards helpful so its easier to put in order so I don't have to number them.
   <u>Tell two</u> that you need to get better at, and what you will do to use them better next time.
   I needed to be better at writing conclusions that are really explained. I need to be better at writing anecdotes so next time I'm going to make observations and turn them into anecdotes.

2. Was your research effective (feel successful)? Why or why not.
   My research felt successful because I know the main facts about their life.

3. Did you put the information you found into your own words?
   Yes I did. I read the sentences over and then wrote it over.

4. Do you feel you know your hero as a person? Tell anything you have in common with them.
   I don't feel like I know my hero as a person because I'm missing her childhood and middle life. My hero and I are both black and living.

5. If you could meet your hero in person, what questions or comments would you have for them?
   Did you have a happy childhood? What schools did you go to?

Figure 11.7.   Biography self-evaluation worksheet for African American Heroes study.

The last questions focused on the social-emotional learning that was an important part of the unit. Stacy had thoughtfully matched individual students to people they were researching, and she wanted to know the effect those choices had on their learning.

- Did you feel you know your hero as a person? Tell anything you have in common with him or her.
- If you could meet your hero in person, what questions or comments would you have for him or her?

The questions and responses demonstrated both teacher and student understanding of evaluation. The questions reflected Stacy's increasing capacity to connect teaching, learning, and assessment, while maintaining focus on the emotional aspects of student learning. For example, she smoothly integrated her skills in teaching self-management skills with the content she wanted the students to learn. She developed products that demonstrated the students' learning of content, research skills, self-organization skills, and social-emotional learning. Finally, she designed tools that helped the students self-evaluate their learning and opened a window into their growing abilities to self-evaluate their work.

The African American Heroes study brought out the best in the students. Comments from students reflect the depth of their project work and ability to apply evaluation to their own work. Cassie, who created the biography of Myrlie Evers-Williams, is an example. Her responses to two of the questions show how the students articulated their thinking and learning. In the question asking students to evaluate the research and writing skills that were most helpful, Cassie wrote, "Using topic sentences was helpful because the wording sounded better. I also found using note cards helpful because it's easier to put [the information] in order so I don't have to number my notes on a piece of paper."

Cassie was clear about where she needed improvements in her research and writing. "I need to be better at writing conclusions that are really explained. I need to be better at writing anecdotes so next time I'm going to make observations and turn them into anecdotes."

In the last questions focusing on social-emotional learning, Cassie's responses show her understanding of the relationship between knowing *about* someone, and actually *personally* knowing an individual. "I don't feel like I know my hero as a person because I'm missing her childhood and middle life." Nevertheless, Cassie felt a kinship with Myrlie Evers-Williams. "My hero and I are both black and living." Recognizing the gap in her knowledge of Myrlie Evers-Williams, Cassie knew exactly what she would ask Ms. Evers-Williams if she met her, "Did you have a happy childhood? What schools did you go to?"

Performance Assessment

The second African American Heroes assessment tool focused on the performance portion of the project. As with the research and writing assessment, the performance evaluation included both a check-off evaluation of the original criteria set at the beginning of the unit and questions that required short answers (see figure 11.8).

Cassie's self-evaluation shows consistency throughout her self-evaluation. In the evaluation using the research criteria, Cassie felt that she could have done better in telling anecdotes. She gave herself a check minus for the criterion, *I told interesting anecdotes.* In her previous evaluation of writing skills, she had written, "I need to be better at writing anecdotes, so next time I'm going to make observations and turn them into anecdotes." She was happy with her performance in all of the other criteria, giving herself checks or check pluses. In the final question, she returned to the anecdotes, saying, "I would like to tell more anecdotes and write a speech."

The performance self-evaluation, like the research and writing evaluation, gave the students an opportunity to think critically about their presentations. Using the criteria they helped develop at the beginning of the unit, the students were able to make reasoned judgments (Paul, 1995). The students were able to see where they did well and where they would plan to improve the next time. There were no mistakes, only opportunities for learning.

Metacognition

The third evaluation tool used in the African American Heroes project addressed metacognition. It assessed the students' ability to think about their thinking. Stacy wanted to know how the students could use the TIEL language to describe their thinking and social-emotional learning involved in the study. How did they get information (*cognition*)? What connections did they make (*memory*)? How did they plan and self-evaluate (*evaluation*)? How did they use *convergent* and *divergent thinking*?

The assessment sheet included the five thinking operations—*cognition, memory, evaluation, convergent thinking and production,* and *divergent thinking and production* (see figure 11.9). Stacy used the word *emotion* to represent care, appreciation, and reflection so that students would be aware of their social-emotional learning as well as their cognitive learning. For example, Shawnell wrote about *evaluation*: "I planned my outline by choosing three different topics for each part of my biography." Shawnell's complete assessment of thinking processes used in her project is shown in figure 11.9.

Name _____**Cassie**_____ Date _____**March 9th, '98**_____

AFRICAN AMERICAN HEROES CONFERENCE
Self-Evaluation #2

Performance Criteria:

Mark the correct box to show how well it was met	√ -	√	√ +
I had an appropriate costume			√
I told important facts			√
I told interesting anecdotes	√		
I could answer questions			√
I spoke clearly		√	
I made eye contact		√	
I stood up like I was proud (had good posture)		√	
I listened nicely to others			√

What did you do to prepare for today?

I practiced speaking clearly. I read over my report a lot.

What did you do during your presentation to make sure the listeners shared your excitement about your hero?

I made sure I answered all questions.

What would you like to do differently next time?

I would like to tell more anecdotes and write a speech.

Figure 11.8. Self-evaluation worksheet for African American Heroes conference.

Name _____*Shawnell*_____ Date_____*March 9th, '98*_____

AFRICAN AMERICAN HEROES STUDY
Self-Evaluation #3
Metacognition

Tell how you used each kind of thinking in this project.
Use complete sentences and try to be explicit.

COGNITION (observing, naming, discovery, gathering facts, knowing)	*I gathered information like: Sojourner Truth died in 1883 for my biography.*
MEMORY (remembering, making connections, historical context)	*I remembered some of the facts I learned about Sojourner Truth so that I could add facts to my biography.*
EVALUATION (analyzing, planning, making decisions, using criteria)	*I planned my outline by choosing 3 different topics for each part of my biography.*
CONVERGENT PRODUCTION (putting information in order, one right answer, one right way)	*I put my note cards in order of what happened in Sojourner Truth's life.*
DIVERGENT PRODUCTION (creative thinking, imagination, taking risks, many possibilities)	*I created anecdotes to make my biography more interesting. Isabella was a religious person and had very strong beliefs.*
EMOTIONS (expressing care, appreciation, reflection)	*I was sad that Isabella (Sojourner Truth) and so many other black people were slaves.*

Figure 11.9. Metacognition self-evaluation worksheet for African American Heroes study.

GRADING RUBRIC

Name	Biography includes all pieces (cover, biblio-graphy)	Gives a complete view of hero's life with facts	Uses anecdotes so we get to know the hero	Clear, well organized writing (revision)	Follows conven-tions (editing)	Total
Cassie	2	2	2	1	2	9

Cassie,

You created a wonderfully interesting and informative biography. It was not easy to gather usable information about this hero, but your research skills proved to be tremendous. Your writing, crafting, and "acting" all show your thoughtfulness and learning.

Congratulations.
Ms. Silver

Figure 11.10.   Grading rubric for African American Heroes study.

Teacher Tools

In addition to the self-evaluation materials designed for student use, Stacy created a grading rubric for the biography (see figure 11.10). Based on the original criteria set with the students at the beginning of the project, she used the grading rubric to assign numerical value to their work. The rubric includes five general criteria for the completed project with each criterion worth two points for a total of ten points. Taking into account the students' self-evaluations, Stacy gave a numerical grade. She shared the rubric evaluation and written comments about their work with the students.

PROJECTS AS ASSESSMENT OF SELF-ORGANIZATION SKILLS: TIMELINE PROJECT

Teachers often use projects to assess subject matter content. Projects, however, can also be used to assess how well students are applying self-organization skills to their project work. How do students make decisions about the topic for the project? How do they decide which content to include? Do students consciously use criteria to make decisions? Can students make an orderly plan? Does the plan help them complete the project? Can students use their original criteria to help evaluate the final project?

Stacy was now a fearless risk-taker. As the year drew to a close, she wanted the students to create one last project that would demonstrate what they had learned about decision making, planning, and self-evaluation within their project work. She wanted an end-of-year project that addressed content, yet put the students in charge of processes. After much consideration, Stacy decided to have the students work in small groups within the discipline of history. The students chose a person or event from the history timeline in the classroom, designed their own projects, and developed their own planning tools to guide the production of their projects.

Timeline of History

All year long the students had been adding to a timeline of history. The timeline was made from a strip of butcher paper that was two feet in height. Placed above the chalkboard, the timeline spanned the full length of the wall. It took a turn into the corner to the right and continued at the same height onto the next wall. The timeline was marked off in intervals of fifty years. When the students studied a period of history, they illustrated the event with a name, date, and picture on a 5 × 8 index card. They attached their cards to the appropriate time periods on the timeline. The timeline card of Christopher Columbus is similar to one the students made during the Explorers unit (see figure 11.11).

1492 – Christopher Columbus

Columbus (re)discovered America in 1492.
The native Americans were here and others had explored the western hemisphere before Columbus.

Figure 11.11.   Timeline card example for history timeline.

Choices

The students had choices in each phase of the History Timeline project. They named ten time periods from history with little, if any, teacher guidance. After the students formed groups according to their common interests, each group chose the style of their presentations, drawing on previous experiences during the year. Most of the projects included posters similar to those made during the United States study. Several projects included costumed skits as in the African American Heroes presentations.

Presentations

The day of the presentations featured all the nerves and excitement of a Broadway opening night. Students bustled about the classroom gathering their props and setting up scenery. Some busied themselves with the costumes that had been prepared at home with the help of parents. "Is my dress too wrinkly? Do you think it's too long? No, no! You look great! What if I forget my lines!" could all be heard as they prepared for the show.

A presentation about the 1960s focused on President Kennedy. Two groups of boys, both planning to present the war in Viet Nam, combined their groups. They shared their information about the war by performing a skit and showing a poster. Nigel, a talented artist, drew an eighteen-inch soldier dressed in fatigues and mounted the cutout figure on the poster.

Two different groups of girls were inspired by a recent fourth grade trip to Philadelphia. Not inclined to join forces as the boys had chosen to do, each group presented a version of the signing of the Declaration of Independence. One group dressed in black suit coats, pants pulled up to look like knickers, and homemade wigs made of cotton. Impressed by the musical *1776*, shown in class as part of the preparation for the Philadelphia trip, this group combined singing, dancing, acting, and a poster in their presentation.

The other group studying the Declaration of Independence also included a dramatization. They acted the roles played by John Adams, Thomas Jefferson, and Benjamin Franklin in the establishment of the United States. However, their presentation was more sedate, lacking the singing, dancing, and musical score.

Planning

Raya's group chose the theme of moving west. Dressed in long pioneer dresses, neatly tied bonnets, and holding baskets over their arms, they presented a mini-play illustrating daily events in the lives of early settlers. A small tombstone made of cardboard symbolized how the pioneers risked death as they settled new lands. Raya's group planned the presentation of their trip west using many of the strategies that Stacy had taught them. They developed criteria for evaluating their skit, which included

- Learn
- Teach
- Interesting
- Use your brain
- Creative/fun
- Shows effort
- Can do

The criteria, "learn" and "teach," meant that the skit had to show both what the group had learned from their research and what they were teaching the class. It was to be interesting to themselves and to the audience. The presentation needed to show evidence that the group had "used their brains." It needed to be creative, fun, and show effort. The last criterion, "can do," meant that each of them pulled together to accomplish the work that they had to do.

Drama is complicated. Clearly understanding the complexities of the theater, Raya and her group organized a list of props. They carefully organized the props according to the scene in which each prop would be used (see figure 11.12). The example shows how they used this list to check off the props they found and would use in the skit. They also placed X's by items they decided they did not need. The horse, thankfully, received an X. They also carefully outlined the steps that they would follow to complete their project.

Learning by Example

Einstein said that there were three ways to learn: by example, by example, and by example. During the History Timeline project, the students certainly demonstrated how they had learned self-organization skills by example. Raya's group placed their planning tools together in a booklet just as they had seen their teacher do for earlier projects. They set criteria for themselves. They created a way to manage the inventory of props. They defined the steps they needed to complete the project and identified who was in charge of each step.

The History Timeline project showed that the students had an understanding of content, process, and product that reflected Stacy's learning throughout the year. The script and the prop list reflected the content—the research made visible—that make up the more tangible elements of learning. Their planning sheets that listed criteria, materials, and the list of steps reflected their understanding of the self-organization processes, those elements of learning that are intangible and most often remain invisible. Raya's group placed all of these materials together under one cover sheet entitled, "Our Script, Criteria, and Other Stuff We Used to Help Us" (see figure 11.13).

Oregon Trail

Criteria	skit essay
Learn	√
Teach	√
Interesting	√
Use your brain	√
Creative/fun	√
Shows effort	√
Can do	√

Things we need

Scene 1.	fake money √	chair/table
	text book √	cash register **X don't need**
	paper √	
Scene 2.	horse **X**	watches √
	food sample √	
Scene 3.	canteen √	fruit basket √
Scene 4.	gravestone √	
Scene 5.	pencil/paper √	bag √

List of steps

1. Decide who does what chapter √
2. Help edit – spelling, punctuation, etc.
3. Make script together based on information √
4. Ask parents for food and clothes

Figure 11.12.   Student planning sheet for History Timeline project.

Our:
Script,
Criteria,
and Other
Stuff We
Used to
Help Us.

By,
Amanda, Meredith
And Raya

Figure 11.13.　Sample cover sheet for History Timeline project.

Providng Extra Help

While some students showed deep understanding of self-organization processes, others needed more structure in organizing their projects. Stacy worked with these groups on the areas of planning they needed. Although the purpose of this project was to assess self-organization skills, it was also another opportunity for students to practice these skills. For the students who needed extra help, Stacy mediated the assessment (Cognitive Research Program, 1999), teaching them the skills they need while assessing what they know. She reviewed how to set criteria for evaluating their project, how to begin the research, and how to sequence the steps of a plan.

At the end, all students had learned more about organizing their own learning, while learning about history from each other. Vonda tried to describe how the discussion, application, and awareness of thinking processes so permeated the learning in the classroom that there was a palpable feeling of being surrounded by thinking. Finally, she described the environment in Stacy's classroom. "Sometimes it feels like you were *around* that thinking."

SUMMARY

As the year progressed, Stacy planned increasingly complex project-based units using the TIEL model. Her students met the challenge. The African American Heroes project included two culminating projects that demonstrated the students' understanding of important African Americans in history. Each student researched the life of an African American who has made a remarkable contribution to American life. After careful planning, the students wrote biographies of the person they studied. The African American Heroes Conference was the second culminating project where students presented their research through dramatization. Using teacher-designed evaluation tools, the students evaluated their biographies, conference presentations, and the thinking and social emotional learning involved in the project. Energized by her students learning, Stacy planned the final unit of the year to assess her students understanding of planning a project independently. Many were able to make their own plans, while Stacy helped those who needed more assistance. Students chose a topic from the history timeline they had constructed throughout the year. They did research on their topic and planned projects that included charts, dramatization, and musical theatre.

12

Transformations in Thinking

I think the only thing that's really changed in my view of them is that I'm stunned by how high they can fly! The students took so much responsibility that I merely guided them and pushed them along to get it done.

—Stacy, fourth grade teacher

By the end of the research year, much had changed in Stacy's classroom. There were indications that Stacy's thinking about curriculum had changed as well as how the students thought about their learning. Where earlier the students had not thought about their learning, now the students were aware of their thinking processes and enjoyed talking about thinking.

TRANSFORMATIONS IN STUDENT THINKING

The students in Stacy's classroom were thinking, creating, and working together. They were mastering content, understanding the processes involved in learning, and producing projects that Stacy could not have imagined just one year previously. The students also showed care and respect for each other that created an emotionally safe environment where they felt safe to take risks. This feeling of safety made it possible for the students to take social and academic risks involved in trying new partnerships and exploring new content.

The students' creativity increased as their autonomy increased. The more passive behaviors that came from listening to instructions on how to do a project had given way to the behaviors of self-motivation as students followed their own plans. Students worked on their projects in various parts of the classroom and often spilled out into the hallway. While on the surface there appeared to be a lack of sitting-at-your-desk structure, the invisible structures of self-organization empowered the students to maintain a personal, meaningful, and more responsible structure for their work.

Descriptive Language

The students' transformation of thinking was clear in their conversations about learning the self-organization skills they would need throughout their lives. They absorbed the discussion of decision making, planning, and self-evaluation that flowed through Stacy's classroom and used colorful phrases to describe their understanding of self-organization processes. Raya, a talented poet, said that without decision making, planning, and evaluating, projects would not come together. It would be like "a snake without a spine."

Harry aptly described the green *evaluation* thinking as the "seasick thinking." He waved his hand toward the TIEL bulletin board referring to all five of the thinking operations and emphatically added, "Out of all these, the seasick thinking makes you the most . . . SICK!" Not convinced that Harry's explanation was sufficiently clear, Raya jumped in to add, "You have to do it over and over and over again." Harry's insightful description illustrated the back and forth movement of decision making and evaluating as well as the often unstable process of planning.

The discussion of thinking had become so natural to the students that they did not realize that it was happening. As I interviewed Harry, Raya, and Vonda, they told me that they had not discussed thinking processes in class. Even as fourth graders they seemed to intuitively know that teachers do not like to know that they have no impact whatsoever. Sensing my disturbance, they all began talking at once in an effort to make me feel better.

Harry took the lead, "I think we used like the same . . . what should I call it?"

I supplied the words, "thinking processes."

"Yeah," Harry replied. "We used the thinking operations." He now remembered the words on the TIEL Curriculum Design Wheel in the classroom. He did not realize that the term *thinking processes* and *thinking operations* were two different terms used to describe the same thing.

Recognizing Project Similarities

As we sorted out the vocabulary, Harry had an epiphany about the projects. "I just figured it out now!" he exclaimed. As he connected the classroom talk about thinking, the processes involved in their projects, and the interview questions, he recognized that there was a fundamental pattern of thinking operations common to each of their projects. His idea got the other students thinking.

Vonda commented on the States project, "The States project was kind of the same as the other projects because we had to do kind of the same things like plan. We had to look up stuff, like in books and inside the computer and encyclopedias."

Reinforcing the importance of planning as a commonality among the projects, Raya mentioned peer editing and using criteria. In each project the students checked each other's work. She lauded the efficiency of peer editing, "Two kids can get each other's things done at once. You had to use some of the same criteria. You had to *really* plan what you were going to do and make sure everything was great because you only had one chance."

I was intrigued by the concept of having only one chance. Instilling perfectionism was not one of my objectives for teaching self-organization skills. When I asked Raya to elaborate, she explained that there was one paper to write and that "you couldn't change the whole thing again."

Vonda clarified, "You *could* change your planning sheet, but if you're doing a project already, you can't really change it [the project itself]."

Therefore, using criteria to make sound decisions was also important. Often students start, stop, and change their minds about projects. Most teachers have had experience with students who jettison projects numerous times until there is no time to complete the project. Setting clear criteria at the beginning of the project helps ensure that students make more solid decisions. Before starting projects, Stacy discussed with the students the availability of time, materials, and resources to complete the project. When the students considered these common criteria, they made more reasoned decisions about their projects. They proceeded in a more focused manner with less mind changing.

Recognizing Project Differences

Planning

While the students noticed many similarities among the projects, they also saw some clear differences. Vonda shared an observation about planning, "We had to plan, but some of it we had to plan a little different. On our State project we had to draw how we were going to make it. On our other projects we had to plan just like what we're going to write. Like how we're going to do it and when we're going to finish it."

Different kinds of projects require different kinds of planning. Two projects involved formal writing products. The Explorers study involved a research paper including a bibliography, and the African American Heroes study included a written biography for the class anthology of great lives. These projects required detailed plans that focused on research and writing.

Planning for the States unit required multiple plans. The culminating project was an individually designed collage sharing information about one of the United States. The state collage project required an overall plan and guidelines for the research. In addition, the students made an illustrated plan that showed the visual organization of the collage poster.

Assistance

Harry and Raya both experienced differences in the amount of help they received in the States unit. Stacy did not discourage parents from helping their children and, at times, asked for specific help. Since Stacy supervised the planning of the projects at school, she was confident that the parents would be acting primarily as assistants instead of project managers.

Harry's parents did not usually help him, but when his father saw the plan for the state poster, he offered to assist. Harry thought that perhaps the magnitude of the project drew his parents into the work. He said, "I think that I got more help from my parents because . . . it's a big thing . . . it's a big collage. And all the other things are just a small book, smaller than my notebook."

Raya's family also helped with research for the States unit. Having lived in Illinois, Raya's father shared his personal experiences of his former home and places he remembered visiting. Her mother found information on the Internet. Excitedly, Raya told how her mother shared her discoveries as she downloaded information. "Here, I've got a great place for you! Here! Oh! There's more. You could go here. 1800s. There's a timeline that is completely *full* of information."

Creativity

Raya noticed another, more subtle, difference between the projects. She observed that there was more creativity displayed in the States projects. She explained her perception, "Each one [poster] has a different sort of thing about it. So you can kind of find out how that person thinks." Indeed, some posters were organized in straight linear order with captions produced on the computer, while other posters were creatively arranged with artistic drawings of the state flower or famous tourist sites within the state. Concrete two-dimensional visual posters provided the students a wide range of options in making the product for the States unit. Drawings, handwriting, computer printing, photographs, and professional pamphlets were some of the methods students used to tell about their state.

There were other similarities and differences in the projects. Two of the projects—African American Heroes and the History Timeline project—both involved dramatization. In three of the units—the Explorers, the United States, and the African American Heroes—the projects were completed individually. The History Timeline project was completed in small groups. Yet, all involved research, decision making, planning, and self-evaluation.

TRANSFORMATION IN TEACHER THINKING

The planning materials developed by the students in the History Timeline project reflect the transformations in Stacy's learning and teaching. Before the professional learning process, the processes of self-organization had been invisible in her teaching. While sensing the importance of students organizing their own learning, she did not understand how to teach these processes more explicitly. Now at the end of the research year, the students themselves were able to make the invisible processes of planning and evaluation visible. This section shares how Stacy transformed her thinking about her students, the curriculum, herself as a teacher, and how she thought about the teaching of thinking.

Thinking about Students

Stacy was amazed by the "astounding work" that the students could do. She always believed that students could learn the skills of self-organization, but she did not know how to teach them. When the students completed the anthology of African American heroes developed from the biographies they had written, Stacy was ecstatic about their work. Enthusiastically, she said, "I think the only thing that's really changed in my view of them is that I'm stunned by how high they can fly! The students took so much responsibility that I merely guided them and pushed them along to get it done."

Self-organization skills empower students. Stacy believed that learning self-organization skills was not just for the student who already possesses a fair amount of self-management skills. Learning to make decisions, plan, and self-evaluate is perhaps even more important for the student who struggles with learning and frequently experiences failure.

Vonda, who had also been in Stacy's third grade classroom, had cried often when she did not do well at a task. She continued this pattern of crying well into fourth grade. When Vonda began to show a significant increase in her coping skills, Stacy attributed her progress to learning self-organization skills. At the conclusion of the States unit, Vonda discovered that she had not met some of the criteria. She decided herself that she had not done everything well, but this time, she did not cry. Stacy said, "Before, she would have just lost her marbles because [she thought] it meant that she failed or that she just wasn't smart. There was no perspective. Now when sometimes she doesn't do well, she doesn't cry about it."

Vonda was in the student interview group and I also noticed her growth in confidence and perspective. When she was struggling with the state collage, I helped her organize her work. She did not complete the project on time, but she was proud of her work and, this time, she was not upset that it took her longer to finish. In the final interview, her comments were insightful as she articulated her knowledge of decision making, planning, and self-evaluation when talking about her work.

Thinking about Curriculum

Stacy's thinking about curriculum had changed over the course of the year. She knew the importance of having students understand the criteria that guide their work. She was beginning to see possibilities for teaching thinking more explicitly in other subjects as she began thinking more divergently about curriculum.

Criteria for Evaluation

Stacy now felt accountable for the students to be involved in the decision making surrounding their work. She could no longer teach without feeling a responsibility to provide full disclosure of the learning experiences she planned. Surface instructions would no longer do; she felt compelled to help the students understand the underlying structures of assignments. She could not say, "Here's a sample essay, now go write."

Criteria setting is beneficial for the student and the teacher. While it is unfair to the students not to know the criteria by which their work is evaluated, Stacy saw that as a teacher she also benefited from clear criteria. Including the students in setting criteria for evaluation made her job less difficult because it made the assessment process easier. She gave an example of assigning an essay to the students without giving them clear criteria, "It [the essay assignment] really wouldn't make any sense. I guess I would grade it [the essay] based on my impression of it, and the students would have absolutely no framework with which to write it."

Other Subjects

Stacy saw the possibilities of teaching thinking across subjects. Because of her success with decision making, planning, and self-evaluation in social studies, Stacy wanted to expand this kind of teaching for understanding to other curriculum areas. She said, "I'd like to do more of that kind of work with math, but frankly, I don't know how." She had a clear understanding of her own strengths and limitations that prevented her from trying to change all areas of the curriculum simultaneously. Wisely, she stated, "It's OK with me that I wait until everything else is sort of settled." When she had mastered more complex teaching in one area, then she would be ready to make changes in another.

Divergent Thinking

Stacy now thought more divergently about curriculum. Learning to teach self-organization skills increased Stacy's ideas concerning how to teach particular topics. With more ideas, came a need to make choices for the most effective way to present concepts. She said, "I have more ideas about how things can get done. Before, I used to think that this is what I have to cover. It didn't really occur to me that there are different ways to cover it. Now I'm starting to think about all the ways that a topic can be taught, as well as the rationale of one over the other."

Student Responsibility

The History Timeline project is an example of thinking of different ways to transfer responsibility to the students. Before starting the unit, Stacy wanted to involve the students in thinking about their choices for a topic. For homework, she asked the students to choose a time period in history for their final project and state the criteria that helped them make their choice.

She said to the students, "Your homework is to go home and decide by what criteria you would choose one [a time period], and then choose one. And if you already know which one you want to study, you need to be able to tell what criteria you used to choose that one."

One of the students asked, "What you're saying is, '*Why* are you choosing it?'"

"Exactly. If you're going to make an important decision about what you're going to study, then you should have some reasons."

Stacy wanted to make sure that all the students thought critically about their choice of topic. The students could set criteria and then choose their topic or, if they had already made a decision, they were required to state why they made that choice. Either way, the already-decided and the not-yet-decided knew they were to think critically about their choices.

Two elements of this homework assignment illustrated the changes that had taken place in Stacy's thinking about curriculum. First, she included the students in her thinking. She said, "Today I started a conversation with the kids . . . their homework last night was to pick out a time period." Where previously Stacy would have given direct instructions for a homework assignment, now the students were drawn into a larger conversation about their work.

Second, the homework assignment itself involved expanded thinking. Instead of more easily managed convergent work, Stacy felt comfortable asking the students to carry out a homework assignment that specifically involved elements of critical thinking. The next day, the students brought in a variety of choices based on multiple criteria that established the platform on which to build the History Timeline unit.

Thinking about Herself as a Teacher

Learning to use an explicit language of thinking altered Stacy's beliefs about herself as a teacher. "I feel more confident and more competent as a teacher. I have a clearer sense of what I'm doing and why. I don't think I really had much of a sense of either of those before." Using the TIEL framework made "teaching easier and more interesting."

In an educational system that often ran counter to her beliefs about teaching, the TIEL Model offered welcome validation. She explained how this way of teaching fit naturally into her political views, "It suits me that children are treated with respect, that they treat their own thinking with respect, and that they understand that their own work is not happenstance."

Stacy gave some examples of when students might need to make practical decisions about their own work. They should feel empowered to do better work if they choose, as well as afforded the opportunity to "cut a corner" when needed. A student might be in a position to make such a choice about a project if she has a piano recital and a soccer tournament at the same time that the social studies project is due. The student needs to have the skills to make an informed decision about how she might most effectively use her time.

Thinking about the Teaching of Thinking

The students were learning to plan and make decisions within the curriculum. Yet, Stacy wanted the discussion of thinking to be more organic. Too often it seemed that talking about thinking was something they did on the "periphery of everything else." Although it was clear from the conversations with the students that the discussion of thinking had gone well beyond "the periphery" in Stacy's classroom, she wanted to make sure that the talk about thinking involved more than labeling.

> I'd like to seek out ways to do different kinds of thinking. Maybe that just needs to be part of the projects next year. I'd like to suggest to the students, "You know what? We just want to spend the day observing. How many ways can we find ourselves naming things and researching? And . . . I don't think we're using our memories enough. How can we bring our memories with us?"

The students needed to recognize that they were already planning and making decisions every day. Yet, they did not see any of that as thinking work. Stacy wanted to make use of the opportunities in the immediate environment to make the invisible processes of planning more visible.

> Maybe I need to sit down with them at the end of the day and say, "Did you plan anything today? Was there anything you knew you were going to do in advance? Did you know who you were going to play with on the playground? Did you agree with them [their ideas for playing]? Did you know what game you wanted to play? Did someone interrupt your plan—such as someone else wanting to play? Maybe you weren't planning for them to play and then you had to set criteria to help you make a decision. One criterion might be 'you can play, but only after my turn.'"

CHALLENGES

Stacy made great progress in transforming her curriculum over the year. She taught her students self-organization skills and, at the same time, made thinking and social-emotional learning more explicit in her discussions with the students. While much had been accomplished, there were notable challenges. Class size added to demands of planning and organization. The increase from twenty-one students in third grade to thirty-one in fourth grade required adjustments.

Materials needed to be developed carefully and instruction had to be clear and concise. For example, the planning calendar for the African American Heroes study provided a clear reference for the students as they progressed through the project. Stacy constructed the calendar with the students on a transparency, transferred it to paper, and gave copies to the students to guide their work.

Developing curriculum that included the teaching of thinking skills requires more time to plan. There are many components to consider. What content will be included? What criteria for evaluation will help students understand what they are to do? Will a planning calendar or a planning worksheet that includes criteria for evaluation, materials, and steps be most effective for this project? Yet, with practice, Stacy found that her planning became more manageable.

Stacy saw the importance in developing curriculum that promoted student thinking and social-emotional learning. Planning more complex curriculum benefited the students and had a positive effect on the students. As the students developed their self-organization skills and became more responsible for their learning, classroom management improved accordingly. There were, of course, inevitable disagreements between students and occasional frustration with projects. Yet, as the students learned to manage their work, they developed coping skills and learned to solve problems. Vonda, for example, developed the ability to cope with constructive criticism. She no longer cried when her work was not what she expected. Having clear criteria helped her understand what she needed to improve. The more self-reliant the students became, the more invested they were in the work they had planned.

Time in the classroom was a challenge. While time for planning was tight, time in the classroom for project work and teaching the self-organization skills required was also at a premium. Standardized test preparation required a large amount of classroom time. At the fourth grade level, the students took tests in English language arts, math, and science. Just as the students finished one test, preparation began for another. Yet, knowing the importance of planning curriculum that provided engaging, thoughtful learning experiences for her students, Stacy carved out the time needed to teach four project-based units. Careful planning and clear deadlines helped her manage project work with her students. With the students motivated to work on the projects they had participated in planning, they used their time more effectively. They worked to meet their deadlines. As Stacy stated, "The kids are swept up in it, and I don't have to drag them on this heavy sled."

SUMMARY

Stacy, a fourth grade teacher, was traditional in her approach to curriculum development. She liked having control in the classroom and was fearful of teaching thinking skills through project-based learning. Yet, her worst fears did not materialize. During the course of a year, she used the TIEL Wheel to develop four project-based social studies units. She designed self-management tools to teach her students the skills of decision making, planning, and self-evaluation within the context of their projects. As she incorporated the teaching of self-organization skills into her curriculum, her instructional approach changed from directing to guiding, while maintaining focus on the content.

The students changed also. Motivation and creativity increased as the students learned how to manage their project work. As the students participated in the setting of criteria for evaluation, planned steps to complete projects, and evaluated their work at the end, they became more autonomous learners. In addition, they were able to discuss the thinking processes involved in their learning.

Committed to the social-emotional aspect of teaching and learning, Stacy appreciated the qualities of character components of the TIEL Model. She planned curriculum to include opportunities for reflection, discussion of ethical decision making, and consideration of how people show care for others. The qualities of character made the TIEL Model initially valuable to her. Indeed, the social-emotional aspect of the TIEL Model invited Stacy in to the hard work of teaching self-organization skills through project work.

V

CONNECTIONS

con·nec·tion (kə nek'shən), n. 1. the act or state of connection. 2. the state of being connected. 3. anything that connects; connecting part; link; bond: an electrical connection. 4. association; relationship.

—Webster's Unabridged Dictionary

The TIEL model helps both teachers and students make connections to their learning. Understanding fundamental thinking processes helps teachers make connections that lead to changes in their teaching. When students understand their thinking processes, they become more empowered learners.

CHAPTER 13: THEORY AND THINKING

This chapter tells how the TIEL Model helped Brian, a second grade teacher, make connections to theory, to his personal thinking, and to the thinking of his students.

CHAPTER 14: CONNECTIONS AND APPLICATION

Chapter 14 begins with a description of the routines, structures, and learning activities at the beginning of the research year in Brian's classroom. The chapter shares how Brian used the TIEL Model to incorporate the teaching of thinking skills into his planning and how he taught self-organization skills to his second graders.

13

Theory and Thinking

> I want to know how I can integrate this more into the classroom . . . making it sort of a seamless part of everything I do in here. I can do that sometimes, but maybe now with a more concentrated effort . . . I can be more consistent.
>
> —Brian, second grade teacher

Intuitive teachers connect to teachable moments. They stop the math lesson to let the children watch the long-awaited birth of the baby hamsters. They direct all eyes to the window sill to witness the last gasp of the geranium (Cullum, 1971). When teachers connect to the immediate moment they enrich the lives and learning of their students. Yet, there are more connections that teachers need to make in the classroom.

Making connections to thinking helps teachers extend memorable learning far beyond the occasional teachable moment. When teachers connect to their own thinking they become more aware of the thinking processes that they use each day in the classroom and in their daily lives; they observe the thinking of their students more consciously; and they make new connections to their teaching. They consider what they do to encourage thinking through the lessons and activities that they plan, and they begin to see what more they can do.

MAKING CONNECTIONS

Brian, a second grade teacher, was like many intuitive teachers who understand the importance of a thinking classroom, but lack specific tools that can make the teaching of thinking more explicit. Tall, large in stature, philosophical, and deeply thoughtful about teaching, Brian expanded my image of a second grade teacher.

He came to teaching from working in the business world. He was a part-time musician who combined the holistic thinking of an artist with the no-nonsense approach of business. In his three years in the classroom, he had developed a balanced approach to teaching. Just as a chef balances a variety of flavors letting none overpower the others, he maintained the various aspects of teaching—content and process, intellectual and social-emotional, humor and seriousness—in equal measures.

Prior Knowledge

Brian joined the research project with no prior knowledge of the TIEL Curriculum Design Model. In the beginning, he was quiet in group meetings because he felt that all the others were far ahead of him in learning the concepts involved in the research. However, none of the teachers, including Erica who had participated in the pilot study, had been formally introduced to the TIEL Model before the research began. Yet, I knew each of the other teachers and they knew of my interest in integrating thinking skills and social-emotional learning into curriculum planning.

Brian experienced the feelings associated with learning something new. He admitted to handling his feelings of intimidation by sitting back in the group meetings, hiding his confusion, and thinking "OK, so what was *that* about?" At the end of the year, he shared those early feelings,

> You bandied around phrases like metacognition, and I really didn't know what I was getting into and what it was about. And for most people, if you're confused about something the tendency is not to raise your hand. You sit back and listen and ask yourself, "Can I get this?" Maybe if I can get it on my own like this, they'll all believe that I really knew it at the beginning.

Nevertheless, Brian was committed to learning how to integrate the teaching of thinking into his teaching. "I want to know how I can integrate this more into the classroom . . . making it sort of a seamless part of everything I do in here. I can do that sometimes, but maybe now with a more concentrated effort . . . I can be more consistent."

Using the TIEL Model to Make Connections

Brian used many teaching strategies that promote student thinking, but he had not really thought about explicitly naming and teaching thinking processes in his classroom. Yet, he turned any event, incident, or comment, no matter how mundane, into an opportunity for the students to think. Whether students were trying to spell a word, put on boots, or tie their shoes, each situation offered an opportunity to think.

The TIEL Model helped Brian draw on his prior knowledge and experience to make connections to theory, to his personal thinking, and to the thinking of his students. These new insights helped him expand the possibilities for teaching and learning in his classroom. First, learning about the TIEL Model helped him make connections to theories of teaching and learning he had learned in teacher education. Second, the TIEL visuals that named thinking and social-emotional processes made Brian aware of his own thinking processes, while the terminology helped him articulate his thinking. Third, Brian became more conscious of student thinking in the classroom and developed a deeper understanding of those students who had little experience with self-organization skills.

CONNECTIONS TO THEORY

Brian's thoughtful learning style contributed to his ability to make connections to the theory he learned in his teacher education program. In science, theory is defined as "a coherent group of general propositions used as principles of explanation for a class of phenomena such as Einstein's Theory of Relativity" (Webster's Dictionary, 2006). The scientific definition focuses on describing phenomena that exist. A theory explains but it can also guide further exploration or problem solving.

Understanding Theory

Brian defined theory as a practical guide. He explained theory and practice together, "Theory is an accepted, by some, way of approaching a problem or task . . . an idea to give *insight* into a way of doing things, while *practice* involves the *doing* represented by the principles of a theory. I guess theory drives my practice hopefully. I don't want to be doing something that I don't know what the theory behind it is."

Brian's definition of theory focused on improvement of practical instruction. Theory was something that helped him evaluate and improve his teaching practice. In this, Brian leaned toward Jerome Bruner's ideas about a theory of instruction. Bruner (1966) explains how a theory of instruction differs from learning and developmental theories that are found in psychology, "Theories of learning and of development are descriptive rather than prescriptive. They tell what happened after the fact. . . . A theory of instruction . . . is concerned with how what one wishes to teach can best be learned, with improving rather than describing learning" (p. 40).

Connections between TIEL and Classroom

Practical about teaching, Brian quickly saw the connection between child-centered classrooms and the self-organization skills of decision making, planning, and self-evaluation. The principles of child-centered education he had learned in his teacher preparation program were similar to those represented by the TIEL Curriculum Design Wheel. Teaching that focuses on the experience of the child involves opportunity for choice and helping children make those choices (Dewey, 1938). Brian wanted to learn more about the theory behind these teaching practices that influenced his own work in the classroom. He wondered how it all fit together,

> I sort of have my own theoretical ideas about whether this [TIEL Model] is useful or not . . . and I think it is. Part of it might be, how do people organize information? Are there certain styles? Gardner's Seven Intelligences? Are there things I want to be playing into in terms of helping them [the students] understand their thinking within a certain structure?

Brian did not recall specifically discussing thinking in his teacher education courses. The purpose of a child-centered classroom is to support the intellectual and social-emotional development of young children. Yet, the thinking and social-emotional processes that can guide teachers' conversations in ways that maximize a child's development were not explicitly addressed in his coursework. Brian did, however, recall educational theories giving examples of the place of thinking in learning activities. As we talked about theory, he said, "I guess some of these things certainly do inform what I do in the classroom. I think about Vygotsky's zone of proximal development. You want to help . . . say guide . . . you're getting them [students] to push into areas that are in some ways uncomfortable for them. But that's where learning takes place."

Brian shared a practical application of Vygotsky's (1978) theory from their reading work. He taught his students the Goldilocks method of choosing independent reading books. He wanted the students to be aware of their own reading level and to make choices accordingly. If some books are too hot, and some books are too cold, how do you know which book is just right? He expected them to explain the thinking that went into making those choices.

> In terms of Vygotsky, you get to a book that would be good for you, [but] something that is difficult. With possibly some help from the teacher they can help themselves. What have you done before? What are your strategies? Maybe I'll skip it [a word] and come back. Maybe I'll think about what happened in the story before, make a guess, and infer it from the text. Do that and try to get them farther than they would be on their own. Rather than giving them the answers, I'm just giving them the strategies.

Brian was interested in the best ways to help his students learn. Since the concept of explicitly teaching thinking processes involved in learning was new to Brian, he needed to find ways to connect the concepts he saw in the TIEL Model to his own beliefs about teaching and learning. Brian believed the job of the teacher is to help children make sense of things and that this is best accomplished through communication. "How can I provide sense in the world for them? I think what drives the whole thing about learning is communicating. Whether it's yourself or whether it's with somebody else or whether it's communicating a number or communicating a feeling. This whole endeavor is what we do in school, and why we learn."

As Brian began to understand how discussing thinking and social-emotional processes was an important, yet neglected part of teacher–student communication, he saw how the TIEL Model could potentially help him communicate with his students about their thinking.

Theory and Practice

Brian continually connected theory to practice. Brian was reading William Glasser's book *Control Theory* (1985) at the same time he was learning to teach his students self-organization skills. In the book, Glasser describes the teacher's illusion of control. When the playground attendants began complaining about the behavior of Brian's class during recess, the illusion was shattered. Brian seized the opportunity to connect theory to practice, bringing the children into the process of solving the problem as Glasser recommended. To help the students gain some insight into their behavior, Brian posed a question, "Why do you think this happened out there when we just had a great morning inside?"

The students gave their view of the midday madness. Brian summarized, "The people out there they just yell at you. They don't listen and so you don't want to do it for them. And if you get yelled at and it wasn't really your fault you think I'm just going to do something to get back at them. The adults just sit in one area and we know that so we can go crazy in another area."

Brian would not allow his students to simply take an uninformed stance or make excuses for unacceptable behavior. He wanted his students to be more responsible, more specific when describing problems, and to think about how each person can make responsible contributions.

Brian saw the connections to the self-organization skills included in the TIEL Wheel. Solving the playground problem required the students to self-evaluate. When children are brought into the problem-solving process, they are given the opportunity to reflect on their contributions to the problem. With insight into what happened and why it happened, the students began to understand their behavior and think of possible ways to change the situation. To help the students reflect on their responsibilities, Brian designed a survey that addressed these questions (see figure 13.1).

The questions addressed both individual and community issues. The first question put the problem in a larger context by asking students to reflect on what bothers them during school. The second question focuses on community responsibility. Questions three and four are more personal and require self-evaluation. In these questions he asked students to give evidence of their personal responsibility and think of ways in which they could show more

THE SURVEY

Please answer the questions.
Be honest with your answers.
We will talk about the answers during meeting.

1.   Do things happen in class, or school that bother you? What are
     they, and how do they make you feel?

2.   How can we help everybody to be responsible and to learn?

3.   What do you do in the class that shows you are responsible?

4.   What can you do to be more responsible for yourself?

5.   What do you like in class and want to do more of?

Figure 13.1.   Classroom survey.

responsibility. The last question gives the second graders an opportunity to suggest ideas that their teacher can use to reward positive changes in their behavior.

CONNECTIONS TO PERSONAL THINKING AND LEARNING

In order to teach self-organization skills, teachers need an understanding of their own thinking processes. As the research began, Brian explained how he used the processes of making decisions, planning, or self-evaluating when he had a goal in mind or desired to accomplish a particular task.

The Piano

Brian used the example of learning to play the piano to explain how he personally applied the processes of self-organization. "I would visualize how I would see this [the goal] at its completed stage in the future. Then I'd take that goal and break it down into pieces, [defining] the steps I need to make that happen. The steps to playing the piano are to get a piano, get a piano teacher, find time for myself to practice, and logistics that go along with that."

In describing self-organization skills, Brian began with describing the steps involved in planning to learn to play the piano. He did not describe the decision of choosing the piano over another instrument. Why not a guitar or an oboe? What criteria did he use to decide on the piano? In his example, he did not explore the criteria guiding his decision, but the steps of his planning are clear. The choice to play the piano was taken for granted.

While Brian did not talk about decision making, he did discuss possible ways to evaluate himself as he learned to play the piano. First, he might evaluate his progress throughout his work to determine if he were meeting his goals. He made clear that he would hold himself to realistic standards. He explained that he certainly wouldn't say, "I'm not playing the piano perfectly, so this is a failure." Instead, Brian would confidently state, "I'm better than I was and not as good as I will be."

Second, he might evaluate his work to determine where to focus his effort. Do I need to spend more time on practicing my fingering or more time on note reading? Third, he may evaluate the validity of the goal itself. Is there a desire to continue on a certain goal? "Sometimes," he said, "you might choose a goal and get into it, and once you get on your way you realize—hey! This isn't for me."

Embedded Thinking

Brian understood that he performed the thinking operations described in the evaluation section of the TIEL Model as he made decisions and planned, but he had never intentionally analyzed it. "It [self-organization] has been embedded in me in the way I go about making decisions," he explained.

As with many of us, Brian's process of decision making and setting criteria to make decisions was deeply embedded. It did not occur to him to discuss the criteria for choosing the piano over another instrument. While he mentioned that he would evaluate himself with realistic standards, he did not mention what those standards might be. Brian did not have to think about specific criteria that guided his decision making or his evaluations. They were automatic processes.

However, automatic decisions and judgments are not always the best ones. Critical thinking, the ability to use criteria to make decisions, evaluate, and judge, lies at the heart of decision making, planning, and self-evaluation. How we use criteria to make reasoned judgments determines the quality of critical thinking (Paul, 1995). Yet, as Paul points out, most people do not dig deeply into their own thinking to consider carefully the criteria for their choices.

Teachers, however, must do this digging. Teachers who are preparing students for an uncertain world of decisions need to be clear about the importance of criteria in thinking. In order gain a better understanding of thinking processes that need to be taught in the classroom, it is essential that teachers can unpack their thinking. With this understanding, they can then help their students develop the skills of using carefully considered criteria that form the foundation of self-organization skills.

Decision Making in Context

Brian was concerned about the effects of changing social contexts on decision making. He knew his students would be making decisions in a world inundated with choice. He gave the example of his father who had the opposite experience in choosing to go law school when the United States was involved in the Korean War. His options included (1) go to law school, (2) leave school to enlist in the war effort, or (3) leave school and become drafted into the military. The contextual factors at the time heavily influenced his decision to become a lawyer.

Brian's father's experience contrasts the clearer-cut options of yesterday, with the overwhelming choices available today. He explained, "For people these days there are so many different choices. You can't use the old way of eliminating something [in order to choose]. It's so splintered and everything's so specialized that you can't make a decision if there's four thousand things to choose from. If there's two things then I can make a decision."

Brian's teaching reflected his understanding of the centrality of choice in today's world, even though analyzing his own decision-making processes was unfamiliar. As a teacher, he felt a strong responsibility to help prepare his students for the choice-filled world in which they will become adults. He continued, "You have to explore and know what all the options are. Know what you're going to miss. Know what's going to happen when you take road 2 and not road 4. And how do you compare those things? What criteria do you use for comparisons?"

Gaining a better understanding of his own thinking helped Brian in teaching the students. He realized that teaching children to manage choices had to be approached judiciously. Since providing too many choices can result in paralysis and confusion, Brian set careful parameters for his students. "As you are beginning to [make decisions], that wide array of choices begins to paralyze you. You sort of have to be given certain options within parameters. Then the student can make a decision from four options." What is important is for children to have the opportunity to make decisions. Teachers need to skillfully guide the setting and using of criteria needed to make good choices and to make these reasons visible to the student.

Why, What, How

The professional learning process provided Brian with a framework that made him aware of thinking processes—his own and his students'. The TIEL framework helped him understand his teaching by stating the *why*, defining the *what*, and serving as a guideline for *how* to make observations in the classroom. Brian saw the TIEL Wheel as representing parts of a "singular process" that were interconnected. He explained, "If you're going to come up with a convergent product, you're going to have to evaluate, gather information. All those things can be embedded in different processes or broken down according to what you're doing."

The visual aspect of the TIEL Model was helpful. Brian thought that the TIEL Wheel provided for thinking what a visible monitoring system provides for increasing the fairness of calling on girls and boys in class. Something concrete to observe and assess performance was better "than trusting your instincts that you are being fair." Similarly, the TIEL Model was a concrete tool that helped him more purposefully include a wide range of thinking processes in his curriculum planning. It clarified the why, what, and how of teaching thinking in the classroom.

CONNECTIONS TO STUDENT THINKING

Brian developed a deeper awareness of the students' thinking as he became more conscious of his own thinking. Learning to teach decision making, planning, and self-evaluation helped him observe the students more carefully. He was able to distinguish between those with proficiency in using self-organization processes and those who lacked this proficiency.

Students' Lack of Experience with Self-Organization

Teachers are well aware of differences in the organization skills of their students. Given a project, some students are able to decide what to do and immediately begin to carry out their internal plans. These projects typically are completed on time and meet the objectives set by the teacher. Some students, however, struggle, not knowing where to start. Others jettison projects barely begun. These students try to begin again or, in some cases, give up.

New Perspective

Learning to teach self-organization skills gave Brian a new perspective. He had experienced similar situations with students, but now he saw problems with organization in terms of thinking skills that can be taught. Learning about his own thinking helped him understand why students needed to learn about their thinking. As Brian became aware of his own thinking, he became aware of the presence or absence of thinking and learning schemas in his students.

He wondered, "Do they have a 'way' of doing thinking—or is it just random?" Using the TIEL Model as a lens for observing his students, Brian developed an understanding of why it is important to explicitly teach students the processes involved in self-organization. He explained that he was concerned about the gap "between children who unconsciously have a way to plan, evaluate, and do (gather information, etc.), and those who don't, and the environmental factors that contribute to this."

Brian's empathy grew for "those who have not, for whatever reason, developed an internal way to think or make decisions." He found that students who lacked these internal self-organization skills seemed to lag behind in academic areas. He offered a hypothesis based on his observations:

> You can tell kids who sort of have it [ways to make decisions, plan, self-evaluate], do it without thinking about it. And kids who don't have it, face everything again for the first time. You're not looking back to memories and you don't have any schema of thinking. You don't have any way to think [about thinking]. If you have it without realizing you have it, well fine, but if you know about it and you can talk about it, to me that always helps in being able to do it better.

Environment and Self-Organization

The professional learning process helped Brian think about the environment from which students came into his class. He had always been concerned about culture and background, but learning how to teach self-organization processes within the context of the TIEL Model gave him further insight. How had his students' thinking processes been developed before Brian met them as second graders? He said, "Some students have been given the opportunity to make decisions, gather information, evaluate in their lives since they were born. And if they come from a background in which they have not had that same environment, [then] you're working with a whole different type of learner."

Brian questioned the assumption that some students learn better under direct instruction rather than through the kind of participatory learning that provides opportunities to make decisions, plan, and evaluate. He suggested that perhaps some students learn better through direct instruction because of their prior experience, but still he questioned, "Is that the best way for them actually to get knowledge in the long run? Can you make them aware of a different way where they are much more involved and have control in the process of learning?"

Historical Questions

Brian raised questions that have been asked in American education for well over a century. Could more purposefully involving students in their learning yield better educational results than assuming that some students are incapable of that involvement? He questioned the attitude of lesser expectations when he said, "Oh, well, you [the student] were never really taught how to make decisions and you were mostly told [what to do] all the time by your parents or whoever you grew up with, so that's the way we're going to teach you now. And you'll learn to read and you'll learn to write, but you won't learn to think."

Teaching Self-Organization Explicitly

Brian wanted to make the processes of self-organization explicit to those students who did not fully grasp the concepts. Due to environment and ability to process information, Brian said some students found it easy to identify their thinking. Others, however, were puzzled when asked to discuss their thinking. Brian imagined aloud how such students might feel, "What do you mean 'how do I think'? I don't think. I react. You tell me to go and do something and I do it."

Brian noticed that students who lack a sense of personal ownership have experienced predominantly external evaluation. When others set criteria and impose judgment, leaving little opportunity for self-evaluation, students are placed in the position of pleasing others. They gain little awareness that their thinking and feelings are also important.

Brian wanted students to gain a sense of power and control over what they do. He wanted students to become conscious of their choices and be responsible for setting their own criteria.

He was well aware of how students who feel powerless effect their environment. He shared his insights on behavior:

It's difficult because the kids who are in that mode [feeling powerless], they have sort of given up power and then the power they have is, "I can do this to please you." Or, "I can do this to piss you off. If you *don't* want me to do this, I can control you by doing it to piss you off." That's where the sense of power comes from. "You want me to do something? I'm not doing *that*. Watch. Watch what happens when I do *this*. You go all crazy."

The student may not be able to meet classroom or academic or family expectations. He may not meet his own expectations, but the student "can make the teacher go crazy!" A better way is to help students learn how to positively affect themselves by explicitly teaching them how responsible choices are made.

Developmental Considerations

Examining his own methods of evaluation helped Brian understand the processes that the students might use. He wanted to teach them how to evaluate their work, yet he was aware of their development as seven-year-olds. He hesitated to use self-evaluation fearing that the students might become too self-critical. Sensitive to the needs of second graders, he said, "This is a time where they have to be free in what they're doing to learn. They have to be free to fail." He did not want young students to become overwhelmed feeling that "the teacher is judging me, I am judging me; I need to work on this, I need to work on that."

Brian addressed his concern about overjudgment by structuring occasional student self-evaluation in nonjudgmental ways. Second graders needed to focus on their feelings about their work. He explained how he set criteria with the students, "I make sure that it's not ever a judgment of good or bad. I don't tie it to others' opinions. Do you feel that you worked hard? Do you like it? I try to make it personal and outside the realm of mastery."

Gentle Evaluation

Evaluation is thought of as comparison to others. Standardized assessment most often focuses on comparing groups of students within grade levels to students in other schools, or to students in other states. Brian, however, thought of self-evaluation in terms of self-comparison. He did not want students to compare themselves to others thinking, "Oh, I'm a good speller, or I'm a bad speller." Nor did he want them to think tensely, "Did I spell that properly?" Rather, he wanted them to consider, "How am I doing this? What do I need to do to get better at spelling? How did I do compared to MY skill?" For example, Brian would not set a criterion stating that the student cannot have over five mistakes. He saw the danger in giving a student the message that "you can't." In second grade, he was less interested in their mistakes than how they felt about their learning and their work.

Criteria that Open Thinking and Feeling

The setting of criteria prior to beginning a project is necessary for evaluation to take place. Setting criteria provides students, including second graders, with signposts along the way as they work on their projects. Brian considered the developmental needs of second graders as opposed to those in higher grades. He reemphasized that the early childhood years that include kindergarten, first, and second grade are still a time when exploration and making observations are important. He suggested a list of criteria that would be appropriate for young children:

- I explored my topic.
- I tried lots of ideas.
- I was surprised at how many things I learned.
- I discovered something new.
- I cared about what I was doing.
- I shared my materials.
- I learned something new to wonder about.

For Brian, the issue was not so much about *when* the criteria are set, but *what* the criteria are. He contemplated the setting of criteria saying, "When you are deciding criteria, you or they are deciding what is important. Is what's important that it was neat? Is what's important that it had four paragraphs? Or, is it important that I liked what I was studying, or that I did more than I could have done to finish the project? Certainly, mastery is important, but maybe at the higher-grade levels." Brian felt that criteria can close down or open up thinking and feeling. Criteria used by young children to evaluate their projects need to focus on celebrating and supporting ideas, being positive about learning, and building curiosity.

SUMMARY

Brian was a connection maker. He joined the research group with no previous knowledge of the TIEL Model, but he was curious about how to teach thinking to second graders and interested in learning. The TIEL Curriculum Design Wheel helped him see connections to theoretical concepts that he learned in his teacher education courses. He also saw important areas, such as the teaching of thinking, that were missing from his preparation for teaching. He recognized that child-centered learning involved self-organization skills, but he needed to be explicit in teaching the thinking skills to his students. TIEL helped Brian make connections to his personal thinking. Becoming more aware of his own thinking gave him a new perspective on the thinking he observed in his students. He realized that students who lack self-management skills can learn the thinking skills that can help them gain more control over their learning.

14

Connections and Application

You should evaluate more and more every year. Because every year, I've heard, that when you get older you do more stuff. Like, maybe in two more years you'll be dissecting a human and you'll have to evaluate like not to eat it.

—Nan, second grade student

At baseline, Brian was ready to integrate the teaching of thinking more explicitly into his teaching practice. The atmosphere in Brian's classroom was one of order, calm, and control within an atmosphere that encouraged creativity and imagination. The organization of the classroom was designed to promote student independence. He supported his second graders' lively imaginations and showed unfailing respect for their differences. His discussions with the children consistently encouraged thinking and connection making.

Brian did not yet have the tools he needed to teach thinking skills more explicitly, yet there were many opportunities to make connections to the TIEL Curriculum Design Model. At the baseline assessment there were no three-dimensional projects going on in the classroom. There was no explicit teaching of decision making, planning, or self-evaluation. That would come later. Over the year, Brian became more aware of his teaching practice, discussed thinking more explicitly with the students, and introduced more options into his curriculum and teaching. At the same time, his students exceeded his expectations in learning about their thinking and developing self-organization skills.

CLASSROOM ROUTINES

Classroom structures and routines encouraged self-management. The morning routines included journal writing, centers, and math. Each student was assigned

263

Monday

Red   Journals
Green   Math Problems at Board
Brown   Centers

Figure 14.1.   **Example of classroom assignments on blackboard.**

to a group designated by a color. When the students came into the classroom each morning, they read the instructions on the chalkboard (see figure 14.1). On Monday, the red group went with Brian to write in their journals. While Brian worked with a group of eight students at a horseshoe-shaped table at the back of the room on journal writing, the students in the brown group worked on activities chosen from among the center activities. The third group, green, solved math problems written on a white board on the ledge of the chalkboard in front of the room.

The physical space was organized in ways that supported student autonomy. Materials were placed where the students could access them easily; desks were arranged in groups of four to six. The carpeted area at the front of the class was large enough to accommodate the class comfortably. Visual references were important in the classroom. Charts with word families generated by the students were attached to the closet doors at child level. Students wrote out words they were learning to spell and attached them to the word charts. This became a ready reference to use during writing.

Creativity and Imagination

Brian's classroom was a place where creativity and imagination were honored and students were respected as individuals. On my first day to visit Brian's classroom, I observed Brian's supportive response to Layla's story about a fish. Following the morning routines, Brian called his class to the carpet. Layla began telling about a fish that visits her at Cape Cod and brings her presents.

Brian asked, "When does the fish bring you presents?"

A student asked, "Is the fish in costume?"

Layla's story was treated with respect and acceptance. Only one student asked if the story was true. There seemed to be nothing unusual about a fish leaping out of the ocean randomly dropping off presents. Einstein said, "Imagination is more important than knowledge. For knowledge is limited to all we now know and understand, while imagination embraces the entire world, and all there ever will be to know and understand" (ThinkExist, 2008).

Empowering kids with the ability to make decisions, plan, and self-evaluate within the context of their own work is important, but only to reach the end goal of releasing their imaginations to more freely soar to new heights.

Respect for Differences

Brian had a deep respect for the differences of his students. One way he differentiated curriculum was to make sure each student's list of spelling words came from his own writing and was appropriate to the level of the student's learning. One day a student asked, "Why does she have different spelling words?" Brian quickly reversed the question, "Why do you not all have the same spelling words? Do you all have the same size shoes? 'S-T-E-P-H-E-N' for some people is too easy, for some too hard, and for some just right. If you practice something and it's too hard, do you get better? If it's too easy do you get better?" It was important to provide content that was appropriate for each student, but it was also important that the students understood why their learning tasks were often different.

Brian gave another example that illustrated his sensitivity and compassion to individual students. During his first year of teaching, Brian had a very intelligent student whom he recommended for the gifted and talented program. Tom was able to sustain a sophisticated conversation about the Hoover Dam and hydroelectric power, but he had a problem sitting still. When Brian explained a game to the class this student would call out, "We got it already! We got it already!" Brian felt that a gifted and talented classroom would be better for Tom because continually waiting for everyone else put an undue burden on him. Brian described his behavior, "We'd be sitting on the carpet and he'd take his shirt off and chew on it. I told the parents about it and they had seen doctors who had had some recommendations but didn't want to put him on any drugs. Now, I really didn't feel like that's what he needed anyhow."

Brian decided to talk to Tom. He understood that students who are intellectually gifted do not always receive straight As nor are they necessarily the most compliant children in the classroom. Noticing that the behavior occurred in certain situations more than others, Brian asked Tom to identify those times when the negative behaviors happened most frequently. Tom replied, "I have a feeling that comes up through my body that I can't stop and I have to . . . move." This could occur when the classroom was quiet or at other times when it was loud and Tom was concentrating. Brian reported that Tom's "attention had to almost always be filled with something. He had no ability to wait."

By approaching the student with respect and concern, Brian learned information about the behaviors that helped Tom address the problem. He suggested, "If you need to move, give me a signal and you come over here and you move. How about if we can just get it down to moving your hand?" A plan emerged whereby he could leave the meeting area to write in his writing notebook or "zone out when nothing was going on." What was important was that Brian helped the student gain a feeling of control over his own behavior.

Thinking Talk

Classroom discussions that promoted thinking were a part of the fabric of Brian's classroom. While he lacked the tools to discuss thinking processes explicitly with the students, he had a natural ability to lead discussions that promoted thinking. The most minor discussion became a vehicle to promote student thinking in Brian's classroom.

Recognizing Patterns

One day, early in the research, Brian was taking attendance during morning meeting. As he called out the names, some of the students began to shout out "HERE!" before he got to their names. After repeatedly telling them not to call out, he turned the experience into an opportunity for thinking and learning.

> *Brian:* Why do some people say "here" before I say their name? How did Samantha know to say her name early?
>
> *Xavier:* Because she knows the name that she comes after.

Brian grabbed the teaching moment, pointing out that Samantha was recognizing a pattern. "She knows what her name is and she remembered what came before." He connected this example of a pattern to the patterns they would explore later that day in math.

Morning Meeting

Brian used the morning meeting to encourage students to be curious, ask questions, and make connections. The students took turns leading the meeting. After he or the student read the agenda, Brian asked the students if they had any questions. From that point "the meeting can go on with questions. The leader chooses who answers and the meeting can almost run itself." Brian stood by to answer questions and probe for deeper thinking. One day the agenda included *Author Study* and several students asked what it meant. Brian began questioning to help them figure out the answer for themselves.

> "What do you think that is?" If they don't even start down that road, kids might think . . . author study? Maybe we're going to watch some guy write a book. That's possible . . . not so far off. Let's get them at least to try to figure it out because I think that if they [the students] are able to sit back and not attempt it—that's what

they do when there's nobody around—they won't even try. [They think] I'll just wait until somebody comes and tells me.

Self-Reliance

Brian turned any event, incident, or comment, no matter how mundane, into an opportunity for the students to think and build self-reliance. Whether students were trying to spell a word, put on boots, or tie their shoes, each situation offered an opportunity to develop responsibility for themselves. He came to the realization in his first year of teaching that while it takes less time for the adult to *do* something for them, children need to learn to do it themselves. He gave an example from spelling,

> "How do you think you should spell it? Think about it. Let's try the sounds first. What does it end with? Have you seen it before?" Now, it would take less time to just spell it out for them. You get to a point as a parent or teacher and you just [think] . . . get it over with . . . I'll put your shoes on . . . let me tie them for you . . . I used to do that at the start of my teaching and then I said, "Why am I doing it?" All these things are a sort of learning.

MAKING THINKING EXPLICIT WITH SECOND GRADERS

Teaching students explicitly about their thinking allows them more control over their thinking, decreases their confusion, and helps them make sense of the world. Over the course of the year, Brian became more proficient at discussing thinking with his students and seeing more reasons why it was important. He commented, "I think I was good about talking about these things [thinking] before, or at least embedding them without necessarily talking about them."

There were two reasons he had not been explicit in his discussions of thinking earlier. First, he did not have the knowledge. Nowhere in his education had he been explicitly taught about thinking. Second, it seemed strange to him to talk about thinking.

Yet, the strange became increasingly familiar as Brian learned to name thinking processes along with the students. He placed the TIEL bulletin board on the wall in the back of the room where he could clearly see it as he worked with the students on the carpet. He referred to the bulletin board as he was teaching to remind himself to discuss thinking with the students.

Brian placed a large TIEL Curriculum Design Wheel with no labels at the front of the classroom in the carpeted area where the students could clearly see it during group teaching. After the students participated in an activity that focused on one of the components of the TIEL Wheel, Brian introduced the name and added the label.

Benefits of Teaching a Language of Thinking

Brian knew that the ability to break down thinking into component parts helped him talk about thinking with his students. Yet, being able to discuss thinking with the students and understanding why you should are two different things.

> Talking about thinking is going to help the students. It certainly can't hurt. They go through those processes, but they do it without naming it. There are certain things that you need to do, for example, to make a decision, to solve a problem. In terms of good thinking—you can't leave out chunks. You can't just say, "Oh! I don't need to gather information because I'll just make this decision using whatever information I have." That information may be erroneous or old.

While at first Brian was somewhat hesitant, he soon was having metacognitive discussions with his students.

Using Constructivist Principles

Brian applied constructivist principles to teaching the TIEL language. Lambert defines constructivism as patterns of learning where "individuals bring past experiences and beliefs, as well as their cultural histories and world views, into the process of learning" (Lambert et al., 1995, p. xi). Brian knew that the learner constructs learning based on prior knowledge. Therefore, before naming the thinking processes, Brian made sure the students first had experience with the thinking processes. How did he do this?

Teaching Convergent and Divergent Thinking

One day Brian taught the concepts convergent thinking and divergent thinking. As the students sat on the carpet, Brian explained that they would be doing two tasks. Half the students would be given blank paper to draw anything they wanted. The other half of the class received worksheets with math facts. Brian gave them a specified amount of time to work at their tables. When they reassembled on the carpet, they discussed the thinking they had experienced in each task. Brian asked the following questions, "How was the thinking similar? How was the thinking different? How did their thinking feel as they carried out their particular task? Would anyone have preferred to do the other task? Why?"

After the students had experienced both *convergent* and *divergent* thinking, he placed the names on the large laminated TIEL Wheel—*convergent* thinking in the yellow section and *divergent* thinking in the orange section.

Naming Promotes Understanding

Brian discovered, as he continued to integrate the teaching of thinking into learning experiences, that naming the thinking processes assisted him in helping his students understand concepts. He named thinking processes involved in project work, but he also used the TIEL language to clarify concepts in other subjects. He explained, "I can make thinking much more concrete in that its part of their projects and work that they need to do. And so it doesn't have to be so esoteric. I can actually talk about thinking rather than talking about something else that they may not get. Naming the thinking, I think, helps."

Brian shared an example of how he used the terms *convergent* and *divergent* thinking to help students understand math concepts. In second grade, math generally involves convergent thinking where the goal is to find "the one right answer" to a problem. While the math program used in Brian's class involved problems with one answer, it also encouraged students to use a variety of ways to solve those problems. When the students were unclear about how you could use multiple ways to find one answer, Brian used the TIEL Wheel and the terms convergent and divergent to help the students understand the two kinds of thinking involved in their math problems. "What's another way to get this? Who has another way? There are *divergent* ways of getting to the answer in a *convergent* problem. And so you can have a couple of different ways and still get to one place—strategies. This is a different strategy now, and this is a different strategy."

Students' Understanding

The value of teaching students about thinking was clear to Brian. Yet, the students' ability to understand and discuss thinking processes exceeded his expectations. Alternating between skepticism and surprise, he commented, "It's hard. You say, 'Talking about thinking . . . oh . . . with second graders?' How are they going to get it? But some of them show great ability to say—'Hey, that's green thinking and that's this . . . and I have to do this kind of thinking.'"

Brian's discussions of thinking were having an effect on the students. When I talked with them, I reminded them of the charts hanging in their classroom, "Cognition is pink, memory is blue, evaluation is green, and yellow is . . ." They finished the sentence, shouting, "Convergent! And orange is divergent." They explained that they were learning about their thinking so that they could understand what kind of thinking they were using in their work.

CURRICULUM AND TEACHING OPTIONS

At the beginning of the research year, Brian's focus was topics and subject matter. He used Socratic questioning, which fostered his students' thinking, but he gave little conscious attention to the actual processes of thinking that the students needed to develop and how they connected across subjects. Two examples, one from writing and one from social studies, showed the many opportunities for teaching thinking more explicitly that were embedded in Brian's curriculum.

> We just started an author study. We'll do that throughout the year . . . looking at different writers and maybe examining our own writing, looking at author's similarities, looking at things that they've written. We might be looking at habitats . . . like New York City as a habitat or a rural environment. You might look at a rural representation of life and things that might go on in an urban one. You might look at [topics] through an artistic sense too.

Learning Activities at the Beginning of the Year

In the author's study, Brian used two books by Chris Van Allsburg, *Garden of Abdul Gasazi* (1979) and *The Widow's Broom* (1992). After reading both of the books, he developed a chart that helped the students see the characteristics of one author's work (see figure 14.2). After learning about the author's writing, the students created an original story in the style of Chris Van Allsburg.

Brian welcomed input about the curriculum from the students. When he introduced the social studies unit on urban, suburban, and rural environments, the students became interested in modes of transportation. Seeing their motivation, he proposed that they research different kinds of transportation. "Shall we do an extensive study of land transportation? Water transportation? We might look at how different countries approach transportation."

Curriculum Connections to TIEL

These two examples show that Brian began the research project with learning activities in place that connected to several of the thinking operations found in

The Author's Study	
Garden of Abdul Gasazi	The Widow's Broom
• strange things happen • interesting • story seemed like it could happen • black-white pictures • pictures look old	• pictures look old • pictures are black, white, and scary • people played tricks in the story • dog in the story • beginning didn't seem real • mysterious

Figure 14.2.   Chart analyzing Chris Van Allsburg books.

the TIEL framework. The author study encouraged student thinking in several ways, including observation *(cognition)*, comparing, setting criteria *(evaluation)*, and using imagination *(divergent production)* to create their own stories. The students gathered the information they needed to develop the comparison chart by listening to the story and looking at the pictures *(cognition)*. "How can you tell a book is by a certain author? Are there signs that give you hints?"

Using the Van Allsburg books, Brian helped the students analyze and compare the two *(evaluation)*. In noticing the similarities and differences between two works by the same author, the students further solidified the characteristics of books by this author. Creating their Van Allsburg–style books also involved *divergent production* as the students used their imaginations to write and illustrate their stories.

In exploring transportation, Brian needed a wide variety of transportation options, the high interest came from their prior experience *(memory)* with different ways of getting from one place to the next. Brian divided the class into groups and let them choose *(evaluation)* from ten subtopics within the subject of transportation. Each group was responsible to gather information *(cognition)* on their subtopic and then come back together to share what they had learned with the whole group.

Opportunities for Teaching Thinking

Both of these learning activities offer opportunities to teach thinking more explicitly, help the students think critically, and introduce them to simple planning. For example, both the author study and the transportation study include places to set criteria. In the author study, students can set simple criteria for writing their stories by selecting common characteristics from the chart comparing the two Van Allsburg books:

- Black and white pictures that look old
- A feeling of mystery
- A story that could happen

These criteria provide students with guidelines for writing their stories and drawing their pictures. When the students are finished, they can use the criteria for evaluating their stories (see figure 14.3).

The transportation lesson included an opportunity to set criteria for making decisions about the method of transportation to research. While the students had a choice, it was an unconscious choice for the students. At this time, Brian did not make the students aware of their decision making by asking them how or why they made their choices. Brian needed a deeper understanding of thinking processes to take advantage of those spaces in his curriculum where he could more purposefully help his students develop their thinking processes.

Story in the Style of Chris Van Allsburg

CRITERIA FOR EVALUATION

1. black and white pictures that look old

2. a feeling of mystery

3. a story that could happen

Figure 14.3. *Story in the Style of Chris Van Allsburg,* example of criteria for evaluation.

Teaching Self-Organization to Second Graders

As Brian learned more about how to teach thinking, his teaching options increased. Like the other teachers, he first connected self-organization skills to the writing process with which he was familiar. Brian began teaching self-organization processes by making the planning portion of the writing process more explicit. Using his recent trip to the Pocono Mountains as an example, he had the following discussion with his students,

Brian: If you start a new piece what do we need to do?

Xavier: Plan.

Brian: The topic. What's it about? Let's have a refresher on this. [Brian wrote *Poconos* on the white board. He was careful to clarify that the Poconos are mountains located in northeastern Pennsylvania. Next, he wrote that the audience for his story was class 202. (see figure 14.4).]

Brian: How do I go about planning? What can help us get an idea about what to write?

Hal: You can make a list.

Tina: Make a web.

Brian: I'm going to do a list this time. Remember the plan is for yourself. Just enough to organize your thoughts. [Brian wrote in the five main points he wanted to include in his story.]

Brian: Now that I have a plan, I'm ready to begin writing.

Topic: Weekend in the Poconos (Poconos are mountains in Pennsylvania).

Audience: Students in 202.

Plan:

1. Car ride to the Poconos.
2. The house we stayed in.
3. Skiing
4. Hot tub
5. The trip home

Figure 14.4.   Weekend in the Poconos story planning chart.

In this lesson, Brian taught the planning process more explicitly. In earlier writing workshops, he had talked to the students about possible ideas for their stories. However, as he began this lesson, he introduced the word *plan*, wrote the topic, the audience, and listed the steps to use in writing the story. He asked, "What is the purpose of a plan?" He helped them discover that a plan helps them organize their thoughts. After developing the plan for his story, Brian asked the students five questions that established criteria appropriate for second graders.

- Is my topic interesting or important to me or my audience?
- Will it make sense to my audience and to me?
- Does my plan include the big ideas?
- Does my story have a beginning, middle, and an end?
- Will I be able to write this? Is it possible?

As the students wrote, Brian used these questions to help them evaluate their own stories using each of the criteria stated in the questions (see figure

Name _____ Date _____

EVALUATION OF YOUR WRITING

Criteria for Judging	A lot 3	Kind of 2	Not really 1
1. Is my topic interesting to me or my audience? Is it important to me or my audience?			
2. Will it make sense to my audience? Does it make sense to me?			
3. Does my plan include all the BIG IDEAS?			
4. Does my plan have a beginning, middle and end?			
5. Will I be able to write this? Is it possible?			

Figure 14.5.   *Evaluation of Your Writing,* self-evaluation checklist for writing project.

14.5). Brian was now explicitly teaching his students the skills of planning and self-evaluation, whereas at the beginning of the year the opportunities were missed.

Brian developed self-organization tools that were developmentally appropriate for second graders. One of the last projects of the year was making scarves from strips of white cloth that the students stamped with shapes dipped in tempura paint. Before they began the project, Brian established the criteria for evaluating the scarves. Two of the criteria evaluated the patterns on the scarves; the other two criteria focused on the feelings the students had about their work. The evaluation worksheets included a place to rate each criterion using a rating scale of 1–3 (see figure 14.6).

STUDENTS MAKE CONNECTIONS TO THEIR THINKING

As Brian became more explicit in teaching thinking skills, the students became very aware of their thinking. At the final interview, they could not wait to talk about thinking processes and how they made decisions, planned, and evaluated their projects. I had hardly finished telling them about the questions, when one student eagerly added, "About cognition? Getting information?"

Name _____ Date _____

CHECKLIST FOR SCARF PROJECT

Criteria for Judging	A lot 3	Kind of 2	Not really 1
1. My scarf has a distinct pattern. It is not a picture or words.			
2. I thought about how to make my pattern before doing it.			
3. I like the way it looks.			
4. I feel I created what I planned and wanted to.			

Figure 14.6. *Checklist for Scarf Project*, self-evaluation checklist.

Juan, who had been quiet during our first interview, found his voice and shouted out, "Divergent!"

Explaining the Scarf Plan

The students had recently completed making their scarves using white fabric. Using rubber stamps, they printed designs on the fabric with colored paint. However, before working with the cloth, they practiced printing designs with black paint on white paper. I asked what kind of thinking was involved in these two projects, expecting them to answer with the term *divergent thinking* since every scarf was different from all the others.

However, Rick confidently said, "Evaluating." He explained how they made the prototype before tackling the final scarf. "We planned it. First we had a big piece of paper. We all had big pieces of paper. We were planning with black and white. We were making different kinds of . . . of . . . of things [designs]. We were planning what we were going to do on our scarves."

Rick clearly understood that planning was a component of the thinking operation *evaluation* and that planning was an important part of the scarf project. He also understood that assessing the final product was also evaluation. He added, "Evaluation means you're planning or you're judging something. Like when we were doing the scarves, we had this sheet. It had 5 for very good, the middle was kind of, and the end was not really. Like . . . uh . . . no good. And the lowest number you can get is 1."

Recognizing Connections to other Projects

The students now recognized patterns of thinking used in their projects. Just as the older students had learned to do, the second graders connected their new learning about thinking to earlier projects and used the TIEL vocabulary to describe the similar patterns they saw. Before the scarf project, the students had created stained glass windows. They cut shapes in construction paper and mounted colored tissue paper on the back. When taped to the window, the light flowed through the shapes that framed the tissue paper, giving the illusion of stained glass.

The students first recognized that the two projects involved divergent thinking in the diversity of shapes and color. Rick mentioned *symmetry*. Nan saw *flexibility* as a common characteristic in both projects. In both the scarves and the stained glass, all the products could be different and adjustments could be made. Juan, for whom making choices was important, pointed out that they could use lots of colors in both projects.

Rick told of using his *memory* in the production of both projects. Showing that he took his work home with him, Rick shared a dream in which he considered how he would make the scarf and the stained glass window. When he woke up, the dream had vanished. "Then I used my memory and then I thought of it again!" he announced triumphantly.

Good Feelings about the Projects

The students were pleased with their projects. Juan wanted a pattern and he made a pattern. Nan liked the colors. Yet, how do you determine success? What does *successful* mean? What did it mean to *succeed*? What does the word *criteria* mean? Nan offered to explain criteria,

> It was like . . . you would know what to do. I think that criteria help you to know if it's nice. Because if you don't have criteria, you don't know if it's nice or not. In an art contest I guess you just say it's done so you give it to them [the judges] and they do it [evaluate]. And if they don't like it, there's no second chance. But you could do it [evaluate it] and if you don't like it you could do it over, and then you do it again.

Looking into the Future

While fifth graders enjoy sitting in the hallway with a tape recorder all day, second graders have limited stamina for interviewing. Nevertheless, I wanted to ask one more question, "Now that you understand more about thinking, how will you approach future projects differently?" From her second grade vantage point, Nan looked deep into the future and explained, "You should evaluate more and more every year. Because every year, I've heard, that when you get older you do more stuff. Like, maybe in two more years you'll be dissecting a human and you'll have to evaluate like not to eat it." For second graders, fifth grade is impossibly far into the future. While her plans for medical school were premature and a bit confused, Nan understood the importance of making wise decisions.

The students had become increasingly articulate about choice, planning, and evaluating. Nan moved quickly from the future to the present. She commented, "If you can make choices, then you can choose what's best for you. Like maybe the teacher says you have to read this big book, but it's too easy for you so you have to pick something yourself."

CONNECTIONS TO CHALLENGES

Brian recognized the challenges in teaching student self-organization skills. Like the other teachers, he mentioned class size, time, and experience as the factors that most affected his teaching of self-organization processes. Since he knew that with experience he would develop his ability to teach thinking skills, Brian was more concerned about class size and time.

Class Size and Time

Class size and available time can affect the quality of teaching and learning in any subject area. Yet, Brian saw how the relationship between class size and time had a more severe impact on teaching self-organization processes. Teaching the analytical processes of self-organization is talk-intensive, requiring significant amounts of discussion time. Large class size meant diminished amounts of the time needed to talk, listen, and analyze responses. "You really have to talk about what they're thinking, what are the decisions that they're making. It's hard to keep track of that. You have to talk about what they did, you know, it's not a teacher-directed sort of classroom."

While not teacher directed in the traditional way, teaching self-organization skills requires very careful teacher planning and direction to maximize the time in the classroom. Brian felt that without the time to clearly name and discuss the thinking processes involved in a project, the students just do what the teacher asks with little understanding of what is being asked. If the students do not know why they are making decisions, planning, and evaluating, it can seem to students that "here comes another thing that I just do because the teacher told me to do it." Students lose the benefit that comes from understanding the how and why of making choices, planning, and evaluating in conjunction with their own work.

Assessment

Assessment was a concern. How could you assess student proficiency in understanding and applying self-organization skills? Realizing that teachers, parents, and administrators all have "some sort of objective criteria" by which to assess students, Brian foresaw the difficulties in assessing self-organization skills. He wondered how to objectively test that elusive element of "how they learn" that is embedded in processes of self-organization. With characteristic humor, he noted the limitations of the bubble test format. "I don't think you can test this [self-organization] objectively . . . how they learn . . . that's more of an essay question than a multiple choice."

Brian was also concerned about his assessments of student work. Would teaching self-organization skills to students give too much responsibility to the students for their own assessments? Would student self-assessment take away from his assessment of students?

Yet, Brian saw the advantages in having the students participate in evaluating their work. They had grown in confidence, independence, and had gained a sense of empowerment over their learning. As he saw the benefits to his students, he became more confident that their self-evaluations would not take away from a more objective assessment that he might do. He explained how both student and teacher assessment can coexist beneficially in the classroom.

Student assessment wouldn't replace anything. It would just become part of the way of thinking in the classroom. I need to do some sort of an objective test and I just do that and this other self-evaluation and group evaluation. I could ask the class, "How did we do that? Could we have done better? This happened. Why do you think we did that?"

Role of the Teacher

Brian was concerned about the role of the teacher in other ways. What is the critical role of the teacher in teaching thinking and self-organization skills in a child-centered classroom? In order to learn thinking skills, children need experiences. In order to learn self-organization skills, students must have something to decide, plan, and evaluate. Yet, Brian could foresee the dangers of relying too much on the students for their insights and assessments. How much guidance does the teacher provide? How many choices are offered to the students? The greater the number of choices, the more time is needed to help students manage those choices.

Dewey had similar concerns about the role of the teacher in a classroom that features experience-based learning. Like Brian, Dewey was interested in balance. He cautioned against perceiving a reduced role for teachers in a classroom that encourages student choice. While traditional education, according to Dewey (1938), neglected personal choice, progressive education should not abandon the teacher's responsibility to plan, guide, and assess students.

Complex teaching makes complex learning possible. Clearly, teachers must carefully plan the experiences and the lessons that teach students the thinking skills involved in decision making, planning, and self-evaluation. Yet, openings to teach students the important skills of self-management exist in every classroom. There are opportunities to teach students how to consider criteria for the decisions they make. There are spaces in the curriculum for teaching students how to plan and evaluate their own creative work. There are places for students to learn empathy, appreciation, and how to be reflective.

SUMMARY

Brian's ability to make connections to a large number of factors pertaining to teaching and learning supported the changes he made in his teaching. At the beginning of the research, because of his child-centered philosophy, he had many structures in place where thinking could be more explicitly taught. Yet, Brian needed skills and language that would provide more support for the teaching and learning in his classroom. From not knowing and feeling a bit uncomfortable about how to teach thinking, he became explicit, planful, and articulate about teaching self-organization skills to his second grade students in a developmentally appropriate way. As his students learned more about their thinking through their projects, they also became articulate in discussing their thinking and learning.

Conclusion

In April 2008, twenty-five years following *A Nation at Risk,* another report, entitled *Democracy at Risk* (Darling-Hammond & Wood, 2008), was released by the Forum for Education and Democracy. This report urges the federal government to commit much-needed resources to the repair of our educational system, which is not currently, in any consistent way, preparing students for the complex society in which we live. A recurring theme throughout the report focuses on the thinking and social-emotional skills that all students need to succeed in the new economy and take an active role in building and maintaining democratic communities. Included in this theme is the importance of "higher order thinking skills, such as the ability to apply knowledge to complex problems, communicate and collaborate effectively . . . find, manage, and analyze information . . . critical thinking and problem-solving [skills] . . . deep knowledge . . . creativity and originality (pp. 15, 19, 38).

These are the intellectual skills described in the TIEL Curriculum Design Model. Communicating and collaborating with others, especially those who are perceived as different from us, require social-emotional as well as intellectual skills. The TIEL Curriculum Design Wheel synthesizes and describes a wide range of intellectual and social-emotional abilities that students need in order to succeed in our complex society. Making visible the fundamental components underlying twenty-first-century skills, the TIEL Wheel is a valuable tool teachers can use as a guide in creating curriculum and planning instruction that leads to complex learning.

CODIFICATION

In codifying fundamental intellectual and social-emotional processes, the TIEL Model brings balance between two historic purposes of American education that have kept the pendulum swinging. One is preservation and transmission of our cultural heritage and "cultivation of the intellect" (Hutchins, as cited in Taba, 1962, p. 20) through the transmission of knowledge focused on classic disciplines and basic skills.

The other focuses on social-emotional or moral development. This second purpose is a synthesis of two important elements of Dewey's (1964) philosophy: social reconstruction and individual development. Progressive educators hotly debated the merits of social development versus the child-centered education that emerged from the individual development philosophy. However, as Taba (1962) points out, child-centered education, grounded in intellectual and social-emotional concerns, is education that can transform society. As individuals develop the characteristics that make a democratic society possible, including reflection on cultural knowledge from the past, their influence can change society itself.

The TIEL Model brings these two purposes together to help teachers develop the knowledge and skills needed to be effective in preparing students in this century. The TIEL Model clarifies intellectual skills that go beyond an emphasis on right answers to include problem solving, creative thinking, and a deeper understanding of critical thinking. In the TIEL Model, equal space is given to acquiring content knowledge in the disciplines and using memory to make connections as well as recall. While the TIEL Model expands the conception of thinking processes, it includes the "humanizing possibilities" (Greene, 1988, p. 13) of appreciation, mastery, ethical reasoning, empathy, and reflection that prepare students to take their places in a democratic community.

CONSCIOUSNESS

To be conscious is to be awake and aware. TIEL opens the minds of teachers to new possibilities and provides the tools to implement ways of teaching that lead to complex learning. It is critical that preparation programs help new teachers become conscious of the physical aspects of classroom organization and teaching strategies. Yet, teachers also need to be conscious of the invisible intellectual and emotional structures that provide the foundation for effective instruction and give richness to the teaching and learning process. Like Ted, veteran teachers need to become aware of the opportunities that exist in their classrooms to teach thinking and social-emotional skills more explicitly.

The TIEL Model provides a framework for reflection. It helps teachers become more awake to the intellectual and emotional facets of their own teaching and learning. It gives teachers a framework for reflecting on their practice, asking themselves, "Where are my strengths? Where do I need to work? How can I expand my curriculum and instruction in ways that will prepare students with the complex skills they need to develop?"

COMMUNICATION

TIEL provides a way to communicate about thinking and learning. It supports metacognition. When students understand their thinking, they have tools to help them put order into their learning world. Michael learned more about his ability to manage his own behavior when Ted decided to let Michael participate in evaluating his behavior chart. Daniel referred to the TIEL component *mastery* as he explained the importance of not giving up.

TIEL supports communication between teacher educator and teacher. If teaching is difficult, Darling-Hammond (2006) points out that "teacher education is more impossible than teaching itself" (p. 8). TIEL helps teacher educators better communicate the intellectual and emotional components that make teaching and learning more complex. Erica learned to teach self-organization skills more easily and in greater depth after she was introduced to the TIEL framework.

CURRICULUM

The TIEL Model helps teachers balance their curriculum and instruction between the intellectual and social-emotional, content and process, and convergent and divergent aspects of learning. Stacy changed from a very teacher-directed style of teaching to planning project-based curriculum that included opportunities for students to make decisions, plan, and evaluate their work. Where delivery of content had been the main focus in Stacy's classroom, she learned to explicitly teach the higher-order thinking processes of self-organization while not minimizing content.

The TIEL Model supports constructivist teaching and learning by providing visual knowledge of important building blocks. Twenty-first-century education requires that students construct an understanding of not only content knowledge, but also of the processes of learning that make understanding possible. TIEL helps make these intellectual and social-emotional building blocks accessible to teachers and to their students.

Achieving balance is not easy. Recognizing the learning differences in their students, the teachers often experienced an inward battle over teaching methodology. Both Brian and Ted asked themselves, "Was the progressive constructivist style of teaching the most effective for the struggling students? Or would a more 'back to basics' approach better help them learn?" The TIEL framework helped Ted see that the more divergent thinking commonly associated with constructivist teaching could coexist and, indeed, must coexist beside the kinds of convergent thinking usually involved in back to basics teaching.

The TIEL Model provides ways to differentiate curriculum for all learners. Using the TIEL Model, the teachers discovered that all of their students, advanced learners as well as those who struggle academically, benefited from "active, independent, self-directed learning" where they "gather[ed] and assess[ed] data rigorously and critically" (Paul, 1995, p. 45). As they planned their projects and evaluated their work using clear criteria, the students showed more motivation and more responsibility for their work, and began to develop the critical thinking skills described by Paul.

At the same time, the TIEL Model reinforces mastery of basic skills and the learning of disciplinary content. The teachers recognized that teaching self-organization skills within project work not only enhanced the learning of content, but provided motivation to work on the basic skills of reading and writing that were necessary in developing their projects.

CONNECTIONS

The TIEL Model helps teachers make connections. It may remind them of effective ways of teaching that have been abandoned in the relentless emphasis on standardized test scores. It may remind them of the need for art and music in the classroom. It may remind them of the value of placing social studies and science at the center of the curriculum with all the possibilities for teaching self-management skills through project work that these subjects offer. It may help them see more deeply into the standards or even into standardized test preparation, allowing them to discover opportunities for teaching thinking or social-emotional processes that were previously hidden.

The TIEL Model provides a framework that helps teachers understand the structures that support complex teaching and learning. Teacher educators can use TIEL to help students see the invisible structures of thinking and social-emotional learning that lie below the surface of theory and practice. As Erica pointed out, TIEL offers multiple entry points for making connections. It helps the student who is beginning a teacher-preparation program with only memories of her own schooling to serve as a model for teaching. This deeper understanding can help prospective teachers break through the boundaries formed by a vision of education constructed over a lifetime in school and decades of history.

Most important, the TIEL Model connects the intellectual to the social-emotional aspects of teaching and learning. It validates what teachers have always known—that students need to learn intellectually, but anchored with qualities of character. Many students who have excelled academically grow up to be leaders in business or government, but they are missing important characteristics of ethical reasoning, empathy, and appreciation for others. Other students, who have had limited intellectual opportunities or emotional support, need ways to increase their chances of developing their thinking as well as social-emotional capabilities. TIEL helps teachers look more deeply into the needs of all their students and develop curriculum and instruction that helps each student reach his or her optimum potential in a complex world.

These four teachers experienced how using the TIEL Model changed their teaching and benefited their students within the classroom. What might be the effect of a generation of thinking, ethical, and compassionate people on their families, neighborhoods, communities, and the wider world? The prospect makes the teaching of thinking and social emotional learning worth the effort, even if it were not absolutely necessary.

Appendix: Research Methodology

This book is based on my doctoral dissertation research. I came to the doctoral program from many years of teaching that included deaf education, preschool teaching, gifted and talented programs, and general elementary education. While teaching in deaf education and gifted and talented education, I learned how use thinking processes to develop curriculum. When I began my doctoral program, I brought my experience in using Guilford's structure of intellect theory as a guide for designing curriculum and instruction.

During my doctoral work, I became interested in principles fundamental to the understanding, maintenance, and regeneration of progressive democratic education. Recognizing that this included social-emotional learning and development of character as well as cognitive abilities, I merged the work of Guilford and Dewey to form the TIEL Curriculum Design Model.

PURPOSE

The purpose of this qualitative research study, which included an intervention, was to follow four teachers, and their students, as they learned to integrate the teaching of self-organization skills into their daily classroom curricula. I spent a half day each week in each classroom for one full school year teaching the four teachers how to integrate the self-organization processes of decision making, planning, and self-evaluation into their curricula. The teachers, in turn, evaluated the professional learning process and gave me suggestions on how best to facilitate their learning. The term *professional learning process*, used by Ann Lieberman (1991), expresses the collaborative nature of the research in which we were all learners.

RESEARCH PROCEDURE

The overall research procedure included teacher selection, baseline assessment, the ongoing professional learning process, and a final assessment. I patterned my overall research procedure after research by Baum, Renzulli, and Hébert (1995) on student underachievement that included four phases: (1) teacher selection, (2) familiarization, (3) treatment or intervention, and (4) assessment. The following sections describe the four phases in my research.

Teacher Selection

I selected the teachers based on their interest in child-centered and project-based teaching, their ability to articulately evaluate the professional-development intervention, and their potential as leaders in their schools. I knew three of the teachers prior to the research. I supervised Erica as a student teacher in Ted's classroom, and I knew Stacy from college courses. Brian, whom I had not met, was selected through a type of "snowball sampling technique" (Bogdan & Biklen, 1992, p. 70) as I discussed possible choices with Ted.

Three of the teachers were interested in how to better incorporate thinking processes into their curriculum, and Brian was curious. They each felt that there were strategies for teaching self-organization to students that they would like to know, and each had expressed interest in learning how to get students to be more responsible for their own work.

The four teachers came from two schools in Manhattan. One of the schools is a K–5 school with about 550 students. It is an ethnically mixed school with access for students with physical disabilities. The student population includes high ability students as well as students with academic challenges. The other school is also an ethnically mixed school with approximately seven hundred students. The population includes academically advanced students and those with academic challenges.

In order to understand what the teachers were learning, I needed to know what the students were learning. Therefore, I asked the teachers to select three children from their classes to participate in the baseline and final assessments. The students represented students who had success with projects and those who had difficulty. During the baseline and final assessments, I interviewed the selected students from each class in small groups.

Familiarization and Baseline Assessment

The second phase concerned familiarization with the teachers and their classrooms. Although I knew three of the teachers and had been in their classrooms previously, we were beginning a new, and somewhat different, long-term relationship where I would be in their classrooms regularly. Working in this close reciprocal relationship, it was important that we trusted each other. During this second phase, I immersed myself in the classrooms, learning their routines and the names of the children.

I conducted baseline assessments with each teacher and the selected students during this phase of the research. The baseline and final assessments included five different data-gathering instruments—classroom observation, teacher interviews, student interviews, teacher materials analysis, and student project analysis. Teacher-made materials include the self-management tools found in this book. Many of the student projects are also described. I tape-recorded the interviews and took handwritten notes for observations. Both were transcribed following the visit to the class.

I conducted baseline assessments with Ted, Erica, and Stacy during the final weeks of school preceding the research year in order to see what projects were in place at the end of the year. Brian's baseline, however, was completed in the fall of the research year. Since it was a new year with new students, I interviewed the selected students in Ted's and Stacy's classes in the fall as well. Because of looping, Erica had the same students from the previous year.

Professional Learning Process

The third component was the professional development intervention or professional learning process. The professional learning process consisted of group meetings and individual work with teachers. Since I chose to focus the book on what the teachers and students shared about learning self-organization skills, there are few details about the professional learning process included in the chapters.

Once a week, I visited each teacher's classroom for a half day, staying through the morning or the afternoon. We had individual meetings during lunch or at the end of the day to discuss my observations and work on curriculum. The professional learning process was individually tailored to meet the needs of each participating teacher. Some teachers needed to focus on the techniques of teaching self-organized learning; others needed to recognize how to optimize existing opportunities for teaching decision making, planning, and self-evaluation. The baselines established for each teacher before beginning the professional learning process provided preassessment information that helped me formulate plans with each teacher.

For the first month of the research, the teachers and I met as a group each week. I introduced the scope of the research and the teachers shared what they hoped to learn from the research project. I introduced them to the TIEL Curriculum Design Wheel in order to place the self-organization skills of decision making, planning, and self-evaluation within a larger context of thinking and social-emotional processes. We also developed a schedule for visits to their classrooms and for future group meetings that occurred approximately once a month.

After the first month, we held group meetings once a month. During these meetings, the teachers told what they were doing in their classrooms to integrate self-organization skills into the curriculum, shared tools they developed to teach students decision making, planning, and self-evaluation, and offered suggestions about how to use the TIEL language to discuss thinking with their students. They also helped each other develop curriculum units. The monthly meetings were usually held in my apartment with tea and cookies served. In the last months of the research, we rotated classrooms for the group meetings. The teachers were able to see how the other teachers were using the TIEL visuals with their students. They received valuable ideas from the materials developed in each classroom.

Final Assessment

The fourth phase of the research involved the final formal assessment. This assessment was conducted at the conclusion of the professional learning process. The baseline and final assessments provided data needed to assess the impact of the professional learning process on the practices and strategies of each of the participating teachers as well as providing information on the professional learning process itself. The data collected through classroom observation, teacher and student interviews, teacher materials analysis, and student project analysis form the basis of this book.

References

Bain, K. (2004). *What the best college teachers do*. Cambridge, MA: Harvard University Press.

Baum, S. M., Renzulli, J. S., & Hébert, T. P. (1995). Reversing underachievement: Creative productivity as a schematic intervention. *Gifted Child Quarterly, 39*(4), 224–235.

Bloom, B. (1956). *Taxonomy of educational objectives: The classification of educational goals*. New York: D. McKay.

Blumenfeld, P., Soloway, E., Marx, R., Krajcik, J., Guzdial, M., & Palinsar, A. (1991). Motivating project-based learning: Sustaining the doing, support the learning. *Educational Psychologist, 26*(3, 4), 369–398.

Bogdan, R., & Biklen, S. (1992). *Qualitative research for education: An introduction to theory and methods*. Boston: Allyn & Bacon.

Bruner, J. S. (1966). *Toward a theory of instruction*. Cambridge, MA: Harvard University Press.

Campbell, J. (1967). *The children's crusader: Colonel Francis W. Parker*. New York: Teachers College Press.

Chiarelott, L. (2006). *Curriculum in context: Designing curriculum and instruction for teaching and learning in context*. Belmont, CA: Thomas Wadsworth.

Cognitive Research Program. (1999). *Mediated learning in and out of the classroom*. Thousand Oaks, CA: Corwin Press.

Cremin, L. (1961). *The transformation of the school: Progressivism in American education*. New York: Random House.

Csikszentmihalyi, M. (1992). *The evolving self: A psychology for the third millennium*. New York: HarperCollins.

Cuban, L. (1993). *How teachers taught: Constancy and change in American classrooms 1890–1900*. New York: Teachers College Press.

Cullum, A. (1971). *The geranium on the window sill just died, but teacher you went right on*. London: Harlin Quist.

Darling-Hammond, L. (1997). *The right to learn: A blueprint for creating schools that work*. San Francisco: Jossey-Bass.

Darling-Hammond, L. (2006). *Powerful teacher education*. San Francisco: Jossey-Bass.

Darling-Hammond, L., & Wood, G. (2008). *Democracy at risk: The need for a new federal policy in education*. Amesville, OH: The Forum for Education and Democracy.

Dewey, J. (1938). *Experience and education*. New York: Collier Books.

Dewey, J. (1964). *John Dewey on education: Selected writings* (R. D. Archambault, Ed.). Chicago: University of Chicago Press.

Dewey, J. (1991). *How we think.* Buffalo, NY: Prometheus Books.

Doll, W. E., Jr. (1993). *A post-modern perspective on curriculum.* New York: Teachers College Press.

Doyle, W. (1990). Themes in teacher education research. In W. R. Houston, M. Haberman, & J. Sikula (Eds.), *Handbook of research on teacher education: A project of the Association of Teacher Educators* (pp. 3–24). New York: Macmillan.

Emerson, R. W. (1990). *Ralph Waldo Emerson: Selected essays, lectures, and poems.* New York: Bantam Books.

Erickson, H. L. (2006). *Concept-based curriculum and instruction for the thinking classroom.* Thousand Oaks, CA: Corwin Press.

Fiske, E. B. (2008, April 25). A nation at a loss, *New York Times,* p. A27.

Folsom, C. (2005). Exploring a new pedagogy: Teaching for intellectual and emotional learning (TIEL). *Issues in Teacher Education, 14*(2), 75–94.

Friedman, T. L. (2005). *The world is flat: A brief history of the twenty-first century.* New York: Farrar, Strauss & Giroux.

Gardner, H. (1985). *Frames of mind: The theory of multiple intelligences.* New York: Basic Books.

Glasser, W. (1985). *Control theory: A new explanation of how we control our lives.* New York: Harper & Row.

Goals 2000: Educate America Act of 1994. (1994). Pub. L. No. 103–227.

Greene, M. (1988). *The dialectic of freedom.* New York: Teachers College Press.

Guilford, J. P. (1968). *Intelligence, creativity, and their educational implications.* San Diego, CA: Robert R. Knapp.

Guilford, J. P. (1977). *Way beyond the IQ.* Buffalo, NY: Creative Education Foundation.

Hansen, J. B., & Feldhusen, J. F. (1994). Comparison of trained and untrained teachers of gifted students. *Gifted Child Quarterly, 38*(3), 115–121.

Hargreaves, A. (Ed.). (1997). *Rethinking educational changes with heart and mind: 1997 ASCD yearbook.* Alexandria, VA: Association for Supervision and Curriculum Development.

Highet, G. (1954). *The art of teaching.* New York: Vintage Books.

Hirsch, E. D., Jr., & Trefil, J. S. (1987). *Cultural literacy: What every American needs to know.* New York: Houghton Mifflin.

Hoffman, M. L. (1991). Empathy, social cognition, and moral action. In W. M. Kurtines & J. L. Gewirtz (Eds.), *Handbook of moral behavior and development* (Vol. 1: Theory, pp. 275–301). Hillsdale, NJ: Lawrence Erlbaum Associates.

Hollingsworth, S. (1989). Prior beliefs and cognitive change in learning to teach. *American Educational Research Journal, 26*(2), 160–189.

Hollingworth, L. S. (1926). *Gifted children: Their nature and nurture.* New York: MacMillan.

Jersild, A. T. (1955). *When teachers face themselves.* New York: Teachers College Press.

Johnson, D. W., Johnson, R. T., & Holubec, E. J. (1994). *Cooperative learning in the classroom.* Alexandria, VA: Association for Supervision and Curriculum Development.

Kagan, S. (1994). *Cooperative learning.* San Clemente, CA: Kagan Publishing.

Kilpatrick, W. H. (1918). The project method. *Teachers College Record, 19,* 319–335.

Kliebard, H. M. (1992). *Forging the American curriculum: Essays in curriculum history and theory.* New York: Routledge.

Kliebard, H. M. (1995). *The struggle for the American curriculum: 1893–1958.* New York: Routledge.

Kohn, A. (1998). *What to look for in a classroom: . . . and other essays.* San Francisco: Jossey-Bass.

Lambert, L., Walker, D., Zimmerman, D. P., Cooper, J. E., Lambert, M. D., Gardner, M. E., & Slack, P. J. F. (1995). *The constructivist leader.* New York: Teachers College Press.

Lieberman, A. (1991). *Teachers, their world and their work: Implications for school improvement.* New York: Teachers College Press.

Lindley, D. A., Jr. (1993). *This rough magic: The life of teaching.* Westport, CT: Bergin and Garvey.

Mager, R. F. (1984). *Preparing Instructional Objectives.* Belmont, CA: Lake Publishing.

Martin, J. R. (1995). *The schoolhome: Rethinking schools for changing families.* Cambridge, MA: Harvard University Press.

Marzano, R. J. (1993). How classroom teachers approach the teaching of thinking. *Theory into Practice, 32*(3), 154–160.

Mayhew, K. C., & Edwards, A. C. (1936). *The Dewey school: The Laboratory School of the University of Chicago.* New York: Appleton-Century.

McNamee, A. S., Zakin, A., Saravia-Shore, M., Ross, A. L., Peloso, J. M., Dubetz, N. E., Folsom, C., Mercurio, M., Morales-Flores, J., Fairbank, H., & Iurato, J. P. (2008). A renaissance of the arts in classrooms: A collaboration between a college, a public school and an arts institution. In C. J. Craig & L. F. Deretchin (Eds.), *Imagining a renaissance in teacher education. Teacher Education Yearbook* (Vol. 16, pp. 328–347). Lanham, MD: Rowman & Littlefield Education.

Meeker, M. (1979). *A structure of intellect.* El Segundo, CA: SOI Institute.

National Center on Education and the Economy. (2000). *Report of the Commission on the Skills of the American Workforce, America's choice: High skills or low wages!* Retrieved from the Commission on the Skills of the American Workforce website: www. skillscommission.org/pdf/High_SkillsLow_Wages.pdf.

National Center on Education and the Economy. (2006). *Tough choices or tough times: The report of the Commission on the Skills of the American Workforce.* San Francisco: Jossey-Bass.

National Commission on Excellence in Education. (1983). *A nation at risk.* Portland, OR: USA Research.

National Council for Accreditation of Teacher Education. (2000). *Program standards for elementary teacher preparation.* Retrieved from the NCATE website: www. ncate.org/standard/elemstds.pdf.

National Council for Accreditation of Teacher Education. (2002). *Professional standards for the accreditation of schools, colleges, and departments of education.* Retrieved from the NCATE website: www.ncate.org/2000/unit_stnds_2002.pdf.

New York State Education Department. (1996). *Learning standards for social studies.* Retrieved from the University of the State of New York, State Education Department website: www.emsc.nysed.gov/ciai/socst/pub/sslearn.pdf.

No Child Left Behind Act of 2001. (2002). Pub. L. No. 107–110, 115 Stat. 1525.

Noddings, N. (2003). *Happiness and education,* New York: Cambridge University Press.

Ogle, D. M. (1997). *Critical issue: Rethinking learning for students at risk.* Retrieved October 28, 2002, from North Central Regional Educational Laboratory website: www.ncrel.org/sdrs/areas/issues/students/atrisk/at700.htm.

Ornstein, A. C. (2003). Critical issues in teaching. In A. C. Ornstein, L. S. Behar-Horenstein, & E. F. Pajak (Eds.), *Contemporary issues in curriculum,* (3rd ed., pp. 77–93). Boston: Allyn & Bacon.

Paul, R. (1995). *Critical thinking: How to prepare students for a rapidly changing world.* Santa Rosa, CA: Foundation for Critical Thinking.

Perkins, D. N. (1995). *Outsmarting IQ: The emerging science of learnable intelligence.* New York: Free Press.

Piaget, J. (1948). *The moral judgment of the child* (M. Gabain, Trans.). Glencoe, IL: The Free Press.

Ravitch, D. (2000). *Left behind: A century of battles over school reform.* New York: Simon & Schuster.

Sarason, S. B. (1982). *The culture of the school and the problem of change.* Boston: Allyn & Bacon.

Schacter, D. L. (1989). Memory. In M. I. Posner (Ed.), *Foundations of cognitive science* (pp. 683–725). Cambridge, MA: Massachusetts Institute of Technology.

Slavin, R. E. (1995). *Cooperative learning: Theory, research and practice.* Needham Heights, MA: Allyn & Bacon.

Smith, R. (2007, August 13). Elizabeth Murray. 66. artist of vivid forms, dies. *New York Times.* Retrieved March 22, 2008, from www.nytimes.com.

Sternberg, R. J. (1985). *Beyond IQ: A triarchic theory of human intelligence.* New York: Cambridge University Press.

Sternberg, R. J. (1988) *The triarchic mind: A new theory of human intelligence.* New York: Viking.

Taba, H. (1962). *Curriculum development: Theory and practice.* New York: Harcourt, Brace & World.

Tannenbaum, A. J. (1986). Giftedness: A psychosocial approach. In R. J. Sternberg & J. E. Davidson (Eds.), *Conceptions of giftedness* (pp. 22–51). New York: Cambridge University Press.

ThinkExist.com. (2008). Retrieved March 21, 2008, from thinkexist.com/quotation/imagination_is_more_important_than_knowledge-for/260230.html.

Thomas, J. W. (2000). *A review of research on project-based learning.* San Rafael, CA: Autodesk Foundation.

Tomlinson, C. A. (1999). *The differentiated classroom: Responding to the needs of all learners.* Alexandria, VA: Association for Supervision and Curriculum Development.

Tyler, R. W. (1949). *Basic principles of curriculum and instruction.* Chicago: University of Chicago Press.

Van Allsburg, C. (1979). *The garden of Abdul Gasazi.* New York: Houghton Mifflin.

Van Allsburg, C. (1992). *The widow's broom.* New York: Houghton Mifflin.

Vygotsky, L. S. (1978). *Mind in society: The development of higher psychological processes* (M. Cole, V. John-Steiner, S. Scribner, & E. Souberman, Eds.). Cambridge, MA: Harvard University Press.

Webster's New Universal Unabridged Dictionary. (2006). New York: Barnes & Noble.

Weiner, L. (1999). *Urban teaching: The essentials.* New York: Teachers College Press.

Wiggins, G., & McTighe, J. (1998). *Understanding by design.* Alexandria, VA: Association for Supervision and Curriculum Development.

Yarger, S. J., & Smith, P. L. (1990). Issues in research on teacher education. In W. R. Houston, M. Haberman, & J. Sikula (Eds.), *Handbook on research on teacher education: A project of the Association of Teacher Educators* (pp. 25–41). New York: Macmillan.

Zeichner, K. M., & Liston, D. P. (1996). *Reflective teaching: An introduction.* Hillsdale, NJ: Lawrence Erlbaum.

About the Author

Christy Folsom teaches in the Childhood Education Department at Lehman College of the City University of New York, which is located in the Bronx. She uses the TIEL model in teaching curriculum development courses, student teaching seminars, and supervision of student teachers. She received her EdD from Teachers College, Columbia University, and has a broad and deep background in education. A former Oregonian, her teaching experience includes preschool, deaf, general, and gifted education. In addition she has worked as a staff developer and as an administrator. Based on her experience as an educator and a parent, she developed the conceptual framework of Teaching for Intellectual and Emotional Learning (TIEL). She has presented her work nationally and internationally. She also directs the TIEL Institute through which she works privately with students, schools, and districts. Dr. Folsom now lives in New York City.